MISSISSIPPI RIVER MAYHEM

Disasters, Tragedy, and Murder on Ol' Man River

DEAN KLINKENBERG

Essex, Connecticut

Globe Pequot

An imprint of Globe Pequot, the trade division of The Rowman & Littlefield Publishing Group, Inc.
4501 Forbes Blvd., Ste. 200
Lanham, MD 20706
www.rowman.com

Distributed by NATIONAL BOOK NETWORK

British Library Cataloguing in Publication Information available

Library of Congress Cataloging-in-Publication Data
ISBN 978-1-4930-6072-6 (paper)
ISBN 978-1-4930-6073-3 (electronic)

∞™ The paper used in this publication meets the minimum requirements of American National Standard for Information Sciences—Permanence of Paper for Printed Library Materials, ANSI/NISO Z39.48-1992.

In memory of all those who lost their lives along the Mississippi River, especially those who took a chance on starting over but who found death instead.

CONTENTS

INTRODUCTION

Sickness and Death

Perhaps there is no river in the world, whose waters and borders witness as much sickness and death as the Mississippi.

—S. L. LATHAM, 1834[1]

Late in the night of April 27, 1865, the steamer *Sultana* pulled away from Memphis and headed upriver. The boat was overloaded and dangerously crowded. Designed to carry 376 passengers, on this trip, the *Sultana* carried over 2,000, most of whom were Union soldiers eager to get home after being released from Confederate prison camps.

Around 2:00 a.m., one of the *Sultana*'s boilers exploded, then another. Fire engulfed the boat, which broke up and sank in a matter of minutes, killing more than half of the people on board. It is still the worst maritime disaster in US history, yet one that many people have never heard of. Few people today would even guess that the worst maritime disaster occurred on the Mississippi River.

The Mississippi occupies a big place in our cultural imagination. Stories of nineteenth-century steamboat life resonate so strongly with us that even today we build boats that transport us back to that era. These contemporary boats provoke feelings of nostalgia, but they do so without the dangers faced by people who traveled on the river 150 years ago.

While pictures of the opulent decorations on many of those old steamboats evoke images of elegantly dressed passengers relaxing in lounges and smoking cigars, people who boarded those boats were well aware of the risks. Debris floating in the river (limbs and trees called snags), fires, and boiler explosions happened far more often than we realize today. While everyone on board was vulnerable when a steamboat wrecked, the people who suffered the most extreme consequences weren't the ones in the opulent cabins, but the passengers crowded on the deck who were seeking a new life in a new location.

If those nineteenth-century travelers survived the steamboat trip, they faced other dangers that people didn't understand very well at the time. Diseases such as cholera, malaria, and yellow fever killed thousands of people in the Mississippi Valley. Steamboats sometimes carried infected passengers who spread those diseases to communities along the river. Once introduced into a local community, mosquitoes often transmitted malaria and yellow fever from person to person and transformed an isolated outbreak into an epidemic.

Floods, like disease outbreaks, wreaked havoc on communities and did so unpredictably. While the Mississippi typically rose and fell in regular, seasonal patterns, no one knew just how high the river would rise in any given year. Long periods of relatively minor spring rises created a false sense of security that led many people to build in areas that were within the river's reach. As the Mississippi Valley's population increased, more people lived in the bottomlands, so when the river reached unusually high levels, chaos and panic ensued. No Mississippi flood was more consequential than the Great Flood of 1927, which covered thousands of square miles and killed hundreds of people. We're still dealing with the consequences of that disaster today. Other major floods (1965, 1993) have led to soul-searching about the wisdom of building so extensively in the Mississippi's traditional floodplain.

Natural disasters along the Mississippi haven't been limited to floods. The river cuts through a part of the country that experiences highly variable weather. Changes can sometimes happen in a matter of hours, as they did in 1940 when a blizzard unexpectedly developed over the upper Midwest and paralyzed big cities and stranded hundreds of hunters in desperate conditions. Spring storms occasionally spawn tornadoes that can destroy communities in the blink of an eye, like they did to the neighboring Minnesota cities of St. Cloud and Sauk Rapids in 1886. And, unknown to many people, the Mississippi Valley sits atop an ancient fault line that triggered some of the strongest earthquakes in US history when they shook the Midwest in 1811 and 1812.

Many of the disasters along the Mississippi, though, have been entirely of our own making. (Much of the damage from floods would fit in that category, truth be told.) A massive fire destroyed much of central St. Louis in 1849. When a mine shaft collapsed along the Mississippi River in northern Minnesota, forty-one men drowned. A busy interstate bridge over the Mississippi at Minneapolis crumpled during rush hour in 2007.

The river's dense and isolated backwaters and islands are ideal places for nefarious activities. Prostitution thrived in river towns and on the river itself. Some brothels set up shop on barges and tied up on riverbanks just beyond the reach of local law enforcement. When they got in trouble, they just cut loose and floated to a more accommodating location. During Prohibition, the thick, isolated islands of the Mississippi were convenient places to hide stills and store liquor. The web of connected channels where the Mississippi River merges with the Gulf of Mexico was an ideal entry point to smuggle illegal booze into the United States.

The Mississippi River has witnessed great human tragedy. In 1964, anglers stumbled across the remains of two African American men who had been murdered and dumped in the Mississippi. The family would fight for forty years to hold the killers responsible.

The Mississippi River is also the place where some individuals, lost in the dark of night and a haze of intoxication, met an untimely end. Between 1997 and 2010, nine college-aged men wandered into the Mississippi River and drowned after nights of heavy drinking.

These aren't the stories we remember from Mark Twain's books, but they were a part of his river, too. After all, townsfolk assumed Tom Sawyer had drowned. Huck Finn had to outmaneuver the race-based prejudices of his day. And Twain himself lost a brother to a steamboat accident. Samuel Clemens understood the power of the river to please and to destroy.

But let's not get too carried away with these stories. Sure, the Mississippi River can be a dangerous place, although it's not as dangerous as it once was. Every year, people still drown in its waters, usually because they failed to wear a life jacket, and sometimes because they consumed a little too much alcohol. So, yes. The risks are real. But the Mississippi is also an ecological marvel that inspires awe and wonder, a national wonder.

So, enjoy these stories. Remember them. But don't turn down a chance to go out on the Mississippi. Just wear that life jacket. And pay your respects to the ghosts of those who found their end in its murky waters.

The Ground Rolled Like Waves

The New Madrid Earthquakes

THE GROUND TREMBLED IN THE MIDDLE OF THE NIGHT. PEOPLE JUMPED out of bed confused and afraid. As the walls shook, plates crashed to the floor. People stumbled as they tried to get out of their homes, struggling to get a stable footing as the ground underneath them undulated. Noises as loud as thunder cracked the silence as one of the strongest earthquakes in American history rumbled in the night.

While many of us would naturally assume that this scene occurred somewhere in California, it actually happened in the middle of the United States near a small community named New Madrid, Missouri. The tremor that struck in the early morning hours of December 16, 1811, was just the first in a series of massive earthquakes that reshaped the Mississippi Valley and sent people scrambling for safety and explanations.

Brothers Francois and Joseph LeSieur opened a trading post in the early 1780s at the tip of a big oxbow along the Mississippi River during the period that the Spanish monarchy ruled the Louisiana Territory. The LeSieur brothers traded with American Indians who lived in the area. Kaskaskia Indians lived on the east bank of the river north of the trading post. A large community of five hundred Shawnee Indians lived near present-day Cape Girardeau in a place they called Chillicothe, while a group of Quapaw Indians called southeast Missouri home.

In the late 1780s, Colonel George Morgan set in motion ambitious plans for a town called New Madrid that would be the center of the economy for Spanish Louisiana. Around 1800, Francois LeSieur

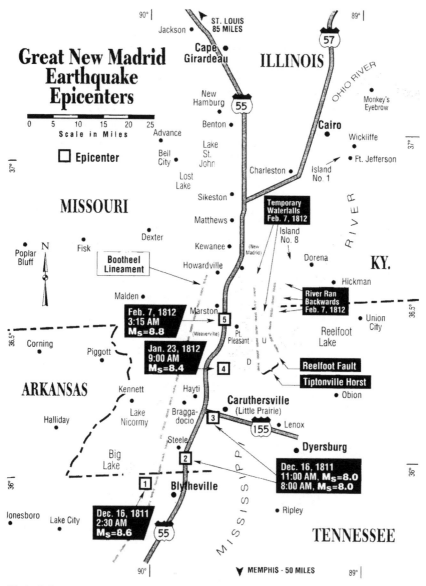

Great New Madrid Earthquake Epicenters

0 5 10 15 20 25
Scale in Miles

☐ Epicenter

MISSOURI

N

ST. LOUIS
85 MILES

Jackson •

Cape Girardeau •

ILLINOIS

57

New Hamburg
55

Benton •

Cairo

Advance •

Lake St. John

Beil City •

Lost Lake

Charleston •

Island No. 1

Sikeston •

Matthews •

Kewanee •

Dexter •

Fisk •

Poplar Bluff •

Bootheel Lineament

Howardville •

Malden •

**Feb. 7, 1812
3:15 AM
Ms=8.8**

Marston •

5

**Jan. 23, 1812
9:00 AM
Ms=8.4**

(Weaverville)

Pt. Pleasant •

4

D

ARKANSAS

Corning •

Piggott •

Kennett •

Hayti •

Halliday •

Lake Nicormy

Bragga-docio •

Steele •

Big Lake

2

**Dec. 16, 1811
2:30 AM
Ms=8.6**

1

Blytheville

55

Jonesboro •

Lake City •

OHIO RIVER

Monkey's Eyebrow •

Wickliffe •

• Ft. Jefferson

**Temporary Waterfalls
Feb. 7, 1812**

(New Madrid)

Island No. 8

Dorena •

KY.

Hickman •

**River Ran Backwards
Feb. 7, 1812**

• Union City

Reelfoot Lake

U

Reelfoot Fault

Tiptonville Horst

• Obion

Caruthersville
(Little Prairie)

3

155

• Lenox

Dyersburg

**Dec. 16, 1811
11:00 AM, Ms=8.0
8:00 AM, Ms=8.0**

• Ripley

TENNESSEE

MISSISSIPPI RIVER

V MEMPHIS - 50 MILES

Photo 1.1
GUTENBERG-RICHTER PUBLICATIONS, 1995. COURTESY OF ANTHONY STEWART.

founded Little Prairie about thirty miles downriver of New Madrid. Within a short time, a hundred people of French descent lived there.

New Madrid eventually grew into a multicultural town, with residents of French Creole, German, and American heritage. One of the early residents of New Madrid was Sergeant John Ordway, who had traveled up the Missouri River with Lewis and Clark. He bought land in the area in 1807 that grew into a thousand-acre farm that bordered the Mississippi River. In September 1809, his old boss, Meriwether Lewis, wrote his will during a stop in New Madrid.

By 1811, several hundred people lived in New Madrid and many more passed through town on flatboats. New Madrid wasn't exactly an easy place to live, though. Residents regularly fought diseases like malaria, and the Mississippi kept eating away at the town's foundation. Eroding banks swallowed three forts and three city streets in the city's early years.

Still, the town had been built on relatively high ground, so at least folks didn't have to deal with frequent flooding. Unfortunately, the reason the ground rose high in that spot was because previous seismic activity had pushed it up. The seismic zone had been quiet for centuries, but it wouldn't be for much longer.

A DEAFENING ROAR

On December 16, just after two in the morning, the folks in New Madrid awoke to a frightening event. "There was a great shaking of the earth this morning. Tables and chairs turned over and knocked around—all of us knocked out of bed," George Heinrich Crist wrote. "The roar I thought would leave us deaf if we lived. It was not a storm. When you could hear, all you could hear was screams from people and animals. It was the worst thing that I have ever witnessed. . . . You could not hold on to nothing. Neither man or woman was strong enough—the shaking would knock you lose like knocking hickory nuts out of a tree. None of us was killed— we was all banged up and some of us knocked out for a while and blood was everywhere. . . . Everybody is scared to death."[1]

Eliza Bryan recalled that "we were visited by a violent shock of an earthquake, accompanied by a very awful noise resembling loud but distant thunder, but more hoarse and vibrating, which was followed in a few minutes by the complete saturation of the atmosphere."[2] The air was frosty and increasingly heavy with a "vapour which seemed to impregnate the atmosphere, had a disagreeable smell, and produced a difficulty of respiration."[3]

As people ran out of their houses (log cabins, mostly), they ran into the dark of night and tried to make sense of what was happening. One neighbor blamed the quakes on a collision between the earth and the moon. Another thought that the quakes signaled Judgment Day.

Smaller shocks rumbled through town the rest of the morning, then bigger quakes hit New Madrid around sunrise. Fissures opened in the ground that were as much as four feet deep and up to ten feet wide. One hole swallowed the contents of a cellar.

The trembling was felt far away. Vincent Nolte was riding a horse through Kentucky when one tremor hit. He recalled that "my horse, as if struck by lightning, suddenly stood still—the trees around us had for some reason exhibited a strange heaving and waving motion."[4]

At New Madrid, residents huddled in encampments of fifty to a hundred people. "I never before thought the passion of fear so strong as I find it here among the people," John Shaw wrote. "It is really diverting, or would be so, to a disinterested observer, to see the rueful faces of the different persons that present themselves at my tent, some so agitated that they cannot speak, others cannot hold their tongues. Some cannot sit still, but must be in constant motion, while others cannot walk. Several men, I am informed, on the night of the first shock deserted their families, and have not been heard of since."[5]

The news wasn't any better at Little Prairie. One traveler reported that "the face of the country has been entirely changed—Large lakes have been raised, and become dry land, and many fields have been converted into ponds of water." As people ran toward open fields, they were blocked by crevasses that opened in the ground: "the earth continued to burst open, and mud, water, sand & stone coal were thrown up the distance of thirty yards."[6]

People fled Little Prairie in search of safety, but they faced a daunting route to escape the chaos. The land around town had sunk and was wet. People had to wade through water up to their waists, not knowing if the next step would sink them in over their heads, and all while watching for snakes and other animals that were also fleeing and confused. When they finally reached New Madrid on Christmas Eve, they discovered a ghost town. Most of the residents had moved to temporary camps about two miles away.

A fifteen-year-old named Walker had left Little Prairie before the quakes to go hunting across the river with Jean Baptiste Zebon. They were camping next to a small lake in Tennessee when the trembling began. "The thoughts of being in a wilderness amongst wild beasts, and the terrors of the earthquake, ran in my head for nearly an hour," he remembered. He had trouble falling asleep again, then later that morning the quakes returned.

"It was awful!" Walker recalled, "first, a noise in the west, like heavy thunder, then the earth came rolling towards us, like a wave on the ocean, in long seas, not less than fifteen feet high." He watched trees bend and heard many crash to the ground. "The whole forest seemed as if an awful hurricane had completely destroyed it."

The lake drained into the crevasses of the earth, and geysers of water and sand shot straight up from the ground. As Walker knelt to pray, Zebon interrupted and told him to focus on protecting themselves. The tremors had completely leveled their camp, and a crevasse had swallowed most of their supplies, including a gun, meat, ammo, flint, and blankets. They gathered what they could and walked back to the Mississippi River, which took most of the day.

Once on the banks of the river, they could see that Little Prairie had been destroyed and abandoned. One boatman who passed Little Prairie around that time remembered that riverbanks there "were all broken to pieces and huge masses were, at short intervals, tumbling into the river." Walker and Zebon tried to build a raft to cross the river, but it drifted away before they could get on it. As they were losing hope of being found, they spotted someone on the other bank. It was Walker's father. He paddled a canoe across the Mississippi to pick them up.[7]

Nature Was in State of Dissolution

Life wasn't any easier for the people who were on the Mississippi River. After the first quake, Daniel Bedinger noticed that the Mississippi "appeared to be much agitated. It was suddenly covered with a thick froth. It rose at least 18 inches in a few minutes time."[8] Boats bobbed around in the water even though there was no wind.

Another traveler, probably on the same boat as Bedinger, saw "a boiling motion in the water, which brought up sawyers and planters, as well as small fragments of wood, bark, leaves, etc. and numerous air bubbles— the water was very muddy and frothy."[9]

"Large trees which had lain for ages at the bottom of the river," William Leigh Pierce wrote, "were shot up in thousands of instances some with their roots uppermost and their tops planted; others were hurled into the air; many again were only loosened, and floated upon the surface. Never was a scene more replete with terrific threatenings of death."[10]

As Bedinger's boat floated downriver, he saw "Many acres of land . . . had sunk to a level with the surface of the river, and some much lower leaving only the tops of the trees above water. Where the banks did not immediately tumble in, vast rents or fissures were made in the earth to an extent unknown."[11]

Water roared out from the fissures. Banks caved along the Mississippi "in such vast masses, as nearly to sink our boat by the swell they occasioned," naturalist John Bradbury wrote.[12] "The crash of [trees falling and banks caving], mixed with the terrible sound attending the shock, and the screaming of the geese, and other water-fowl, produced an idea that all nature was in a state of dissolution."[13]

At a portion of the river known as Canadian Reach, "A great portion of it [the west bank of the river] was sunk beneath the surface of the river so that the tops only of some of the tallest trees were to be seen, and many of them shattered and prostrated by the concussion."[14]

John Davis had been at Island 25 when the first quakes hit, along with forty other boats. The banks caved in near them, and trees fell into the river. They raced to get away as the water began rising around them. They floated thirty-five miles to Flour Island, passing through a river so full of driftwood that it "gave the appearance of timbered fields."[15]

The extent of the devastation became more obvious at daybreak. Canoes and flatboats floated down the river with no one on board. Bradbury stopped along the Chickasaw Bluffs, where he encountered a group of twenty people praying. One person believed the earthquake had been caused by a comet that had appeared in the sky a few months earlier, "which he described as having two horns, over one of which the earth had rolled, and was now lodged betwixt them: that the shocks were occasioned by the attempts made by the earth to surmount the other horn."[16]

The comet was first visible on March 26, 1811, and remained in the night sky until mid-August 1812. It was a giant with a double tail that was hard to miss. Many considered the appearance of the comet an omen of ill times.

The first round of earthquakes echoed east. They woke up President James Madison and First Lady Dolly Madison some eight hundred miles away in Washington, DC. The tremblers triggered landslides in North Carolina and created Big Lake on the Missouri/Arkansas border. But the December earthquakes were just beginning.

THE EARTH WAS IN CONTINUAL AGITATION

The ground returned to relative calm for a few weeks, then a big tremor on January 23, 1812, ushered in the most tumultuous period, when "the earth was in continual agitation, visibly waving as a gentle sea."[17] Another massive tremor shook the area on February 7 and hundreds of aftershocks followed.

The naturalist John J. Audubon was traveling near present-day Hickman, Kentucky, when the second round of earthquakes hit. His horse froze suddenly and "fell a-groaning piteously, hung his head, spread out his four legs, as if to save himself from falling, and stood stock still, continuing to groan." Audubon looked around and "saw a sudden and strange darkness rising from the western horizon. . . . I heard what I imagined to be the distant rumbling of a violent tornado [and] at that instant all the shrubs and trees began to move from their very roots. The ground rose and fell in successive furrows like the ruffled waters of a lake."[18]

Two hundred miles north of New Madrid, the new stone house of Daniel and Rebecca Boone shifted a few inches off its foundation and nearly came apart. In St. Louis, chimneys fell from buildings. The quakes continued to reshape the land. Prairies sunk and filled with shallow ponds. Fissures opened up and shot out water and sand. Some areas became dotted with sand hills from the eruptions. When the land shifted along Reelfoot Creek, a dam formed that created Reelfoot Lake, which still exists today in northern Tennessee.

The solid, dependable ground that everyone took for granted had become liquid and terrifying. On February 8, 1812, George Crist wrote in his journal: "If we do not get away from here the ground is going to eat us alive. . . . We are all about to go crazy from pain and fright."[19]

Like much of New Madrid's population, John Shaw had moved to a tent camp after the quakes started rumbling again in early 1812. He noted an ecumenical enthusiasm for prayer among the refugees as "Catholics and Protestants, knelt and offered solemn prayer to their Creator."[20]

The quakes attracted evangelists, who descended on the area and urged people to repent. "It was a great time of terror to sinners," one preacher commented.[21] While some people gave up their vices (at least temporarily), most didn't change.

Amid the panic from the second round of earthquakes, Shaw was one of the few people who kept his wits about him. Betsey Masters had suffered a broken leg during one quake, so she wasn't mobile. Her family had left her behind in their cabin in New Madrid when they fled to the hills, leaving her with a supply of cornbread and water. Shaw was the only person willing to go back and check on her. He found her in decent condition and stayed long enough to cook for her. She recovered.

All Nature Appeared in Ruins

James McBride passed by Little Prairie on a flatboat and stopped to tour the remains. The spot where he tied up turned out to be a cemetery, but it had been partly submerged in the river and some coffins were exposed.

McBride walked two miles from the river. "The surface of the ground was cracked in almost every direction and stood like yawning gulphs, so wide that I could scarcely leap over them. . . . All nature appeared in ruins, and seemed to mourn in solitude over her melancholy fate."[22]

The earthquakes had wiped out Little Prairie. A smokehouse, granary, and two houses had disappeared into a crevasse and some of the town had slipped into the Mississippi. Most everyone had fled.

The Mississippi River Ran Backwards

The tremors had a curious effect on the Mississippi. "At first the Mississippi seemed to recede from its banks," Eliza Bryan wrote, "and its waters gathering up like a mountain leaving for a moment many boats, which were here on their way to New Orleans, on the bare sand, in which time the poor sailors made their escape from them. It then rising fifteen or twenty feet perpendicularly, and expanding, as it were, at the same moment, the banks overflowed with a retrograde current, rapid as a torrent—the boats which before had been left on the sand were now torn from their moorings, and suddenly driven up a little creek, at the mouth of which they laid, to the distance in some instances, of nearly a quarter of a mile."[23]

Firmin LaRoche was on the Mississippi. He woke up when he felt his boat being tossed around. He cut the boat loose from its moorings, then "so great a wave came up the river that I never seen one like it at sea. It carried us back north, up-stream, for more than a mile, and the water spread out upon the banks, even covering maybe three or four miles inland. It was the current going backward."[24]

For several miles between Islands 8 and 10, the earthquake had altered the elevation of the Mississippi enough to temporarily force its waters to flow north. Vincent Nolte was sitting at a table on his flatboat and sketching late at night "when there came a frightful crash, like a sudden explosion of artillery, and instantly followed by countless flashes of lightning; the Mississippi foamed up like the water in a boiling cauldron, and the stream flowed rushing back, while the forest trees, near which we lay, came cracking and thundering down."[25] Nolte was among the lucky ones. He had tied up with twenty boats at New Madrid. All of the other boats were lost to the Mississippi.

The earthquake-altered Mississippi had one more surprise waiting for boats traveling near New Madrid. William Shaler related a story from a flatboat captain who encountered a waterfall above New Madrid "at least six feet perpendicular, extending across the river, and about half a mile wide."[26] Eight miles below New Madrid, another set of falls had emerged and thundered loudly enough to be heard in town. The captain waited five days for the falls to erode down to rapids before continuing downriver.

Mathias Speed was also on a flatboat lashed to a willow bar during the second round of earthquakes. After the earthquake, the bar started sinking, so they cut loose. As they floated downriver with little control over their direction, the swells were so big that they stuffed blankets into the boat's oarholes to prevent water from coming in. Shortly after that, they "were affrighted with the appearance of a dreadful rapid or falls in the river just below us."[27] Speed thought the cataract was comparable in size to the Falls of the Ohio. He was among the lucky few who rode a boat over the temporary falls and survived.

A CHANGED LAND

The New Madrid area experienced over two thousand earthquakes in five months. February and March 1812 were the most active periods. Large aftershocks continued for another ten years after that.

The earthquakes wiped out five villages, several American Indian communities, a few islands, and Fort Jefferson. Shawnee Indians abandoned Chillicothe and moved to western Missouri. The force of the tremblers rearranged the land, wiped out forests, created lakes, and erased streams. Reelfoot Lake emerged from a forest of cypress and deciduous trees. The quakes broke up the Pemiscot River into smaller bits of discontinuous bayous and swamps.

The quakes emptied New Madrid. Most folks moved away to central Missouri, Arkansas, or other parts of the Midwest. Sergeant Ordway lost almost everything to the quakes. He died a poor man around 1818.

On November 21, 1820, Audubon stopped at New Madrid and found an "almost deserted Village [that] is one of the poorest that is seen on this River bearing a name; the Country Back was represented to us as being good, but the Looks of the Inhabitants contradicted strongly their assertions—they are Clad in Buckskin pantaloons and a Sort of Shirt of the same, this is seldom put aside unless So ragged or so Blooded &

Greased, that it will become desagreable [*sic*] even to the poor Wrecks bear it on."[28]

New Madrid eventually came back, but the city is now located about a mile from the original village site. Little Prairie is long gone. Caruthersville, Missouri, is close to its original site.

Most accounts of the New Madrid earthquakes assert the quakes caused few deaths, but there was no systematic effort to count casualties. David Stewart and Ray Knox reviewed the evidence and estimated that the earthquakes killed five hundred to one thousand people, including flatboatmen, American Indians, and people who lived in the towns. For an area with a population of fifteen thousand, that's a heavy toll.

What We Know Now

The New Madrid earthquakes reverberated over a million square miles of North America. In contrast, the well-known quakes that have ravaged California typically impact about thirty thousand square miles. The New Madrid quakes unnerved people in Savannah, Georgia, and Charleston, South Carolina. The tremors rang church bells in Boston; woke a sleeping President and First Lady in Washington, DC; rattled St. Louis; and shook New Orleans and Natchez.

There's no way to know how strong the New Madrid earthquakes were by contemporary standards. The best guesses initially put them around a magnitude of 8.0 to 8.5, but more recent studies suggest that the biggest tremors were more likely between 7.3 to 7.5. (The 1906 earthquake in San Francisco registered a 7.8 magnitude.) Those are still big quakes, though, enough to level entire neighborhoods in today's cities of the Mississippi Valley.

The seismic zone remains active even today, but it hasn't produced a major tremor since October 31, 1895, when a 6.5-magnitude quake struck east of Sikeston, Missouri, and damaged Cairo, Memphis, and other cities nearby. In 1990, climatologist Iben Browning released an analysis he conducted that suggested a high probability of another major tremor on December 3 of that year. It didn't happen, but his prediction served as a wake-up call for a region that was completely unprepared for a major earthquake, despite its history.

Deadly Winds

Tornadoes

THE MISSISSIPPI RIVER CUTS A PATH THROUGH THE MIDDLE OF THE Great Plains, an area known for wild variations in weather and violent storms. No storm is more notorious or feared than tornadoes. They were impossible to predict for a long time and even today they can form with little warning. And when that funnel cloud drops from the sky, it can change a person's life in a matter of seconds.

People who live along the Mississippi have experienced their fair share of life-changing moments from tornadoes. Two of the three deadliest tornadoes in US history struck Mississippi River towns.

ALL IS SWEPT AWAY

In the years before the Civil War, Natchez was the busiest port on the Mississippi River between New Orleans and Cairo, Illinois. Boats of all shapes and sizes left the banks of the city's river district, known as Natchez-Under-the-Hill, loaded with bales of cotton and products from around the world.

Natchez was the center of social life for the South's genteel planter class. They built mansions on top of the bluffs from the profits they gained from the labor of enslaved Black people who toiled in their cotton fields. Natchez-Under-the-Hill, in contrast, was a spirited place where people from all over the place—including some planters—filled gambling halls, brothels, and bars.

Natchez residents were accustomed to unsettled weather in the spring, so it wasn't unusual when lightning rolled across the sky and heavy rain fell on the night of May 6, 1840. The next day dawned steamy like many May days, but by noon, dark clouds had returned and the staff in dining rooms ran around lighting candles. While people enjoyed lunch, winds grew stronger, and the Mississippi River stirred.

Outside of town, a massive funnel cloud had formed. It touched down about twenty miles southwest of Natchez, then raced toward the city along the Mississippi River. The winds uprooted ancient trees, then spit them out. Waves on the Mississippi rose as high as fifteen feet. As the tornado reached Natchez, a ferry, the *Vidalia*, was midstream. The tornado ripped it to shreds and killed everyone on board.

The tornado then blew directly into Natchez, where it laid waste to the river district. It hit boats tied up along the riverbank first. The steamboat *Prairie* and a wharf boat called *Mississippian* took direct hits. The *Hinds* was badly damaged and presumed sunk. Of the 120 flatboats tied up at Natchez, all but four were destroyed.

On land, the tornado leveled all but two buildings in Under-the-Hill, including the busy Steamboat Hotel. Writer Timothy Flint and his adult son James were among the lucky ones pulled out alive from the hotel ruins. Beams fell over them and had shielded them from debris. A local newspaper lamented that "all, all, is swept away and beneath the ruins still lay crushed the bodies of many strangers."[1]

The tornado rose onto the bluff and continued on its destructive path. It blew the Planter's Hotel off the bluff and into the river, killing all the registered guests. It destroyed homes, churches, and businesses in the central part of town.

Officials counted 317 dead, most of whom had been on the riverfront. It's likely that far more people died, however, as there were reports that many enslaved workers had also been killed on plantations near Natchez. No one counted their deaths.

For days after the storm had run its course, debris from damaged buildings floated down the Mississippi River past Natchez. And a few days after the storm, a badly damaged steamboat drifted into Baton Rouge, Louisiana, 130 miles south of Natchez. It was the *Hinds*, or what was left of it. Inside its wrecked shell, Louisianans found the remains of fifty-one people.

Flying Horses

Twenty years later and 1,100 miles upriver, the good folks of Camanche, Iowa, and Albany, Illinois, were enjoying a warm, late spring day in 1860. A ferry across the Mississippi River connected the two towns, and residents of each community—about a thousand in Camanche and six hundred in Albany—felt bullish about their future. Sunday, June 3 began warm enough so that "the whole town of Camanche lay steeped in Sunday torpor," one writer noted.[2] As the winds picked up and ominous clouds rolled in, that listlessness would transform to terror.

Around 6:30 in the evening, the first wave of the storm hit Camanche. Many folks initially welcomed the rain and the cooler air. The mood changed, though, when large chunks of hail fell from the sky and broke windows around town. Half an hour later, people heard a loud roar "as of a heavy train passing over a bridge."[3]

A funnel emerged from the clouds that looked like a "cloud of murky blackness, with the appearance of a thin white vapor revolving around it."[4] Everyone scrambled to find shelter. Debris flew around the town, including "a horse . . . flying through the air at about twenty feet from the ground, followed by a cow at about the same height."[5]

The tornado next swept into the Mississippi River, where it upended a raft carrying twenty-six men. Only three survived. A local man who worked as a steamboat pilot, Wes Rambo, saw "two thirds of the bottom of the river swept clear as the floor before a tidal wave swept back, lifting everything, including the log raft."[6]

After crossing the river, the tornado wreaked havoc in Albany. A hundred buildings—most of the structures in town—disappeared in the blink of an eye. Even though folks in Albany could see the storm coming from their homes on the bluffs, there wasn't time to get out of the way. Five people died, and another forty-three were injured. The tornado caused more death and destruction as it continued eastward before finally petering out.

The tornado left behind some mind-boggling scenes. It blew a chimney off a house, then set it down on the ground ten feet away but upright and unbroken. The first floor of a building near the river had somehow been blown out, then the second floor dropped into the vacated space nearly intact.

A few survivors raced on horseback to the nearby towns of Clinton and Lyons to secure help. The devastation shocked those who hurried to help. "The ruins strewed around, the hideous distortions of the dead, the mangled bodies of the living, the multitudes of eager, grimy workmen, the peaceful summer night and the clear moonlight overhead" became permanently etched in one person's memory.[7] The tornado had devastated Camanche and Albany, and it had done all that damage in five minutes.

Folks in Camanche placed the remains of their twenty-nine dead in coffins that were stacked in front of the bank. The dead, some too badly wounded to be reliably identified, were buried in a single, mass funeral that attracted two thousand mourners, who grieved among the ruins of Camanche. It would take the town decades to recover from the destruction wrought by the tornado of 1860.

A Sullen Roar and Ceaseless Whirl

North of Minnesota's Twin Cities, St. Cloud and Sauk Rapids grew up next to each other around a stretch of the Mississippi River that is shallow, narrow, and punctuated by occasional rapids. The cities were built around sawmills, granite mines, and railroads. By 1886, St. Cloud was home to several thousand people, while another thousand lived in Sauk Rapids.

April 14, 1886, was a Wednesday like any other, just hotter and more humid than a typical April day. Around four in the afternoon, two funnel clouds dropped near North Star Cemetery "the lower [funnel] writhing along the earth like a serpent, gathering within its fold everything in its path; the upper, a tongue-like cloud, which soon united with the lower monster."[8]

When one resident saw the dark clouds on the horizon, she told her family, "Children, come in the house, we'll have to pray, it's the end of the world."[9] The world did end for St. Cloud's Nicholas Junnemann, the tornado's first victim. His wife, Angeline, suffered terribly—both of her arms and legs were broken—but she survived, as did all nine of their children.

Photo 2.1. A man and child survey tornado damage in Sauk Rapids, Minnesota, after the tornado of 1886.
BENTON COUNTY (MN) HISTORICAL SOCIETY

P. H. Washburn had just left the Manitoba freight depot when the tornado swept through and leveled it. Woodstoves flipped over in buildings around the city, which ignited multiple fires. The tornado raced on to the northeast and toward the city's cathedral, then set its sights on the other side of the Mississippi River and Sauk Rapids.

Peter Daubanton saw the tornado approach the city "turning what had been a black mass of clouds and wreckage into a white swirling mass."[10] As it moved over the Mississippi River, it sucked enough water from it to expose the mud river bottom. The winds slammed into the Mississippi River bridge at Sauk Rapids and wiped out the eastern span.

J. A. Senn left his Sauk Rapids office that afternoon and stepped into an airborne eddy of timber, boards, and other flying debris. The tornado "with a sullen roar and ceaseless whirl . . . moved slowly and unsteadily forward, as if uncertain at times which direction to turn."[11] People scrambled for cover. Girls marching out of St. Mary's Catholic school dove into a ravine for safety.

The winds picked up a flour mill and dropped it back down. They ripped a hole in the courthouse. Winds lifted Thomas Van Etten, who weighed around three hundred pounds, then dropped him in mud. He survived. A pharmacist named Schulter wasn't so lucky. He was sucked into the blackness of the swirling winds. No one ever saw him again.

The tornado totally wiped out the Nieman printing plant in Sauk Rapids. The building was painted an unusual shade of yellow, yet no one found a single fragment of the building. "It is not any one section of Sauk Rapids that has gone," *Harper's Weekly* reported, "it is not the north end or the south end; it is the whole town."[12]

Around St. Cloud and Sauk Rapids, people did whatever they could to survive. Lulu Carpenter was outside when the storm roared through. She picked up her baby sister, then desperately clung to a tree. Flying debris fatally wounded Lulu, but she lived just long enough to safely hand off her baby sister. Little Harry Ziebol was six years old. He had just walked into his house when it collapsed around him. The winds carried him to a pile of lumber, where a neighbor later discovered him. Remarkably, Harry wasn't hurt. Still, it took two days to reunite him with his parents.

The tornado wasn't finished after destroying Sauk Rapids. It continued north on a course parallel to the Mississippi River and terrorized more communities in central Minnesota. On the John Schultz farmstead just outside of Rice, Henry Freitag and Minnie Schulz had exchanged wedding vows in the garden in the morning, then they had moved inside for dinner. Around 5:30 in the evening, as Reverend Gustav Schmidt of the Evangelical United Brethren Church was giving a farewell address to mark his transfer to a new church, the tornado tore through the Schultz's land. Fourteen people at the wedding died, including the Reverend Schmidt, the mother and brother of Minnie, and the man she had just married, Henry Freitag. Minnie was badly injured, but she survived.

Besides the tragic deaths at the wedding, the tornado claimed seventeen lives in St. Cloud and thirty-eight in Sauk Rapids. Within a few hours, help poured into the area. Doctors from Minneapolis arrived on the first available train. Railroad mogul James Hill donated $5,000 to relief efforts. St. Cloud would recover and grow into the biggest city in central Minnesota. Sauk Rapids, meanwhile, struggled to bounce back.

LIKE CHAFF BEFORE A BREEZE

As the nineteenth century ended, St. Louis was a boomtown with half a million residents. Factories employing tens of thousands of people turned out beer, bricks, and shoes. Sturdy structures built of red brick and stone spread from the riverfront to the city's emerging neighborhoods on its western edge. In the Mill Creek Valley, Black residents were developing the ragtime sound that would define the city a decade later. Optimism ran deep like the Mississippi.

Spring in St. Louis always meant unsettled weather, and May 1896 had been no exception. Multiple storms had caused widespread damage throughout the Midwest, but the worst was yet to come.

May 27, a Wednesday, started out warm. Hot, dry winds kicked up in the afternoon and seemed to blow from every direction. Later in the day, temperatures dropped and "huge banks of black and greenish clouds were seen approaching the city."[13] By five, it was as dark as night when heavy rain fell and lightning flashed across the sky. "In every direction the long lines of telegraph poles were flashing pillars of blue flame. The wires were strings of fire and the insulators were blazing bunches of sizzling wires."[14]

There was a lull around 5:30, then greenish-black clouds rolled in from the southwest. The winds picked up again. Buildings swayed. Bricks and fragments of wood flew through the air. Buggies flipped over. The sounds of breaking glass echoed through the city's streets. More rain poured down. St. Louisans ran for cover.

A tornado touched down in the southwest part of the city and tore its way northeast. "Buildings in the track of the storm went over like chaff before a breeze," one newspaper noted.[15] Houses around the city crumbled in the face of the winds, even the mansions in the Compton Heights neighborhood. Two of the city's beloved parks—Tower Grove and Lafayette—suffered widespread damage, as did the city's renowned botanical garden.

The tornado blew down the powerhouse for the Union Depot streetcar company and knocked out one hundred miles of streetcars. Buildings went down at the Liggett & Myers tobacco company complex, killing thirteen men.

St. Louis's large public hospital, City Hospital, took a direct hit from the tornado. Hundreds of patients were inside but because staff had had the presence of mind to move them to safer areas, only one patient was killed. George Wilson was a patient on the hospital's second floor when the tornado hit. "I knew something awful was happening," he recalled, "and thought may be the end of the world had come. There was a roar. The walls in our division fell out. The rain rushed in on us. Then I felt myself picked up in bed and borne out on the ground. I somehow managed to scramble to the basement, although suffering severely from rheumatism."[16]

All around the city, people scrambled for shelter. Lillie Bene was at home with her children when the tornado approached. As the storm raged, she and her children, five-year-old Sylvester and three-year-old Oliver, huddled in the middle of the house. Sylvester got spooked as the storm raged and ran to the kitchen. As Lillie ran after him, flying debris struck Sylvester and killed him, then the house collapsed. For two hours, she was trapped under debris next to her son's body. She could hear Oliver crying, though, so she knew he was still alive. When the family was finally rescued, Oliver was under the body of the family's Irish setter. The dog had provided just enough protection to save his life.

The Rohrbach family was at home when the storm hit. Mrs. Rohrbach and her children were in their second-floor unit, while Mr. Rohrbach was in the saloon on the first floor. When Mrs. Rohrbach realized what was going on, she sent each of her four children—one by one—down to the first floor through the dumbwaiter, where Mr. Rohrbach plucked them out. Once all the children were safely downstairs, she lowered herself down, just before the second and third floors of their building collapsed. The whole family survived, though.

The city's Soulard neighborhood suffered the highest concentration of fatalities. Seventeen people died when a tenement collapsed at the corner of Rutger and Seventh Streets. Fred Mauchenheimer worked in his parent's bar in that tenement. He had just stepped outside when the building collapsed behind him. He survived, but his parents, who hadn't gotten out, were killed.

The tornado roared on to the riverfront where it destroyed warehouses and boats, and "lashed the water [of the Mississippi River] to waves of proportions never seen in this vicinity before."[17] George Simons, the second clerk on the steamer *JJ Odill*, was in his cabin when the tornado hit. Winds ripped the boat loose from its moorings and flipped it over. Simons got out, but he surfaced in the middle of debris. He took a deep breath and went back down. When he came up again, he was clear of the wreckage. He grabbed a piece of wreckage and floated down the river. For two and a half hours he floated at the mercy of the river and the winds, before he washed onto an island. He was rescued the next morning. Five other people on the *JJ Odill* perished, however.

The city's landmark river crossing, the Eads Bridge, took a direct hit from the tornado. While the east approach suffered some damage, the main span held strong. Two trains got safely across the bridge as the tornado hit, although powerful gusts blew one off the tracks as it descended into East St. Louis. Everyone survived, though.

After crossing the river, the tornado roared into East St. Louis and leveled half of the city, including the courthouse and police headquarters. Five of the six boats operated by the Wiggins Ferry Company were destroyed. Wrecked boats littered the levee.

Henry Collins had been standing in an East St. Louis tavern with a glass of booze in one hand when the tornado struck it. It tossed him about a couple of times—he claimed he was completely flipped over—but somehow he landed back on his feet with the glass still in his hand and, most importantly, half full. He finished his drink, no doubt to ease the pain of the broken collarbone he suffered.

The tornado had cut a path of destruction through several miles of St. Louis and East St. Louis and had done so in just twenty minutes. Telegraph, trolley, and telephone wires were down everywhere. Many streetcar lines were disabled. The city morgue was overrun with bodies. Pine boxes filled every available space. Crowds gathered in front, hoping to find out if their loved ones were resting in one of those pine boxes. Police arrived to help maintain control.

Two days after the storm, folks noticed "a parrot in a battered cage, his feathers disheveled and possessing a general appearance of a hard luck tale, was noisily scolding the world for going awry."[18] For many St. Louisans, that parrot symbolized how they felt.

The disaster turned into a major tourist event. Some trains sold half-price tickets for day excursions to St. Louis to view the damage. About one hundred thousand people did so on the Sunday after the storm, overwhelming the city's train station. "Never before in the history of the Union Station had such a large crowd assembled there except on the night of its dedication. Viewed from an elevation the midway seemed a moving, surging sea of hats."[19]

The saloon at Rutger and Seventh Streets reopened to serve all those disaster tourists, many of whom must have surely been thirsty. Stores offered special deals to develop film from one of the recently introduced personal cameras, like the Pocket Kodak. "You can take your own 'pictures' of the horrible results of the tornado and cyclone," one ad read.[20]

Some visitors, a minority of them, went to St. Louis to search for loved ones. The initial reports right after the tornado hit suggested that the city had been almost completely wiped out. All communications went down after that. It took several days for the rest of the country to learn that most of St. Louis was, in fact, still standing.

On Sunday, bereaved family and friends buried their loved ones. At least two hundred funerals took place in St. Louis and East St. Louis, so many, in fact, that "one procession followed another so closely as to make it look like one long, unbroken line, miles in length."[21] The mood remained somber into Sunday night, when "Occasionally, a gong on a cable car would break the stillness of the night. . . . The twisted stumps and broken trees in Lafayette Park made a ghostly sight. Ruins, ruins everywhere."[22]

The official death toll was 137 in St. Louis and 118 in East St. Louis, making it the third-deadliest tornado in US history. For a time, officials believed that a small community of people on shantyboats downtown had been killed by the tornado, but they later discovered that they had cut loose and drifted downriver when they saw the storm approaching.

The tornado flattened three hundred buildings in St. Louis and badly damaged thousands more. The city began putting the pieces back together immediately. A thousand men cleared the streets. Police officers served as employment brokers by connecting companies looking for certain types of skills with the individuals who had those skills.

Relief groups organized efforts to help people get back on their feet. Many offered loans to facilitate temporary repairs to homes to make them habitable again. Still, many people, especially the working poor, had a hard time finding new places to live that they could afford.

A few people found a silver lining in the disaster. William Howe and Helen Edwards of St. Louis were engaged but their parents didn't want them to marry because they thought they were too young. (She was twenty-two, he was "entitled to vote.") After the storm had interrupted all communications, they took advantage of the quiet by speeding across the Mississippi River to Belleville, Illinois, where they married that evening "under the flare of a single gas jet . . . near the witching hour of midnight."[23]

Water from Bluff to Bluff

The Flood of 1844

IN THE DECADE FROM 1840 TO 1850, ST. LOUIS'S POPULATION DOUBLED from 36,000 to 78,000. Over a thousand new buildings went up in 1844 alone, which still wasn't enough to keep up with the demand for housing all those new residents.

Just across the Mississippi River from St. Louis, seventy miles of thick floodplain forests and wet prairies known as the American Bottom were increasingly being cleared for agriculture. New communities coalesced to serve the growing farm economy: Venice, Madison, Six Mile Prairie (later renamed Granite City), Brooklyn (founded around 1830

HIGH WATER AT CAIRO, 1844.

Photo 3.1
LLOYD'S STEAMBOAT DIRECTORY, 1856

by a small community of free Black people led by "Mother" Priscilla and John Baltimore), and Illinoistown (later East St. Louis).

South of St. Louis, villages founded under French colonial rule were adjusting to American life: Cahokia and Prairie du Rocher in Illinois and Sainte Genevieve in Missouri. About sixty river miles south of St. Louis, though, the once-prominent French settlement of Kaskaskia was in decline. Founded in the seventeenth century by a community of Illini Indians, the village eventually became home to French traders, farmers, and missionaries, as well as free and enslaved Black people. Kaskaskia grew into a thriving trade and government center of several thousand residents and even served briefly as the capital of Illinois Territory. Repeated flooding and competition from newer, drier cities had driven most people away, though.

When seven nuns and one postulant from the Sisters of the Visitation arrived in Kaskaskia in 1833, they found "One street intersected the village & that [was] so quiet, & we may say unfrequented, as almost never to be disturbed by the sound of carts or wheels. . . . No press, no rail road, no mill, no smoke of manufacture rising to the blue sky; no bridge,—only a flat-boat drawn wearily by a rope from shore to shore of the Okaw (Kaskaskia) river."[1]

The Mississippi River tied these communities together and linked them to the rest of the United States, and even the world. St. Louis was one of the busiest inland ports. Steamboats, sometimes dozens at a time, lined the riverfront levee. Boats laid out wooden gangplanks over the muddy banks that were busy with roustabouts who moved cargo between the boats and warehouses. A robust fish market thrived on Fourth Street. The Planters House on Fourth Street provided elegant accommodations to visitors, including Charles Dickens during his tour of the United States in 1842.

French traders who lived under Spanish rule had founded St. Louis in 1764. St. Louisans became Americans in 1804 with the Louisiana Purchase and the French character of the city gradually diluted as the city grew.

The founders built the city on a sloping bluff that protected most of the residents from high water, although much of the city's commercial life centered on the riverfront. Variable river levels were part of the rhythm of life, with predictable rises in the spring that came in two pulses: in May from the Upper Mississippi and in June from the Missouri River. Just how high the river got varied tremendously from year to year.

In some years, there was barely any flooding at all, while other times, such as in 1811 and 1827, the water got dangerously high. Many residents remembered the rise of 1785, what the French residents knew as *l'anee de grand eau*, or the year of the big flood. It was the yardstick by which they compared all floods, the event that defined a life-changing flood. Until 1844.

FEARING THE WORST

No one saw it coming. The spring began like most springs, with the river waking from its winter slumber in April. The Mississippi overflowed its banks on May 1 and crested two days later just six inches lower than it had the previous spring. It fell for a few days, then began rising again, enough to cause some alarm around town. One of the local newspapers, the *Republican*, reported on May 17: "The waters were coming down upon us from every quarter. The Mississippi is now as high as it has been known for many years, and is still rising. . . . The whole of the American Bottom, from Alton to Kaskaskia, will be, we fear, submerged. The people are deserting their homes in Illinois towns."[2]

That fear was realized. By May 18, water had spread throughout the American Bottom south of St. Louis, flooding fields where corn had just sprouted. Two days later, the Mississippi had crept up the levee at St. Louis and into stores on Front Street, forcing many of them to move their goods to the second floor. On May 21, though, the Mississippi crested at St. Louis. Over the next two weeks, the river steadily retreated into its banks and people in the area breathed easier. They rinsed mud off floors and streets, and riverfront stores moved their products back down to street level. Their sense of relief wouldn't last, though.

Heavy rains pummeled the Midwest beginning in late May. For ten straight days it rained, and by June 8 the Mississippi was on the rise again at St. Louis. Water returned to the fields of the American Bottom, rising a foot or more every day. Residents grew increasingly worried that this was not just another spring flood. Every river and stream was running high. Across the Mississippi from St. Louis, the houses of Illinoistown were slowly disappearing into the muddy water. The Mississippi "presented a grand but awful appearance. Its current was turbid, and, as it rushed along, it emitted that howling fretful volume of sound peculiar to angry waters."[3]

On June 17, the Mississippi surpassed the May crest and buried a marker known as the directrix, a limestone block on Front Street near the Market House that marked the high-water level of the 1827 flood. St. Louisans wouldn't see the stone again for a month. Once again, riverfront stores moved their goods to the second stories of their buildings.

The next day, the steamer *Missouri Mail* brought ominous news. The Missouri had risen seven feet in twenty-four hours at St. Joseph, Missouri, five days earlier and the river had already submerged the bottom lands under six to eight feet of water. The crew had spent a full day rescuing people from the flood. "Sometimes there would be an entire family clinging to the side of a frame house or the roof of a log cabin that was coming down the Missouri at the rate of eight miles an hour," Anthony Brown, who worked as a cabin boy on the steamer *JM White*.[4]

By June 20, the Mississippi had already covered nearly the entire valley from bluff to bluff for thirty miles. It stretched up to nine miles wide and covered the land up to twenty feet deep. Still, it rose an astonishing seventeen inches overnight at St. Louis. Dr. Benjamin Brooks, who lived south of St. Louis near Jonesboro, Illinois, wrote that "Stock, crops, houses and fences were carried away in the raging waters. The people made great efforts to save their stock, and called to their aid ferry and coal boats and all floating craft, but soon they found they could only hope to save a few of their household effects, and the stock was left to its fate and the people fled to the hills."[5]

St. Louis's Mill Creek Valley had become a backwater lake. Front Street was now water street. The river flooded buildings along Battle Row on Laurel Street to the door hatches. At Pine and Front Streets, water reached the top of warehouse door sills. Much of the new Soulard neighborhood was underwater, too. With the city's boat landing buried under several feet of water, steamboats tied up to buildings. The *Lightner* floated up to Front and Morgan Streets, where it tied up to Henry Davis's store. "I remember very well when the White Cloud ran here in June of 1844," Anthony Brown recalled, "and sidled up alongside the stores on the water front, and was loaded from Commercial alley."[6] The water rose so high that steamboats rose to the tops of buildings. Crew and officers stood on the hurricane deck and carved their names in eaves, a temptation that even the great captain J. M. White didn't resist.

FLEEING TO HIGH GROUND

South of St. Louis, the situation was especially dire. Residents of Cahokia evacuated to the bluffs. On June 21, water rushed into the cellar of the Visitation convent and school in Kaskaskia. That night, most of the nuns and students fled to the home of Amede Menard, who lived on higher ground on the Illinois shore. They joined dozens of other Kaskaskians who took refuge in tents.

That same day, an editor for the *Republican* toured much of the flooded bottomlands in a rowboat with several young men "and had a most pleasant time of it. . . . [W]e passed over several streets of Illinoistown, and went to 'Old Pap's House,' a mile and a half from the ferry landing. Thence we rowed through a cornfield, and an oatfield, to the railroad." His breezy account of the boat trip ended with a note of heartbreak: "Everywhere we witnessed the destruction of whole crops, the year's subsistence of the farmer and his family."[7]

The raging Mississippi wasn't exactly the right place for a day's pleasure boating, though. It ran thick with debris: entire trees, haystacks, the carcasses of cattle and pigs, and even the occasional barn or intact house. Witnesses even reported seeing people float by, often desperately hanging onto a piece of driftwood or wall frame. Most of those people probably drowned.

Other flood victims were luckier. Steamboats ran volunteer rescue missions to flooded Illinois communities, often running across cornfields and through woods. Flood refugees, mostly farmers new to the area, crowded into St. Louis, and at least five hundred of them scattered about in warehouses or temporary camps in open fields. The flood washed away their modest possessions and left them wondering how they were going to rebuild. Many wouldn't.

On June 23, the rapid rise of the Mississippi at St. Louis slowed down. It finally crested on June 27 at 41.32 feet, more than four feet above the city's directrix. An old-timer who lived just south of St. Louis in Carondelet calculated that, based on the marks he had carved in a rock, the crest was six inches higher than the 1785 flood.

After five days as refugees at the Menard home, the Visitation Sisters got a lift to St. Louis on the steamboat *Indiana*, loaded with all they could salvage from their building in Kaskaskia. When they reached St. Louis, they saw riverfront warehouses that were filled with water up to seven feet deep, their entrances blocked by steamboats. The Mississippi covered Second and Third Streets, a few blocks removed from the Mississippi, with water deep enough to float a boat.

It wasn't all doom and gloom, though. During the June flood, a renowned actor called Macready performed *Macbeth* in front of packed houses that were "intent on forgetting that the angry waters of the Mississippi were rising higher and higher."[8] Still, the river proved the bigger draw. Much of the actor's audience raced to the riverfront as soon as his show was over to join their fellow St. Louisans, who had crowded into the upper stories of buildings to watch the flood waters pass by.

STARTING OVER

The river slowly fell back into its banks in July, leaving behind deposits of sand and silt that were several feet deep in places. Some agricultural lands were unfit for cultivation for years. Homes in places like Jonesboro and Illinoistown, if they survived, had been pushed off their foundations.

Meanwhile, the Mississippi continued to rage farther south. Cairo, Illinois, at the confluence of the Ohio and Mississippi Rivers, disappeared into the rivers. Few of the plantations along the Lower Mississippi grew cotton or corn that year. The flood of 1844 motivated folks along the Lower Mississippi to speed up construction of levees.

Many of the flood victims moved back to the bottoms after the waters receded, but their lives didn't get easier. Many who started over would give up after severe flooding covered the bottoms four more times in the next seven years.

Strictly in terms of the volume of water flowing past St. Louis, the flood of 1844 was probably equal to the Great Flood of 1993 and may have been bigger. Still, St. Louisans washed down their sidewalks and storefronts, and the city's boom continued unabated. The city's population would double again between 1850 and 1860 (to 161,000). More people moved into the American Bottom to cultivate land. And as the Mississippi rose every spring, folks had a new yardstick to judge the severity of seasonal flooding—the Great Flood of 1844.

The Unappeasable God

The Flood of 1927

With us when you speak of "the river," though there are many, you mean always the same one, the great river, the shifting unappeasable god of the country, feared and loved, the Mississippi.[1]

—WILLIAM ALEXANDER PERCY

Photo 4.1
NOAA

The lower half of the Mississippi River, the part that begins where the Ohio and Mississippi Rivers merge into a single giant stream, has long inspired wonder and fear. This part of the river flows through wide, flat expanses that were once thickly populated with swamps and forests. Americans moved in and leveled the forests and drained the swamps, which exposed a rich layer of soil that proved irresistible to generations of farmers. The river created that rich soil over millennia by spilling over its banks repeatedly and dumping sand and silt collected from the heart of North America. With no mountains or bluffs to constrain the Mississippi, the river zigzagged its way through the land, continually cutting and recutting paths through the pliant soil as it flowed to the sea.

For the people who lived along this dynamic river, life required the ability to adapt to changing land- and waterscapes. But it also came with rewards. The rich alluvial soil, temperate climate, and rivers abundant with wildlife allowed people to thrive for thousands of years.

Ten thousand years ago, Dalton-era people cultivated plants such as persimmon and cattail, hunted deer and waterfowl, and traveled the waterways in canoes they dug out with stone adzes they invented. Five hundred years ago, thousands of descendants of the great city we call Cahokia, who were carrying on Mississippian traditions, flourished in two dozen villages along the Mississippi and Arkansas Rivers.

As Europeans and Americans moved into the region four hundred years ago, they built permanent settlements in low-lying areas, then looked for ways to keep the water out. French settlers started building the first levee in 1717 to protect a small but growing city called New Orleans. Levee construction has never stopped.

The river, though, regularly poked holes in the levees. After the Civil War, the federal government established the Mississippi River Commission, hoping that its engineers would bring more consistency to flood protection. The engineers decided that the best way to prevent flooding—the only strategy they approved of—was to build more levees. They closed off side channels and forced more water into the main stem of the river. They believed that adding more water to the channel would cause the river to scour a deeper bottom that would increase its capacity to carry more water. The levees, though, cut off the river from water-absorbing marshes, swamps, and back channels.

Problems with this approach were apparent early. In 1850, a levee just under eight feet tall was enough to protect Morganza, Louisiana, but by the 1920s subsequent floods had pushed that same levee up to thirty-eight feet tall. The decision to contain the river by building a wall around it would have enormous consequences in 1927.

THE RAINS CAME

The fall and winter of 1926 were wet and wild in middle America. Rivers rose from Nebraska to Indiana and from South Dakota to Oklahoma, washing away crops and killing dozens of people. All that water poured into the big rivers. In the last quarter of 1926, three of North America's biggest rivers—the Ohio, Mississippi, and Missouri—reached heights unprecedented for that time of year. At Vicksburg, October is usually a low-water month, with the river gauge typically hovering around zero. Until 1926, the record height for the Mississippi in October was thirty-one feet. In October 1926, the Mississippi reached forty feet at Vicksburg. All signs pointed to something worse on the horizon.

And worse it got. In mid-December heavy snows blanketed the upper Midwest, while rain pummeled the South: six inches fell at Little Rock in one day, four inches at Memphis. The Mississippi reached flood stage at Cairo, Illinois, on January 1, an ominous way to begin the new year. And the rain just kept falling. The Cumberland River left its banks and swamped Nashville; the Tennessee River flooded Chattanooga. Water rained down all spring, culminating in a Genesis-worthy torrent on Good Friday (April 15) that put the Lower Mississippi Valley over the edge: eight inches at Greenville, Mississippi; ten inches at Cairo, Illinois; and fifteen inches in New Orleans.

All that water eventually flowed into the Mississippi, and the levees forced it up and up. People grew increasingly worried about the integrity of the entire system. On April 16, the Mississippi River poked a hole in a levee near Dorena, Missouri, some thirty miles downriver of Cairo. Water quickly filled 175,000 acres. Three days later, a levee failed near New Madrid, Missouri. The river was winning.

Still, people fought to keep the river contained. Near Greenville, Mississippi, ten thousand men worked night and day to fill and place sandbags on top of the levee near Mounds Landing. Most were Black sharecroppers, men who were not given a choice about helping with the work. Local police patrolled the streets of Greenville every morning looking for Black men to conscript, who didn't get paid for their labor. In mid-April, the effort got a boost when inmates from Parchman Penitentiary arrived to help on the levee. The work was grueling, and the men often worked in chilly rain. The levee would prove to be no match for the Mississippi.

At 12:30 p.m. on April 21, Bill Jones, part of the crew placing sandbags near Mounds Landing, said the levee "felt like jelly. . . . You could feel it shaking."[2] The river overpowered the earthen structure and broke open a hole that sent a one-hundred-foot-tall wall of water pouring through the gap. Men died. We don't know how many, but dozens of Black men had been piling sandbags near the breach just before the levee's collapse. Many—feeling the trembling levee and seeing water creeping over its top—had initially refused to wade into the endangered area, but their White supervisors threatened to shoot them if they didn't keep working.

The breach eventually widened to three-quarters of a mile long. The force of the water scoured a hole at the spot of the break, forming a lake that still exists today. Water raced across the flat delta landscape. Cora Lee Campbell described the scene as water crept: "And so I run and run and run and when I got home the bells was ringing, the whistles was blowing, and, oh it was a terrible time."[3] She and her family made it to the levee, but many weren't as lucky.

Further south the fight continued. Twenty thousand men worked on the levees between Baton Rouge and New Orleans. Still, from mid-April to the end of May, the Mississippi blew through levee after levee, punching nearly 150 holes in total and reclaiming 27,000 square miles of its floodplain as its waters rolled across the land and covered the land up to thirty feet deep. At its peak, up to three million cubic feet per second of water flowed down the Mississippi just below the mouth of Arkansas River, more than triple its normal flow. And still the Mississippi refused to slip away quietly. For five months, the river stayed high and mighty, causing death and destruction in epic proportions.

Human Tragedies

The levee breaks caught many people unprepared. The authorities had been downplaying the risks of levee failures, so when the river broke through, the floodwaters trapped tens of thousands of people. E. M. Barry was among those who had to make an unplanned escape. "[T]he water was leaping, it looked like, in rapids thirty feet high. And right in front of the break was the old Moore plantation house, a big mule barn, and two big, enormous trees. And when we came back by there [a few hours later] everything was gone."[4]

Minnie Murphy was near Tallulah, Louisiana, when the levee broke on May 3: "Automobiles tore through the streets; trucks thundered by piled high with trunks, furniture, chicken coops, band-boxes, pets, people . . . all headed for the railroad, where passenger coaches, box cars, cattle cars, flats, and locomotives had been stationed for weeks, steam up, ready to rush to a place of safety."[5]

Fred Chaney, who had taken shelter in a boxcar, remembered when the water approached. "At nine o'clock we could hear the rustle of waters in the wood a mile North [sic] of our box car haven. It sounded not unlike the rising rush of the first gust of wind before an oncoming storm and a shiver shot up and down my spine as the rustling noise grew louder and its true significance plumbed the depths of my mind."[6]

After the Mounds Landing levee break near Greenville, the Yazoo Basin flooded over some five thousand square miles, the water rolling across fourteen miles a day "in the form of a tan colored wall seven foot high, and with a roar as of a mighty wind," Louise Cowan recalled.[7] All that water eventually reentered the Mississippi near Vicksburg, which wasn't good news for folks on the other side of the river. The force of the combined flow punched a hole in the levee on the opposite bank, flooding communities in Louisiana.

Herman Caillouet, who lived near Greenville and worked for the Army Corps of Engineers, made multiple trips in his boat to rescue people in the area, saving at least 150. Not every trip was a success, though.

He recalled one trip where he saw a family clinging to a house when the building suddenly broke up: "I searched the boards and things . . . and never saw a soul come up, not a soul. When the house started breaking up and falling, you see, they couldn't come out from under. . . . Seven of them . . . I went round and round, did not see a hand."[8]

Boats of all sizes searched for and rescued people. They floated across cotton fields and past telephone wires and steered around field posts that could puncture a hole in the hull. Planes flew over the area searching for survivors. In northeast Louisiana, American Legion chapters organized rescues. They even bought a Ford truck and converted it to run on rails, then used it to move supplies and mail to people in refugee camps.

Some refugees found temporary housing in railroad boxcars, where they cooked with woodstoves and slept on pallets. Others were lucky enough to find temporary housing with friends or relatives in unflooded areas. Most, though, had to move into emergency housing in refugee camps.

The Red Cross set up 154 camps throughout the Lower Mississippi, their entire operation funded by private donations—there were no federal relief programs in 1927. They raised over $17 million to help flood victims, enough to provide emergency housing for 325,000 people—69 percent of whom were Black. One camp alone—at Forrest City, Arkansas—housed 15,000 refugees. At Greenville, 13,000 refugees packed into tight quarters atop an eight-mile section of the levee, the only high ground for miles around. White people could leave the camps as they wished, but Black people could only leave if they had a pass. The National Guard patrolled the camps to enforce their confinement. Plantation owners were afraid that the Black sharecroppers would move away and few would remain to work the cotton fields.

The loss of life and damage to property was staggering. The Red Cross estimated that 254 people died in the flood, but the real number was undoubtedly much higher. When the river swamped levees, torrents of water ripped through the bottoms, uprooting trees, annihilating houses and barns, and sweeping people away. Flooding displaced over 600,000 people; 350,000 refugees lived in tents for months. In Washington

County, Mississippi, alone, nearly the entire population—185,000 people—had to leave their homes.

Disasters can bring out the best and the worst in people, and the 1927 flood was no exception. The Red Cross operated a relief operation on a scale that was unprecedented, but fraud, theft, and abuse tainted its good intentions, especially at Greenville. Field directors kept donated supplies for their personal use. County-level offices broke national policy by giving supplies directly to plantation owners (at no charge), but many plantations then made their sharecroppers pay for those supplies. White refugees were better off almost everywhere. Black men in refugee camps had to work to get food; White men did not. Black refugees slept on the ground and ate without utensils. White refugees slept on cots and ate with forks and knives.

Downriver at New Orleans, city leaders publicly downplayed the flood's threats, even as they made plans to protect their city at all costs. They pushed through a plan to blow a hole in a downstream levee to release pressure on levees at New Orleans. State and federal officials reluctantly agreed after city leaders pledged financial support to the people they were about to displace. Residents of St. Bernard and Plaquemines Parishes evacuated, many to the homes of family members, and on April 29, the first blasts of dynamite exploded on the levee at Caernarvon. People who didn't have family or friends nearby stayed in New Orleans at the International Trade Exchange warehouse, segregated by race.

ANIMAL TRAGEDIES

When the levees broke, there wasn't much time for folks to gather up their families and go, much less figure out what to do with their animals. Mules, cows, pigs, horses, dogs, cats—all had to be left behind. Some animals found their way to a levee or hill, but many drowned. There were so many panicked animals that rescuers often carried guns to keep them at bay. One boat owner had to shoot a cow that was trying to climb in his boat.

The Red Cross estimated that 165,298 farm animals died in the flood: 26,451 cows; 127,983 pigs; 1,559 sheep and goats; and 9,305 mules and horses. In addition, over a million chickens died. Perhaps half of all farm animals in the area died in the flood, clogging the flood waters with their bloated carcasses.

Eyewitness Jess Pollard recalled: "Water was just rolling in, like you see the waves down in Gulfport. They were high—you saw horses and cows floating. If you were standing on the levee, you could see people floating who had drowned. It was a sight you never forget."[9]

Wildlife wasn't as bad off. Many animals are good swimmers. They got themselves to dry places where they waited until the water receded. Snakes slithered on the water, piling up wherever they could find dry land. People saw predator and prey resting next to each other in some places and looking quite comfortable about it. River historian Lyle Saxon was on a Coast Guard boat during the 1927 flood when they approached an ancient mound built by American Indians. He recalled:

Extending but two or three feet above the surface of the rushing water, the mound rose—a wooded island not more than twenty-five feet long—crowded with animals. There were cows and mules, standing near the edge, looking out toward the rescue boats. Chickens were at the water's edge. 'Coons and opossums filled the trees, and knotted snakes hung from the branches in close proximity to the smaller animals. Crouched upon the ground were wildcats, their tails lashing, their teeth bared. But they made no move to attack the other animals around them, nor did they attempt to escape when the rescue boat came near. They held their ground because they could retreat no further, terrified equally of man and of the water. A black and white cat—some child's pet—stood between the forepaws of an antlered buck. A doe and two spotted fawns cowered behind the larger deer. The grass seemed alive with field mice and wood rats, and there were small black and white animals unfamiliar to me and to the sailors in the boat with me. . . . Our boat was small; there was no way to save any of them. The domestic animals came close to the water, as though asking for help. The wild animals did not move, but stood watching us with wide eyes. Our boat drifted with the current—farther, farther away. . . . The animals were left to their fate.[10]

WANDERING AND HOMELESS

In some places, the Mississippi River stayed flooded for as long as 153 consecutive days. As the water receded, it left behind silt and debris that baked dry in the southern heat and fouled the air with the smells of rotting detritus and flesh. As the land dried out, some farmers got seeds in the ground, only to watch them wash away when the river rose again in June.

Mostly, though, the water took a long time to recede. Well into July, one and a half million acres of land remained flooded. It wasn't until the middle of August that the river would fully recede. Still, life remained hard. Mosquitoes thrived, and cases of malaria spiked. Typhoid fever also spread through the affected areas. Pellagra, a potentially fatal vitamin deficiency, was a common problem because the refugee diet was heavy with corn, molasses, and salt pork, foods that lacked niacin.

Those who returned to rebuild faced a long and difficult cleanup. If your house survived, it had been sitting in water for weeks. Wood doors expanded and sealed shut, forcing many homeowners to break a window to get inside. Interior walls and plaster became petri dishes for mold and bacteria. High water contaminated wells and ruined wiring. Layers of sand and silt covered many fields and had to be removed before crops could be planted again. In other places, the river carved new channels through farm fields.

White officials tried to conscript Black workers again for the cleanup, but they ran into strong resistance. The Black population of the Delta had had enough. While still powerless in most ways, they could at least exercise the choice to leave. Many did.

During the disaster, federal officials repeatedly rejected requests for direct aid to flood victims. Providing relief after a disaster just wasn't seen as a federal responsibility. Instead, the Red Cross coordinated relief efforts with local officials and raised money from private donors to make it work. After relief efforts ended, the federal government even tried to get the Red Cross to pay for the blankets they had loaned to the agency and never returned.

As the region shifted into recovery mode, White authorities in Mississippi wanted to cut food rations in half to encourage Black sharecroppers to get back in the fields and work. In Tennessee, Governor Austin Peay even turned down Red Cross offers to help folks rebuild because he believed people should provide for themselves and not rely on outside help. Once the immediate crisis was over, government officials expected plantations to take care of their own sharecroppers, although the Red Cross provided limited help to some folks who did not have ties to a specific plantation.

Downriver of New Orleans, in the parishes that had been flooded intentionally, residents lost their homes and livelihoods. Total claims from St. Bernard and Plaquemines Parishes reached $35 million, but the board overseeing settlements only approved about a third of them for consideration. The banks and money people ultimately agreed to pay $3.9 million to the people in the intentionally flooded areas, but they deducted nearly a million dollars of that total for the cost of feeding and housing refugees. They also awarded six large companies $2.1 million, which left $800,000 for the remaining 2,809 other claimants to divide up, an average of just $284 each to replace all they had sacrificed to save New Orleans.

WASHED AWAY

The 1927 flood triggered seismic changes in American culture and the landscape of the Mississippi Valley. Many African Americans had migrated out of the South after the Civil War and more had left around World War I, fed up with poll taxes and literacy tests, with laws that prohibited them from shopping their labor to competing farms, with the constant threat of violence against them, and with the lack of opportunity to build a better life.

The 1927 flood, though, inspired an exodus on a new scale. Entire communities left rural sharecropping for good in search of a better life in the cities of the North and Midwest—places like Chicago, St. Louis, Detroit, and Milwaukee. It wasn't easy to get out. Landlords sometimes placed armed guards at train stations to prevent their workers from leaving. Many African Americans had to sneak out of their homes at night and walk several miles to find a train station that was beyond the reach of the plantation.

Washington County, Mississippi, alone—Greenville's county—lost half of its Black residents after the 1927 flood. With fewer people available for manual labor, southern farmers turned to heavy equipment such as tractors and cotton harvesters. As they did, many farms merged into bigger farms, and dramatically reduced the amount of labor they needed. More people moved away.

The disaster also triggered fundamental changes in the role of the federal government in the United States. The most immediate change was that the US government assumed full responsibility for the job of trying to tame the Mississippi River. In 1928, Congress passed the Flood Control Act, which gave the Army Corps of Engineers the authority to build flood control measures along the Mississippi River from Cairo, Illinois, to the Gulf of Mexico. The act also made the federal government responsible for paying for most of that ambitious work. Congress also directed the Corps to move beyond its levees-only policy and develop floodways and outlet channels. The work continues to this day, one of the largest flood control projects ever attempted.

While the federal government focused its immediate attention on remaking the Lower Mississippi, the rest of the river would come under increasing federal responsibility, too. In 1930, Congress authorized the Corps to build and maintain a nine-foot channel for shipping on the Upper Mississippi River. That work would require the construction of a series of locks and dams from St. Paul, Minnesota, to St. Louis. While the most immediate reasons for the upriver construction were to provide a more reliable shipping channel and to create jobs during the Great Depression, the desire to control the Mississippi after the 1927 flood almost certainly played a role, too.

The Ducks Came and Men Died

The Armistice Day Blizzard

WEATHER FORECASTING IS AN INEXACT SCIENCE. I DON'T NEED TO TELL you that. Still, forecasting has improved much more in the past few decades than most of us appreciate. Just ask the people who lived through the tragic Armistice Day blizzard in 1940.

Until 1934, professionals at the Weather Bureau checked their gauges and instruments twice a day, typically at eight in the morning and again twelve hours later. The weather experts then built forecasts, very general forecasts, based on those observations, again twice a day. They didn't have satellite images or computer models to work with and couldn't send weather alerts as text messages. They recorded their observations in notebooks and distributed the forecasts via telegraph.

In 1934, the Weather Bureau started compiling data on punch cards, and a few years later they began distributing revised forecasts five times a day. Still, there wasn't much of a sense of urgency about it. In 1940, the Weather Bureau offices stayed open no more than fifteen hours a day, which is why the Weather Bureau offices were closed when the Armistice Day blizzard of 1940 blew up.

Because weather forecasting was so limited, few people in the Midwest paid attention when steady forty-five mile an hour winds roared through the Pacific Northwest and rocked the Tacoma Narrows bridge until it collapsed. Three days later, the storm moved over the Rocky Mountains, where it bumped into another front and, beginning around 6:30 in the evening, intensified like few land-based storms ever do. In the next twenty-four hours, the air pressure plummeted twenty-nine millibars, and the storm shifted north and raced across the continent at thirty-five miles per hour. Weather experts later labeled this storm an "extratropical cyclone."[1]

As the storm system spun around, winds on its eastern boundary pulled warm air from the Gulf of Mexico up the Mississippi Valley, while winds on its western side dragged in bitter cold from the Arctic. The temperature contrasts were stark. On the morning of November 11, hunters along the Mississippi left their houses wearing light jackets, while blizzards pummeled South Dakota.

Decoyed

November 11, 1940, started as a day full of promise. In the United States, many businesses and schools were closed for the Armistice Day observance, the holiday that marked the end of World War I. Even as Americans marked the end of one war, Adolph Hitler had conquered Poland and France and was moving against England. Mussolini was hell-bent on occupying Greece.

While many Americans feared another world war, along the Upper Mississippi, people were just trying to enjoy the last few days of nice weather before winter settled in. Some people took advantage of the holiday to go shopping. Others were eager to salvage something from what had been a disappointing hunting season.

The fall of 1940 had been unusually mild, and because of that, the waterfowl hadn't yet migrated south. Frustrated hunters wondered when they'd finally get the chance to get out and shoot some ducks. November 11 looked like it would be their lucky day. In the morning, temperatures reached upwards of sixty degrees along the Upper Mississippi River, with the Weather Bureau predicting a cooler weather and snow flurries later in the day.

Light rain fell in the morning, then the weather rapidly deteriorated. A tornado touched down a mile west of Davenport, Iowa. Some places got soaked with two to three inches of rain. The winds picked up.

Still, the hunting was great. The best many hunters had ever seen, in fact. As the winds grew stronger, birds—thousands of them—flew just a few feet above the water. "Hundreds of mallards would come in, flying against the wind. They could hardly move, just going up and down and would land within a few feet of me, completely exhausted and wouldn't get up," Raymond Rice remembered.[2] Easy pickings. Harold Hettifk recalled, "Shooting got good. Hunters were going for their limits, which were big limits in those days."[3] Many hunters couldn't remember a time when they'd seen so many birds.

Twelve-year-old Bill Hawes was hunting with his father and a friend near Winona, Minnesota. "About noon it looked like the weather was clearing with some blue sky showing. The ducks were flocking into our decoys now and the shooting was terrific."[4]

Hunters, lost in the moment, didn't notice how much the winds were picking up. It would be a fatal mistake for many.

THE WINDS TURN

Temperatures plummeted, and rain turned to sleet, then snow. Heavy snow fell in parts of western Minnesota and Iowa. Visibility dropped. Wind gusts stirred up massive waves in the river. The sky turned an eerie orange. Bill Hawes remembered clearly when the fun ended: "The wind came out of the northwest and the temperature dropped like a stone. A flock of bluebills came over me and I found my gun was frozen up!"[5]

The shallow skiffs the hunters used to navigate the river were no match for the wind and waves. The window of opportunity to get off the river safely was quickly closing.

"All of a sudden, dad said, 'Grab the decoys—we're getting out of here,'" Jack Meggers recalled. "But we were throwing an awful lot of ammunition into the air, and none of us wanted to quit. The sky was just full of ducks. Finally dad said, 'Grab the decoys now or we're leaving without them.' That's when we began to see how bad it was getting." Visibility had dropped to just a few feet and was getting worse as the snow fell heavier. "By the time we finally made it to the shoreline, you couldn't even see the shoreline," he said.[6]

Hawes and his father also caught a break. "Fortunately we were going exactly with the wind," he wrote. "I used an oar as a rudder and merely steered the boat the half-mile to our landing. By the time we got there it was dark and only 2pm!" Even though they made it safely back to shore, Hawes still suffered frostbite on his face and hands.

Meggers and Hawes were among the lucky ones. Duck hunters by the hundreds lost their gear and boats as winds up to eighty miles an hour raced across the river and down shallow backwater channels. Waves rose as high as fifteen feet. Many hunters scrambled to create makeshift shelters to stay alive.

In the Twin Cities, ice accumulated before the snow fell. Traveling around town became virtually impossible. Cars stalled and people abandoned them in the street. Streetcars and buses crept from stop to stop, sometimes taking an hour to cover a single block. "Cars were lined up for blocks and the only time we moved [on the streetcar] at all was when motormen from cars behind came up with switch rods and scraped the ice from the rails,"[7] Hamilton Heald remembered. The slow pace of travel gave Heald time to hop off the streetcar to call home and to buy sandwiches. Heald finally walked into his house at six in the morning, over thirteen hours after leaving downtown Minneapolis.

Five-year-old Barbara McKernan and her six-year-old brother had been visiting an uncle and aunt in south Minneapolis when they set out with their uncle to get home to St. Paul. His car got stuck in snow, so they huddled in a doorway on Lake Street as they waited for a streetcar to arrive. When one finally showed up, people crowded shoulder to shoulder. Still, the streetcar crept forward. "I wonder now how it was possible," McKernan said. "How could it have kept on going as far as it did; the tracks must have been covered over and over with blowing snow." Their uncle gripped their hands. When they reached their stop in St. Paul, they huddled close together and sang as they walked the last mile to their home. "I remember Uncle buttoning us up as best he could and holding our hands, one kid on each side . . . the other hand in our pocket."[8] Their uncle, George Guise, got them safely home, then turned around and went back to his job in Minneapolis. He was the city desk editor for the *Minneapolis Tribune*.

Skipping work wasn't an option for most people, including Bob Enerson. "The job was very important to me because we were just pulling out of the depression and during it I had been laid off three or four times from the Honeywell factory,"[9] he said. Gail Lofdahl's father, Clifford, worked at Honeywell in downtown Minneapolis. He stayed for his entire shift, even as visibility neared zero. "When I asked him if he'd left work early," she wrote, "he said that the economy was still emerging from the Depression, and workers just didn't leave work early for a trivial reason like a blizzard!"[10]

Forty-six-year-old Ida Rehbein left home when the weather was still decent, so she didn't see a need to layer up. As she walked from her home to her job in downtown St. Paul, the wind turned bitterly cold and battered her relentlessly. An alert storekeeper saw her staggering down the street and pulled her inside, which probably saved her life.

The storm stranded thousands of people in the Twin Cities. The John W. Thomas & Company department store booked several rooms at the Radisson Hotel for its employees. It also set up overnight shelter on two of the store's floors to house people stranded by the storm.

Around town, people took shelter wherever they could. The lobby of the Radisson Hotel was "Complete chaos," Olive Olsen Early remembered. "Everything available on which someone could sit or lean was in use. I had never been involved in such confusion."[11] The Scott Motor Company took in twenty people stranded by the storm, including a family with four children. The unexpected guests slept on chairs and benches, and even inside a couple of cars. A nearby restaurant provided food for them. They would all be in for a long night.

HELL FREEZES OVER

The storm brought life to a standstill. In Minneapolis, 175 streetcars went out of service. The streetcar company declared it "had work for any man able to swing a pick and shovel."[12] They had pressed every available plow into service to clear streetcar tracks, but it wasn't enough. Cars had pushed and compacted slush, so the tracks had to be cleared by hand.

Nearly half of the long-distance phone lines out of Minneapolis were down, and power went out around town. Repair crews had to fight through tremendous snowdrifts and around abandoned cars to reach downed lines. Newspapers went undelivered. Nearly every road in the state was impassable, and plows couldn't get out to clear them until visibility improved. Even the post office would have to skip delivery for a couple of days in some places because mail carriers couldn't get through.

The Milwaukee railroad's eastbound Olympian train that connected Seattle with Chicago got stuck just east of Granite Falls, Minnesota, when it ran into a massive, quarter-mile-long snowdrift. Passengers watched as the wind blew snow up toward the top of the railcars they sat in. They spent the night stuck on board, then transferred to another train on Tuesday to continue their journey.

The storm didn't paralyze everyone, though. Hormel's team of intrepid marketers continued undeterred. "Many of you people were greatly surprised to find Spam Men and Girls trudging around in the blustering snowstorm," an advertisement read. Throughout the night, they approached people at random and asked if they had a Spam key (a can opener) and a container or two of the popular canned meat. The lucky folks who said yes got a crisp new two-dollar bill, including Mrs. Agnes Fewel, who said "I use Spam for sandwiches for my two sons—I like it creamed, and also in salads."[13]

No one came by to help the hunters stranded along the Mississippi River, though, at least not during the night. The storm trapped hundreds on islands and backwater channels. Some huddled under overturned boats for shelter, while others crawled next to piles of driftwood or downed trees. They burned what they could to stay warm, including pieces of their shattered boats. Survival depended on staying dry. "Anyone who went out that day, fell in the water or got wet somehow, they were done," recalled Oscar Gerth, who was twenty-four years old at the time of the blizzard.[14]

Gunner Miller had been hunting near Winona when the storm blew in. He and three buddies started a fire "with a shotgun blast into gasoine [sic] on wood"[15] and stayed warm by burning two dozen duck decoys they had chopped up. They were afraid to walk more than a few steps from the makeshift camp for fear of getting lost in the blinding snow. In the morning, they found two men frozen to death under a boat just sixty feet away.

The storm's reach extended well beyond the Mississippi Valley. On the eastern shore of Lake Michigan, high winds sank three ships: the

SS *Anna C. Minch*, the SS *Novadoc*, and the SS *William B. Davock*. Fifty-eight people died.

SEARCH AND RESCUE

As the snow stopped falling and the winds slowly died down, bitter cold settled in. In the Twin Cities, temperatures fell into the single digits, which complicated efforts to reopen streets and businesses. Twelve street-cars got stuck on Hennepin Avenue, neatly lined up in a row. Abandoned cars littered city streets, making life difficult for plow drivers trying to clear them. A few buildings burned to the ground when snowdrifts blocked the paths of fire trucks. Cars couldn't start because the wind had blown snow under the hoods and frozen hoses and engines. People looking for missing family members overwhelmed police, hospitals, and morgues with phone calls.

Estelle Smith was about to give birth but couldn't get to a hospital on her own. Two police officers formed a makeshift chair by clasping their hands together, then carried her from her house to a police car, a grueling two-block walk in the middle of the night through deep snow. The trip from her house to the hospital took ninety-five minutes. Less than half an hour after arriving, she welcomed a baby daughter into the world.

Some good news filtered through with the bad. The Great Northern Railroad's Empire Builder train finally made it to Minneapolis, just twenty-seven hours behind schedule. The train had gotten stuck about fourteen miles east of Willmar, Minnesota, after hitting a big snowdrift. Efforts to clear the tracks were complicated by strong winds that just blew snow right back onto the tracks after it had been removed. Passengers passed the time by playing cards, reading, and chatting.

Residents of small towns throughout the region continued to shelter and feed stranded people. Some farm families even took in dozens of school children after their buses had run off the road. One farm family sheltered twenty school kids for three days.

As the sun rose along the Mississippi River, rescue teams began frantic efforts to locate people stranded by the storm. One team found and rescued seventeen men who had survived the night. Game wardens rescued dozens of hunters near Winona.

Abe Kuhns, a bachelor farmer on Prairie Island (near Red Wing, Minnesota) and a hulking six-foot-four-feet tall, got word that some hunters were stranded on an island near his home. He pushed off in his rowboat with a kerosene lamp and quickly discoveredhe had to lie down as he rowed to keep the boat from capsizing. He found four stranded hunters, and got each one back to safety, even though he could only carry one at a time in his boat.

When T. J. Sasser and a hunting buddy realized how much the winds had kicked up, they loaded up their rowboat and pushed off. "We knew our only chance was to ride with the waves downstream and edge to the Minnesota shore," he said. "Within two minutes my mittens had frozen to the oars. We were both sheathed in sleet. I was completely blinded by the storm, and followed Carl's directions, desperately trying to keep the boat from swinging broadside to the waves."

They got within a hundred feet of the shore when a wind gust ripped the oars from Sasser's hands and swamped the boat. "Right then the miracle occurred. What looked like a mountain of water literally hurled us at the shore, and as the boat went down we were able to stumble in through breast-deep water."[16] Sasser and his friend made it to a farmhouse, where they thawed out.

Harold Hettrick found an inventive way to get to safety. He tied all his gear inside his boat, then flipped it over and "held on underneath [in] this air pocket and waded out to deeper water toward shore where the wind picked the boat up and him and moved him to shore." It worked. The winds blew him to shore, where people grabbed the boat as it floated near them. They got quite a shock when they flipped the boat over and found a man underneath. "He was literally a frozen ice stick," one of his rescuers recalled. "We couldn't bend him to walk because his clothes were stiff."[17] They got him to a nearby house, where he warmed up next to the stove. Not every effort worked out so well, though.

Rescuers spotted thirty-eight-year-old Herbert Junneman, a barber from Wabasha, Minnesota, hanging on to the sides of a boat that had overturned. Before they could reach him, though, his strength gave out, and he slipped under the water and drowned.

Another team went in search of two missing St. Paul residents, Carl Iverson and Melville Roberts, who had been hunting on the Mississippi near Red Wing. They weren't successful, but a local farmer, Theodore Samuelson, found them a short time later. Iverson was already dead and Roberts was so close to death that he asked to stay where he was. "I might as well die where I am," Roberts told Samuelson. Roberts died shortly after that.[18]

Not far away from where Jack Meggers had been hunting, a father and his two sons got stranded on an island. The oldest son, an athlete, told his younger brother to jump up and down to stay warm. Every time the younger brother stopped jumping, the older brother punched him. This helped the younger brother stay motivated to keep jumping through the night. When rescuers found them the next day, the younger brother's legs "were frozen hard as wood below both knees." He lost both legs, but he survived. His father and older brother didn't make it through the night, however.[19]

Winonians Herman Pagel and Fred Nytes had probably taken a similar approach to surviving, although it hadn't been enough to save them. When rescuers found the bodies, their "hands were bleeding and their faces black and blue." Bodies of many of the victims were stored temporarily in Winona's bus garage. Most were frozen so solid that authorities had to wait for the bodies to thaw before they could search their pockets for identification.

Rescue teams used every available method to search the area. Pilot Max Conrad flew his Piper Cub over the Mississippi River near Winona. His plane wasn't designed to run in high winds, so just getting it out of a hangar and into the air on November 12 "took ten people, five hanging on each wing, to hold the plane down before the wind caught it and it took off, literally blown backwards."[20] The wind speeds were still dangerously high. The plane plodded along at just twenty to thirty miles per hour when it flew into a headwind. With a tailwind, though, the plane—designed to max out at seventy-five miles per hour—topped out at 130.

When Conrad spotted a stranded hunter, he circled over them to guide rescue teams. Sometimes he'd drop a bucket with supplies that included tins of food, matches, and whiskey. Other times, he'd fly low and signal the stranded men to follow him, then he'd lead them to a spot where rescue teams could get to them. He flew from sunrise to ten at night on the first day after the blizzard, then got up the next morning and did it again.

During one flight on that first day, he passed over an area where he spotted a man who was standing in icy water up to his waist. The man waved, then fell over. "I flew back again," Conrad recounted, "real low, and this time I saw him plainly in the ice, and right behind him a boat, under the ice, and next to it a body. Then when I was over him, I saw another body, and when I reached the willows, there was another man hanging onto the lower branches of one of them."[21]

Conrad had spotted Carl Tarras, his sons, Gerald and Raymond, and Bill Wernecke. Seventeen-year-old Gerald was the one who had waved at Conrad's plane. He was the only one in that group who survived. Later, he recounted what the group had done to try to stay alive. "He [Wernecke] was cold. We boxed each other to keep warm. Bill died. I was holding him. He went 'O-h-h-h . . . and he was gone."[22] After Wernecke died, the three survivors waded through a patch of willows, which is where they were when Conrad spotted them. Journalist Gordon MacQuarrie talked with Tarras while he was recovering in the hospital. "He has not yet come to a full realization of what has happened," MacQuarrie wrote, "for grief is sometimes far in the wake of catastrophe."[23]

Conrad's efforts were heroic and foreshadowed what became a stellar career as a pilot. He would later set multiple speed and distance records, including an around-the-world flight in 1961 that was then the fastest ever completed. Winona named their airport for him.

Conrad wasn't the only person who responded heroically to the monster storm. People throughout the Midwest responded with remarkable ingenuity, generosity, and persistence. Rural residents sheltered strangers. Thousands of people helped dig out cars and trains. And when the work still needed to get done, city residents "straggled to work on the few streetcars and buses that were operating, while others hiked, drove or arrived in the loop on skis."[24]

"It takes an old-fashioned blizzard to bring out the unbeatable spirit of Minnesotans," one newspaper observed. "Total strangers joined forces to share the last available rooms. An oldster in an expensive fur coat rejoiced that he'd found a cot in a Turkish bath. Office girls sat up all night in crowded hotel lobbies. All without one word of complaint!"[25]

The Aftermath

The storm remains one of the most disruptive in the history of the Upper Mississippi Valley. The storm buried some places under as much as twenty-two inches of snow. In the Twin Cities, the wind blew snow into drifts that averaged ten feet high but got as tall as twenty-six feet.

Air pressure fell to levels more typical of a hurricane than a Midwestern storm. Weather Bureau spokesperson William M. Labovich noted that the storm's aftermath wasn't all bad, as the region needed the moisture after a dry fall. Labovich was also directly affected by the storm. The storm closed all the roads near his house, so he had to walk three miles to get to work.

Gradually, the region's transportation system got back up and running. Railroad and airplane services came back first. Local buses and streetcars gradually resumed service. Reopening Minnesota's 11,350 miles of roads took longer. The state employed over 500 plows and 4,000 "blizzard busters"[26] (the plow drivers plus thousands of men with shovels), many of whom worked twenty-six hours without a break. Within forty-eight hours, they had all of those roads open, although some were just a single lane wide. The highway clearing effort cost the state an estimated $260,000 (nearly $5 million today).

The storm killed between 150 and 200 people. Dozens of duck hunters died, and hundreds more suffered frostbite. Livestock were also hit hard. The storm killed a million turkeys just three weeks before the Thanksgiving holiday. The turkeys were unlucky. Their feathers became waterlogged from the heavy rain that fell at the front end of the storm. When temperatures plummeted, they froze. "Many birds I saw were so packed with ice they were as big around as barrels," observed William A. Billings, professor at the University of Minnesota and an expert in the turkey economy.[27]

Pheasants also suffered high mortality rates, although there was a sliver of good news there, too. Wayne Miller's neighbors collected frozen pheasants they had found near their homes in Emmet County, Iowa. Miller stacked the pheasants in the hayloft of the family barn. It turned out that most of the pheasants were not, in fact, dead. As their bodies warmed, they flew around inside the barn, much to the surprise of Miller. "It was quite a sight when all those pheasants flew out of the barn," he said.[28]

The Armistice Day blizzard brought an end to Iowa's apple industry. Farmers replaced fields of neatly planted rows of Red Delicious and Jonathan with corn and soybeans. The big storm also permanently changed weather forecasting. Before the storm, residents of the Upper Mississippi Valley got their forecasts from the Weather Bureau's Chicago office, which closed at night. After the storm, the Chicago office remained staffed twenty-four hours a day and local meteorologists in the Twin Cities could issue forecasts.

One big thing didn't change, though: the reality that we judge the severity of storms primarily in terms of how they affect us. "There is nothing to indicate that the weather gets any worse, or any better, by and large, from century to century," wrote the editorial board of the *Minneapolis Star Journal*. "The fact is that we judge blizzard and flood and hurricane not by their ferocity, but by the extent to which man gets in their way and is caught unprepared to cope with them."[29]

Few people were prepared for a storm as great as the Armistice Day blizzard in 1940, but, given the advances in modern weather forecasting, no such storm would likely sneak up on us today.

The Worst-Case Scenario

The Flood of 1965

FOLKS ALONG THE LOWER MISSISSIPPI RECKONED WITH THE POWER OF the river in 1927. The people who lived along the Upper Mississippi faced a similar crisis in 1965. While there was no major flooding along the Mississippi's first three hundred miles, by mid-April, the Mississippi would essentially be in major flood stage from Fort Ripley, Minnesota, to Hannibal, Missouri, a distance of over 650 miles.

The Mississippi River begins as a modest stream that meanders its way for 450 miles through forests and plains flattened over thousands of years by continental glaciers. At Minneapolis, the river flows through a narrow gorge before entering a deep and dramatic valley defined by tall limestone-faced bluffs. From Hastings, Minnesota, to Cape Girardeau, Missouri, those bluffs confine the river to a floodplain that ranges from one to eight miles wide. When the Upper Mississippi overtops its channel, its waters just can't go that far. It can still inflict plenty of damage when it floods, though.

In 1965, the Upper Mississippi Basin experienced a perfect convergence of natural forces that made history: a rapid melt of thick snow cover, heavier than normal rain, and frozen ground. When all three happened at the same time, the Mississippi rose higher than it ever had in recorded history and, for many communities, higher than it has since.

After an unusually wet September in 1964, the ground was deeply saturated and remained so through the fall. Nature played a trick on people in the upper Midwest in November by blanketing them with uncharacteristic warmth early in the month, then smacking them down with a nasty cold wave a couple of weeks later. Dubuque, Iowa, for example, recorded a high temperature of seventy degrees on November 11, but shivered through a low of two degrees below zero just three weeks later. Many cities in the upper Midwest set record low temperatures in November, and the bitterly cold air kept people bundled up through February.

The first hints of trouble arrived with a warm-up in late February, which melted some snow but not the ground. When two inches of rain fell in early March across parts of southern Minnesota, the Cedar, Zumbro, and Root Rivers—whose waters all flow to the Mississippi—left their banks.

The weather turned cold again, then a massive blizzard in mid-March dumped up to eighteen inches of snow on the northern Great Plains. The snow cover at St. Cloud piled three feet high in March, so high that drivers tied brightly colored pennants to their antennae, a signal that rose above the snowbanks to alert other drivers to their presence.

St. Cloud may have experienced more extreme weather than other communities, but March was wet and cold in many places. Minneapolis was warm enough for rain in early March, but residents still had to dig out from under thirty-seven inches of snow during the month.

Further south, major storms piled up snow in Iowa in early March and again in mid-March. Des Moines, Iowa, recorded the second-coldest March on record. Lake Pepin—the widening of the Mississippi River just south of St. Paul—was a giant sheet of ice that stretched three miles wide, twenty miles long, and up to three feet thick. Because of the late, extreme cold, many smaller streams totally froze over by the end of the month.

In late March, temperatures warmed quickly, and often remained above freezing overnight. Heavy rains fell in the first week of April, quickly melting much of the snowpack. With the ground still frozen, the water ran unabated into the rivers. Smaller rivers rose first.

As the ice cover broke up, chunks of ice clustered together into jams that blocked rivers and made water overflow its banks. In a short time, half of the Crow River watershed (west of Minneapolis) flooded. The

Rum, Sauk, Elk, Minnesota, and St. Croix Rivers also spilled out of their banks before merging with the Mississippi.

In northern Minnesota, eight county roads washed out around Aitkin. At Brainerd, the city hastily erected a temporary six-foot-tall dike to protect a water pumping station and an electric substation. An ice jam formed around a Mississippi River bridge at St. Cloud, flooding areas north of downtown with five to six feet of water. At Elk River, the Mississippi cut across a horseshoe bend, flooding twenty-six houses. Water poured over US Highway 10, so snowplows broke up ice that piled up on the roadway.

Some good news came from the small community of Dayton, where its 450 residents successfully fought back high water from the Mississippi and Crow Rivers with temporary dikes built by volunteers. By mid-April, the smaller rivers of the upper Midwest were falling back into their banks, but the crests were rolling downriver and would threaten the Twin Cities and communities farther south.

WATCHING AND WAITING

By mid-April, a few dozen families in low-lying areas around Minneapolis had evacuated. Flooding forced the closure of two sewage treatment plants in the Twin Cities. Untreated sewage flowed into the Mississippi River. Big chunks of ice clogged the river and crashed into bridge piers, which is generally not a good thing. The ice damaged piers for the Plymouth Avenue and Broadway bridges. Worried city officials deployed fifty people to monitor the integrity of the city's bridges. The floodwaters would eventually undercut one pier of the Stone Arch Bridge, an active rail bridge, forcing expensive repairs once the flooding was over.

In north Minneapolis, residents of North Mississippi Court watched nervously as the river crept closer to the community of twenty-five four-unit buildings. Adults and children alike rallied to build a temporary barrier to protect their homes, a plywood wall that was held in place with piles of sandbags. Nearly a third of the families had already moved out by mid-April. For those who stayed, "It is the waiting that is the bad part,"[1] resident Diane Lundberg said.

On April 14, Dan Hnath, a high school student and gymnast, got more attention than he had bargained for. He and a friend had been jumping on parts of the frozen river near Brooklyn Center when a chunk of ice five feet wide and ten feet long broke free and quickly carried him into the middle of the river. Rather than panic "he crouched surfboard-style and nimbly rode the door-sized floe past hundreds of horrified onlookers."

The fun didn't last, though. The ice glanced off of two bridge piers, but it remained intact, fortunately. When a man on shore tossed a rope in his direction, the rope turned out to be too short. A rescue squad soon showed up that included a Navy helicopter and police, but it was the fire department rescue boat that pulled up next to him that got him off the ice. Back on land, he got a good scolding from rescuers and his mother. He later admitted to feeling "plenty scared," but as the next day was his eighteenth birthday, he said he intended to go back to the river to play around again. At least he promised to stay off the ice.[2]

BURNED TO THE WATER LINE

Downstream of Minneapolis, the evacuations continued, with two dozen families moved out of Inver Grove Township and Mendota Heights. Residents of perennially flooded Lilydale began moving out in early April. The water reached the roofs of many homes, and the force of the current twisted buildings off of their foundations.

By mid-April, eight hundred people had moved out of endangered parts of St. Paul. The city's main train station, Union Depot, was closed because the rail lines feeding it were underwater. Holmen Field, St. Paul's downtown airport, disappeared under nearly eight feet of water and would remain closed for four weeks. The city built a temporary flood wall along Shepard Drive.

The flooding did not interrupt every business. In mid-April, the Minnesota Senate approved a bill that would allow state institutions to serve oleo, a vegetable oil–based butter substitute that is now known as margarine. The oleo prohibition dated to 1921.

On April 14, President Lyndon Johnson stopped in St. Paul to inspect the flood damage. He surveyed the city as a cold drizzle fell, then left to a chorus of thunder and lightning. Earlier that morning, officials had blown up the clubhouse at the St. Paul Yacht Club because they worried the building would break loose and float into boats and bridges downriver. After three blasts of dynamite, the club caught on fire, burned to the waterline, and sank.

Just downriver of the boat club, the stubborn staff of the Golden Garter on Navy Island—the "Twin Cities only Banjo Band Saloon"—finally shut down as waters crept up toward the second floor of the Minnesota Boat Club where the bar was located.[3] The previous day, three musicians had played a few songs on the roof to let folks know the club was still open. The morning after the club closed, the Mississippi washed away a wall that had protected the building.

The river peaked in St. Paul on April 16 at 26.01 feet, 4 feet higher than the previous record set in 1952, and a record that still stands. Concerned about the flow of disaster tourists, St. Paul granted the police the authority to arrest sightseers who interfered with flood-fighting activities. Minnesota Governor Karl Rolvaag banned amateur photographers from flooded areas, because officials worried they lacked the judgment to avoid taking risks while snapping pictures.

THE ISLAND OF WABASHA

As the high water rolled into the wider valley below St. Paul, the problems got bigger. In South St. Paul, flooding knocked the city's sewage treatment plant out of service (it wouldn't reopen for four weeks) and submerged railroad tracks throughout the city. The city raced to complete a three-and-a-half-mile temporary dike to protect the St. Paul Union Stockyards and meat-packing plants, where 260 employees had been on strike for nearly a month.

Meanwhile, long-time river dweller Ed Custer lost the fight to protect his house along Concord Street when the Mississippi moved it off its foundation and carried it away. Custer, who had lived seventy-four of his seventy-five years next to the Mississippi, swore he was finally done with the river: "Custer's last stand is over. I fought long enough," he insisted. The river also took three hundred jars of canned fruits and pickles and his pet cat. "I don't know what I'll do. But I'm through with the river."[4]

Twenty miles downriver at Hastings, the Army Corps of Engineers was scrambling to shield the control station at Lock and Dam #2. A hundred volunteers worked in cold, wet weather to construct a temporary barrier to protect the sensitive electronics that kept the lock open. When high winds added to the challenges, a Naval Reserve helicopter dropped life jackets to the volunteers, in case winds blew them into the river.

Nearby, Hastings resident Peter Mitzuk devised a creative method of protecting his house from the flood: He wrapped it in a sheet of plastic film. Five feet of river water surrounded his home, but the inside remained dry, except for some seepage that bubbled up from underneath.

Another five miles downriver, low-lying areas around Prescott, Wisconsin, struggled against record crests on the St. Croix and Mississippi Rivers, which merged near downtown. The city's sewage treatment plant had to be shut down, and US Highway 10, a vital east–west route, was closed. Red Wing, at the upper end of Lake Pepin, also lost its sewage treatment plant. US Highway 63 was closed, so officials set up a ferry to temporarily move people and cars between Minnesota and Wisconsin. Further downriver at Lake City, Minnesota, ice floes rammed into the shore and damaged fifty homes in the Central Point neighborhood.

For the residents of Wabasha, at the lower end of Lake Pepin, the situation was growing tense. Water surrounded the city and flooded roads into and out of town. "The island of Wabasha, formerly a Minnesota city linked by dry land to the rest of the state, was about one-third water Friday," the *Minneapolis Tribune* reported.[5]

Forty families had already evacuated. Workers piled sandbags on the city levee to add four feet in height. Worries shifted from the height of the river to the large chunks of ice coming out of Lake Pepin. The city had barely avoided disaster when an ice floe a quarter-mile long and hundreds of feet wide crashed into woods north of the city, knocking down trees in the floodplain forest. If a floe that size had rammed into the city's levee, all of Wabasha would have flooded.

The closed highways complicated the delivery of medical care. Mrs. Willard Drysdale was scheduled for major surgery, but she needed an infusion of a rare type of blood. Doctors at St. Elizabeth Hospital requested the blood from the Red Cross in St. Paul, who then had to engage in a creative delivery process to get the blood to Wabasha. A police car drove the blood to Hastings, where the officer handed it off to Norman Jacobson, who flew the blood to Wabasha in a helicopter. Jacobson had trouble locating the landing site, though, so people on the ground waved him in the correct direction until he spotted a red flare marking his destination. Once on the ground, he handed off the blood to Sister Lucretia, who "ran, habit flying in the wind, to the hospital." It took six hours to get the blood to the hospital, but the surgery went fine and Mrs. Drysdale was recovering well the day after.

Nothing but a Cotton-Picking Sandbar

For all the challenges faced by people in the Twin Cities and Wabasha, the risks were relatively minor. The places facing the greatest challenges were downriver, and the city with the most to lose was Winona, Minnesota. The city was built in an area where Mdewakanton Dakota Indians had lived, a place known as Wapasha's Prairie. It's flat. Really flat. Without levees, the city would flood regularly. Winona was, as Harold Breisath, president of the city council, said "nothing but a cotton-picking sandbar in the first place."[6]

As the Mississippi rose in late March and early April, residents of Winona realized they were facing a much bigger threat than usual. In early April, the city organized an effort to add height to existing levees and to build a new dike around vulnerable areas. Unlike other cities that had relied on volunteers, Winona hired experienced contractors. Feeling a sense of urgency, Mayor Rudy Ellings told the press, "We haven't even thought about the cost."[7]

Gerry Modjeski, twenty-four years old at the time and a supervisor at his father's plumbing company, recalled: "All the contractors met at Winona Heating, and we laid out a plan and decided what dikes had to be fortified, what dikes had to be built new and began to construct all these areas with heavy equipment."[8]

Within a week, the city had mobilized twenty bulldozers and a hundred trucks to build an eight-mile temporary levee that would wind its way around the city. The stakes were high. If they couldn't get a strong enough dike built, the river could flood three-quarters of the city and the homes of fifteen thousand people.

In 1965, Ken Morgan was sixteen years old and obsessed with golf. When his high school was closed because of the flooding, he and many of his classmates got jobs fighting the flood. He was paid $1.50 an hour, $0.25 higher than the minimum wage. After a fifteen-minute training video, they went to work. "They'd bring in a pile of sand," he recalled. "You'd have one guy with a shovel and another guy holding the bag open. You'd throw two or three shovel fulls in the bag and then someone else would carry it off and actually lay it down on the dike. It was a pretty good system. It was very well organized."[9]

Ken Bruekse, a sophomore at Winona State University, also worked on the front lines. "We had a chain gang approach from filling the sand bags and then handling them along the dike line. I don't remember the exact number but there were a lot of us. The city workers would line the dike with plastic and we would place the sand bags on the plastic.... The city workers told us that we were going to be the force that saved the city. Let me tell you we all gave 125%."[10]

The crews worked in twelve-hour shifts under hard conditions. It was loud from the constant parade of trucks coming and going. The air had a distinctive smell, too. "I can still smell that combination of wet burlap and diesel fumes," Morgan recalled. "It's a smell I haven't smelled since, but I can almost relive that." And the people on the front lines couldn't escape the raging river. "We were just like a finger of sandbags out there on Prairie Island," Morgan said. "I could look out on both sides of the dike and see water. We had no idea really just how fragile our safety really was."

"It was [a] pretty scary and dangerous situation," Brueske recalled. "The river was running wild and just trying to get the plastic and sand bags in place was very dangerous. One missed step and you were gone."[11]

The river continued to rise. A hundred families left their homes north of town on Prairie Island. High water cut off rail traffic into the city. Downtown businesses piled sandbags in front of doors and basement windows. Pumps were moving forty thousand gallons of water a minute back into the Mississippi. High winds threatened to knock over parts of the temporary dike.

As the river rose, engineers grew concerned that the increased water pressure might cause the storm sewers to explode. A thousand people evacuated endangered areas as the city worked on a risky plan to deal with the problem: They sent divers into the sewers to plug them with inflatable rubber bags. Ray Beyers was one of those divers.

Beyers was thirty-four years old and worked as a glazier for Reinert Art Glass, but he had been a diver when he served in the Navy. Forty years after the flooding, he described what he experienced:

> *There's rungs in there for sewer workers to climb down. I just walked right down like going down a ladder. But it was a little awkward to get all that stuff on. The shoes weigh around 40 pounds, then you have a belt—that weighs 80 or 90 pounds. The last thing you want is to have too much air in there and you float to the top. That's why the lead shoes. You crawl along like a crab on one foot and then one arm, then the other foot and the other arm and you don't know what you're going to walk into. It was only about five or six feet across. There's two or three or four openings. They knew which one was pointing toward the river and we just had to go and make sure the thing was clean, so there was no obstructions in there.*
>
> *We took a garden rake and cut it off, then they bent it so it would fit in a big pipe. I put the rake in there and made sure it was clean. Then I took the bag and put it down in there and then we filled it up with air and that sealed it off. It was like filling up a car tire. Over about six blocks, as soon as you put that in there, they said that the water quit rising.[12]*

Exploding sewers weren't the only threats to the city. Volunteers placed logging pikes on the west side of the levees to deflect ice chunks. The river rose uncomfortably close to the top of the dikes, but a stroke of bad luck for folks on the east side of the Mississippi meant good fortune for the people of Winona.

Gary Evans was a twenty-four-year-old sports reporter for the local newspaper during the flood. He was on Prairie Island on April 16— Good Friday—when he witnessed the remarkable turn of events. "While we're standing on the Prairie Island dike speculating about are they going to pull the flood workers off," he recalled, "all of a sudden the water started—at first it seemed like an optical illusion but all of a sudden you could see the water start to drop. And it dropped about 18 inches in what seemed like just a few minutes. I think in reality it was about an hour."[13]

On the opposite shore, a berm supporting railroad tracks collapsed near the village of Bluff Siding. The Mississippi River poured through the berm and spread out over 7,500 acres of land in Wisconsin. "That took significant pressure off the dikes and probably is the reason that the dike didn't break," Evans said.

City officials in Winona organized nonstop surveillance of their flood protection system to spy weak spots and quickly repair them. The National Guard "had strung a kind of a battle-field phone system along Prairie Island," Morgan said. "Every quarter-mile to half-mile they had a phone set up. They needed someone to man that phone so that if there was a problem we could phone it."[14]

The Mississippi would finally crest on April 19—the day after Easter—at 20.77 feet, three feet higher than the previous record but three feet below the top of the temporary dike. "When the river had finally crested," Brueske recalled, "the dike held and the city was saved. Let me tell you, we were all very happy."

The Mississippi would remain above flood stage for twenty-four days, but the levees held. It was an impressive effort. Fifteen hundred people worked feverishly to place 1.3 million sandbags. Carol Slattery was twenty-two years old when she volunteered with the Red Cross. "I just remember how the whole community joined together," she said. "And how people volunteered, whether it was resources or time."[15]

"There never was any panic or sense of crisis," Morgan remembered. "We were a hundred percent confident that this plan was going to work and we were going to beat the flood. And we did. It only struck me years later that I don't know what our odds really were of having that be successful."

The flood-fighting efforts cost the city $2.6 million but saved multiples of that in damages. For Ken Morgan, the long days filling and stacking sandbags proved to be a lucrative gig. He used the unexpected income to buy a set of high-end golf clubs.

Down toward the Gulf, the water continued to roll, submerging sections of Wisconsin's scenic Highway 35, the Great River Road. By mid-April, only one river bridge remained open in the two hundred miles between La Crosse and Davenport, a bridge connecting Dubuque, Iowa, and East Dubuque, Illinois.

Charlie Hale, a photographer with the *Rochester Post-Bulletin* who worked dawn to dusk during much of the flood, saw "hundreds of homes and cabins along the river had been flooded, some were slashed to kindling by wind-whipped ice floes, and farmers had to use boats to feed their chickens."[16]

In La Crosse, Wisconsin, the city raised five miles of levees. Pumps moved water from storm sewers over dikes and into the river. Two hundred families in low-lying areas temporarily relocated. Water backed up the channel of the La Crosse River and cut off the two main roads that connected the north and south parts of the city. When a railroad dike collapsed, a major street disappeared under several feet of water that submerged cars to their headlights and forced 1,200 people to evacuate. Wisconsin Senator William Proxmire toured flooded areas and advised residents that the best way to get aid was to "complain, complain, complain."[17]

Meanwhile, hopes dimmed that rescuers would locate Northern States Power (NSP) employee Roland Fischer. The forty-five-year-old had disappeared on Friday night when he set out in a boat to ferry employees from an isolated NSP station on French Island. He never showed up. Witnesses last saw him in the boat floating without power as it approached a rail bridge.

Further downriver, a thousand residents of Prairie du Chien, Wisconsin, left their homes. One-third of the city was underwater. All roads into and out of Marquette, Iowa, flooded, and the town's Main Street disappeared under four feet of water.

The Mississippi crested four feet higher than the previous record at Dubuque, Iowa, and remained above flood stage for twenty-eight days. The city built a temporary dike that ran three and a half miles, thanks to the labor of 3,500 volunteers who placed four hundred thousand sandbags. That temporary dike was a key reason their Mississippi River bridge stayed open.

At Clinton, Iowa, folks successfully protected the downtown with a mile-long temporary dike, but businesses in the Lyons District in the north part of the city weren't as lucky. Fifty businesses flooded. Across the river, much of Fulton, Illinois, disappeared into the Mississippi as the river breached several levees. More than half of the city's 3,400 residents evacuated their homes.

People reacted to the hardships in different ways. Many fled their homes for emergency shelters. Others moved in temporarily with friends or family. Seventy-five-year-old Harry Steele—known around town as "Silent Henry"—rode out the flood in a raft tied to a tree that floated above the single-room shack where he lived. He refused all offers of help to evacuate from his home on Joyce's Island near Clinton, Iowa, where he had lived for at least twenty-eight years. "I rode it out in '52 and I'll ride it out in '65—there ain't no man or officer gonna take me off my island," he told would-be rescuers.[18]

Residents of river towns fought the high water for another two hundred miles south of Clinton, all the way to Hannibal, Missouri. Twelve thousand people had to leave their homes in the Quad Cities region of Iowa and Illinois. Homes and businesses in Muscatine, Iowa, flooded when a pump failed for just a few hours. A stack of forty thousand sandbags wasn't enough to protect the business district of Keithsburg, Illinois. Levee breaks in Illinois flooded twenty-eight thousand acres in Henderson County just across the river from Burlington, Iowa. In the riverside town of Gulfport, Iowa, roofs were the only visible sign of the city's neighborhoods. At downtown Hannibal, stores lined their doors with sandbags and temporary walkways kept foot traffic dry, so most stores stayed open.

ASSESSING THE DAMAGE

The river crested on April 16 at St. Paul. Over the next twelve days and 320 miles, the crest rolled downriver and set records that still exist for river towns as far south as Fulton, Illinois. Many tributaries also set records, notably the Minnesota River.

Nineteen people died in the flooding, hundreds were injured, and forty thousand were forced from their homes. The Red Cross assisted 150,000 people, and 3,721 National Guard troops deployed to fight the flood and help with cleanup.

The flood caused $200 million in damages (over a billion dollars in today's currency). The federal government declared 183 counties in five states eligible for federal disaster aid, most of them in Iowa and Minnesota. Damages from the 1965 flood were almost eight times greater than those from the next-greatest flood (in 1952), a difference that had little to do with the amount of water overflowing. A Department of the Interior paper noted that "Perhaps the greatest consideration is the increased occupancy of flood plains. The tremendous property damage that results from major floods points out the need for flood-plain zoning."[19]

After the flood of 1965, cities along the Upper Mississippi got busy building flood walls and levees. Winona got a flood protection system that spanned eleven miles and took twenty years to build. Clinton constructed a tall levee between its downtown and the river. For communities south of the Quad Cities, though, the flood of 1965 was merely a dress rehearsal for the big one yet to come—the Great Flood of 1993.

The River Kept Rising
The Flood of 1993

FOLKS WHO LIVE IN THE MISSISSIPPI VALLEY BELOW THE OHIO RIVER remember 1927 as the year of the epic flood. North of the Quad Cities of Iowa and Illinois, the most consequential flood was in 1965. In the middle part of the river, the biggest flood was in 1844 . . . at least until 1993. The Great Flood of 1993 was remarkable not just for the volume of water that flowed down the Mississippi River but also for the unprecedented time that the river stayed high. People in river communities not only had to fight back high water, they did so for weeks on end.

The 1993 flood challenged people who lived in some of the oldest communities in the Midwest, places that existed before the United States. Missionaries and farmers moved down from French Canada and founded the communities of Kaskaskia (1703), Prairie du Rocher (1722), Sainte Genevieve (1749), and Cahokia (1699). French merchants traveled up from New Orleans in 1764 and founded St. Louis. Many of these places reached their population peak two centuries ago, but they're still around and proud of their deep roots. And while people who live in these communities have long had to cope with the occasional high water from the Mississippi River, no one in living memory could recall a year quite like 1993.

A FOREBODING PATTERN
Floods on big rivers rarely come out of the blue, and that was certainly true in 1993. The summer before had been wetter than normal, and above-average rains lingered into the fall. When the spring also turned

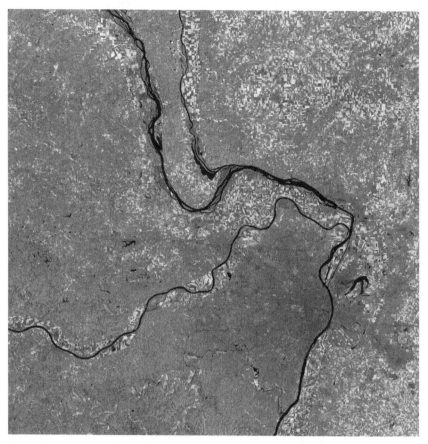

Photo 7.1.a. This photo and the photo opposite are satellite images of the Mississippi/Missouri River confluences in 1992 and 1993.

out to be wetter than average, the soils throughout the Midwest couldn't hold any more moisture. Additional water raining down from the skies simply ran into the rivers.

The Missouri River near Kansas City rose above flood stage in early May. Just a couple of days later, nine inches of rain fell in southwest Minnesota, sending the Redwood River out of its banks and flooding Marshall. Spring floods were nothing unusual, though, and hardly anyone was concerned that the overflows signaled anything ominous, especially when

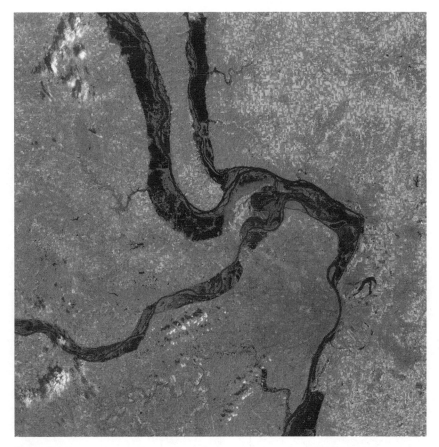

Photo 7.1.b
NASA

the rains slowed down in late spring. Folks who lived in areas that had flooded moved back home in late May and cleaned up.

As summer approached, though, a steady stream of upper-level winds coursed across the Upper Mississippi Valley. Cool, dry air flowed from the mountains into the Great Plains, where it mixed with warm, moist air from the south. This is a typical spring and early summer pattern that brings thunderstorms to the middle of the country. Most of the time, this pattern breaks down after a few days. In 1993, it locked in place for most of the summer.

By the middle of June, the steady, heavy rains had pushed the Minnesota River to record heights. Unusually heavy rains pelted the region nearly every day beginning in late June. On July 1, six inches of rain fell at Craig, Missouri. Seven inches of rain drenched Dawson, Nebraska, on July 5. Three days later, eight inches of rain fell around Jefferson, Iowa. Many of the people who had cleaned up once already had to leave their homes again.

By mid-July, a hundred Midwestern rivers had overtopped their banks. On July 9, extreme rains in northwest Iowa increased the Raccoon and Des Moines Rivers to record levels. When water from those rivers merged in Des Moines, they overtopped the levees around the city's water plant, cutting off water to 250,000 people. It took twelve days to get water flowing again and nineteen before it was safe to drink. Midwesterners realized that this would not be an ordinary flood year after all.

RELENTLESS RAINS ON THE GREAT PLAINS

By the end of June, officials had declared multiple counties in South Dakota, Wisconsin, and Iowa disaster areas. By early July, flooding had cut off access to Mississippi River bridges at Louisiana and Hannibal, Missouri. Waters were getting high enough to attract attention. On July 4, President Clinton toured flooded areas around Davenport, Iowa.

The rains kept falling, though, and soon the levees did, too. On July 7, the Pope Creek levee gave out, flooding Keithsburg, Illinois. For four days in a row, the Mississippi River broke through levees and reclaimed mile after mile of its floodplain. Thousands of people who lived behind those earthen barriers evacuated.

By mid-July, high water closed five hundred Mississippi River miles to barge traffic. Rail lines around the Midwest flooded or washed out. National news anchors stood in front of the rising Mississippi River near the Gateway Arch in St. Louis and featured stories about blown levees and communities fighting the rising waters.

STEADY RISE

By late July, anyone who needed to drive across the Mississippi or Missouri River was in for a long detour. The eight Mississippi River crossings between St. Louis and the Quad Cities were all closed. Along the Missouri River, only two bridges remained open in the two hundred miles between Kansas City and St. Charles, Missouri. National Guard troops patrolled flooded areas to control access.

Even if you didn't have to cross a bridge, getting around sometimes required ingenuity. One resident of Grafton, Illinois, had a daily fifteen-mile commute to Alton. The drive down the Great River Road typically took him less than twenty minutes. After the Mississippi flooded the highway, though, he drove a truck to the water's edge in Grafton, took a boat to other end of the flooded highway, then drove another truck the rest of the way. Getting around that way day after day, a person can have some unusual experiences, like the day shortly after the river swamped the town, when he heard a bunch of smoke detectors going off at the same time.

Volunteers streamed in from around the country. Northwest Airlines flew in employees to help with relief efforts, and other companies also sent employees to help. Volunteers prepared and distributed meals. Others lined up to pile sandbags on top of waterlogged levees at Hannibal, along the River des Peres in St. Louis, in West Quincy, at Ste. Genevieve, at Prairie du Rocher, and at dozens of other places. Residents of Hannibal thought they'd be celebrating the completion of a new downtown levee in 1993, but instead they worried that their new wall might not be tall enough to hold back the Mississippi River as it steadily rose toward the top.

Some volunteers got a pleasant surprise during the struggle. After playing a concert at an outdoor amphitheater in St. Louis, Jon Bon Jovi called a local command center and thanked them over a speakerphone. He then donated $10,000 to local relief efforts.

One challenge faced by people on the front lines was that flood crest forecasts changed regularly. Some of this was because it just kept raining and more water raced into the area's rivers, but forecasting models also proved to be inadequate. The changing crest predictions added to the stress and forced floodplain residents to continually adjust. In West Alton, Missouri, for example, folks knew that the elementary school was going to flood, so staff moved furniture and supplies to the second floor, to a location that was two feet higher than the previous record flood. When the Mississippi rose toward the second floor anyway, the staff scrambled to move everything to the third floor. When the Mississippi finally reached its peak in West Alton, though, it had spread water across those third-floor classrooms.

Residents of West Alton knew they were going to get wet. Officials had given up on reinforcing the levee, so they warned residents that they only had a few days to prepare. Those days turned to hours, though, when Timothy Steinmann rammed his Jon boat into a wall of sandbags on top of the levee. Steinmann later pleaded guilty to first-degree property damage and was sentenced to five years in prison.

Displacement took a heavy toll on people's mental health. Many experienced prolonged depression and grief from their losses. Others felt a persistent anger over their loss of control. Insomnia was common. Family members sometimes turned on each other. Relationships ended. This being the land of stout Midwesterners, many people were too proud to ask for help.

But help came, anyway, in the form of all those volunteers and responses from all levels of government. Even family pets weren't left out. Many shelters didn't allow evacuees to bring in animals, so the St. Charles Humane Society and other animal welfare groups stepped up and created a foster care system for pets.

CRESTS BRING HEARTBREAK

As the floodwaters climbed toward their ultimate crests, the region suffered through a dizzying series of losses while barely avoiding even bigger disasters. On July 22, the levee that protected historic Kaskaskia, Illinois, gave way. A federally constructed levee protected the community on Kaskaskia Island, which was just thirteen years old. Everyone felt confident it would hold. When a sand boil developed on the southern end of the island, though, the river undercut the levee and burst through, and "water blew into the air like small geysers as the collapse tore a 300-foot hole in the southeastern corner."[1] Most of the island disappeared under twenty feet of water, and the hundred residents who had remained on the island evacuated on barges.

The next day, counselors from St. Joseph Home for Boys took a group of their resident teenagers on a hike to Cliff Cave Park in the southern part of St. Louis. The park had been closed after high water from the Mississippi River had flooded low-lying areas. When counselors arrived at the park, they drove around the barricades blocking the road and led the boys on a hike into one of the park's caves. As they were hiking inside it, thunderstorms developed that dumped heavy rains. Water quickly filled the cave and swept away two counselors and five of the boys. Remarkably, one thirteen-year-old boy survived. He had climbed onto a narrow ledge that kept him above the water as it raged through the cave.

That same day, a routine inspection of St. Louis's eleven-mile-long flood wall discovered a scour hole along the northern end. Just like at Kaskaskia, the Mississippi had found a way underneath the flood barrier. It had opened a sixty-foot hole that threatened a busy industrial zone. City workers hurriedly dumped six thousand tons of rocks into the hole to fill it. The hole had caused a piece of the wall to lean about an inch toward the river, but the fill worked and the wall stabilized.

At the other end of the city, the Mississippi River was pushing water up the channel of the River des Peres, a concrete drainage ditch that had once been a natural river. Dozens of people feverishly piled sandbags to build a makeshift levee. On July 18, though, the river pushed through part of the sandbag wall and flooded two hundred homes.

The dominoes continued to fall as July ended. On July 30, residents of Chesterfield, Missouri—an affluent suburb of St. Louis—watched in shock as water poured into the Chesterfield Valley. The Missouri River had poked a hole in the city's levee. Within a few hours, water up to fifteen feet deep submerged a small airport, a county jail, a busy interstate highway, hundreds of businesses, and twenty homes. Fortunately, there had been just enough warning to evacuate the jail and for businesses to move vital items out of the way.

The Mississippi crested at St. Louis on August 1. As curious St. Louisans enjoyed free rides on the region's new light rail line, called

MetroLink, the Mississippi peaked at 49.58 feet on the gage, over six feet higher than the previous record and just two-and-a-half feet below the top of the city's flood wall. Water crept one-third of the way up the steps fronting the Gateway Arch. One million cubic feet of water flowed underneath the Eads Bridge every second—over five times greater than the river's average flow at St. Louis—and people riding MetroLink, including me, looked down in awe at all that water rushing by.

August 1 was a busy day for the people struggling to hold the river back. The Mississippi claimed the water plant in Alton. Residents of that Illinois city would go without water service for sixteen days. South of St. Louis, the Mississippi cut a hole in a levee near Columbia, Illinois. TV news helicopters swooped in just in time to catch stomach-turning images of the Gummersheimer family farmhouse being swept away by the torrent. Virgil Gummersheimer later told reporters, "It [the Mississippi] reclaimed its valley this morning."[2]

As the water rolled across the Mississippi's historic floodplain south from Columbia, flooding overtook more farmhouses and the old community of Valmeyer. Residents of the historic settlement of Prairie du Rocher raced to protect their community. They built a new temporary levee and blew a hole in another to redirect the flow of the oncoming water. It was a risky strategy, but it ultimately worked, at least for those on the right side of the levee.

Another potential disaster was averted later in the evening of August 1 when tourist barges moored below The Arch—a helicopter landing pad, a Burger King restaurant, and the USS *Inaugural*, a World War II–era minesweeper—broke loose from the riverfront and floated down the Mississippi. The Burger King and the USS *Inaugural* rammed into a pier of the Poplar Street Bridge. The bridge was fine, but the boats suffered extensive damage. Tows raced after the renegade barges and corralled them before they had the chance to collide with the city's flood wall and possibly punch a hole in it.

The next day didn't provide any relief. Twelve thousand residents of south St. Louis evacuated when small fires erupted near propane tanks that had broken loose a couple of days earlier. Officials worried about a potentially catastrophic explosion if propane ignited. Waters from the

Mississippi had lifted forty-eight of the site's fifty-one tanks off their bolts. Each tank was filled with twenty-five thousand gallons of liquid propane. Only the thin lines used to fill and empty the tanks held them in place. A team of twenty-six courageous divers went to the site and slowly drained the propane from each tank over several days. "This is definitely the most dangerous diving I've done," Frank Byer told a reporter.[3] People began moving back into their homes a week later.

SAVING STE. GENEVIEVE

As the flood crest passed St. Louis, attention shifted south to Sainte Genevieve, where concerns ran as deep as the Mississippi. Sainte Genevieve is a unique place. Founded by French Canadian farmers in the eighteenth century, the entire community relocated from the bottomlands after a massive flood in 1785. The entire community relocated from the bottomlands after a massive flood in 1785. Many of the buildings constructed after that move are still around today. The city has so many extant French colonial buildings, in fact, that the US Congress created a National Park in 2020 to preserve them.

In the spring, the Mississippi had crested ten feet above flood stage, then slowly fell. People got to work preparing for the busy summer tourist season. By late June, though, the Mississippi was rising steadily again. On July 4, two tourist boats, the *Mississippi Queen* and the *Delta Queen*, made unplanned stops in Ste. Genevieve. High water had blocked the route of their annual race to St. Louis. That would be the last tourist event of the season. A few days later, city leaders made the tough decision to cancel Bastille Days, the city's busiest annual event. Instead of welcoming tourists, the city greeted troops from the National Guard, who helped them build a temporary levee.

The new levee snaked three miles around the perimeter of the city's historic core and rose as high as twenty feet tall. Volunteers came from around the country to help. Even inmates from a nearby prison pitched in. City officials conducted routine patrols to spot leaks, boils, or trouble spots. There were plenty of nervous moments. In the second week of July, a levee break sent water into the bottomlands south of town, closing a highway. The city suffered another loss when water overtopped a levee that protected homes around LaHaye and Biltmore Streets.

On July 15, the Mississippi River rose above its previous record height at Ste. Genevieve and showed no signs of receding. Two weeks later, another levee breach at the southern end of town flooded more farms and homes, including the Bequette-Ribault House, one of only three remaining *poteaux-en-terre* (post-in-ground) buildings in the United States. Still, the temporary levee that protected the historic core of the city was holding up. Folks just wondered how much longer it could do so.

The Mississippi finally crested at Ste. Genevieve on August 6. The city had built the temporary levee to protect against a fifty-foot crest, but it had to be raised one more foot when residents learned that a higher crest might still be possible. Ultimately, the Mississippi peaked at 49.67 feet at Ste. Genevieve, and the levee held. The river fell steadily after that, and folks breathed easier. Another round of storms brought the Mississippi back up to forty feet in late September, but the levee was still solid and the city's historic core remained dry. On October 12, the Mississippi finally fell below flood stage. The city's defenses held, but the cost had been high. The city had lost almost all of its tourist revenue for the year, and fighting back the water had cost millions of dollars. "We've mortgaged our future to save our past," said Bernard Schram, who lived in one of the city's historic houses.[4]

WAITING AND ASSESSING

As the Missouri River fell back, residents of Hardin, Missouri, discovered that six hundred coffins had washed away from the town's cemetery. The town would eventually retrieve most of them, but there was no practical way to identify the remains of those inside, so most of the coffins were reburied in a mass grave.

On August 22, barge traffic returned to the Mississippi. Heavy rains in September brought the rivers—and nerves—back up, but the high water quickly retreated. Residents of Portage des Sioux, Missouri, marked the end of a sixty-two-day stretch during which they had been surrounded by water. At Grafton, Illinois, the Mississippi finally dropped below flood stage on October 11. From March 6 to October 11, the Mississippi had been below flood stage at Grafton for just eighteen days.

As the water retreated, the most striking realization was just how much of the Midwest had been affected by the summer rains. The Mississippi River set record heights on ninety-five river gages. Record flooding occurred on 1,800 miles of Midwestern rivers, while another 1,300 river miles experienced major (but not record-setting) flooding.

Overall, almost 70 percent of the levees failed between the Quad Cities and Cairo, Illinois. Most of the levees that gave way had been built and maintained by local interests to protect agricultural lands, but the Mississippi also breached 40 of 226 federal levees. Nearly 7 million acres flooded in 419 counties.

Most of the flooded areas were farm fields. Corn yields were down 31 percent in the flooded areas. Soybean yields dropped 16 percent. However, the majority of the crop losses (70 percent) occurred in farms far from the floodplains. These were places where water from the frequent storms pooled for weeks on end. Corn and soybean prices rose, which was great news for farmers whose fields had stayed dry.

Flooding damaged one hundred thousand homes, more than half of them beyond repair. High water forced tens of thousands of people into temporary housing, many of them in trailer homes provided by the Federal Emergency Management Agency (FEMA). Most would stay there for months.

Transportation networks suffered widespread damage, too. Hundreds of miles of roads would need repairs. Railroad tracks washed out. Barge traffic halted for several weeks. Even some small airports flooded, although commercial air travel in the Midwest operated normally.

Overall, the Great Flood of 1993 resulted in some $18 billion in damages. The federal government spent $6.2 billion in direct aid to flood victims. State and local governments spent another $1 billion. Fifty-two deaths were attributed to the floods, although many of those fatalities occurred when people drove their vehicles onto flooded roads. The hardest-hit states were Iowa and Missouri, where almost every county was declared a disaster area.

RECOVERY

The Great Flood of 1993 was unusual in many ways. The flood waters rose through the summer and peaked with the summer heat. Rivers throughout the Midwest stayed high for weeks. Flood waters displaced thousands of people, sometimes entire communities. The flooding also exposed weaknesses in public policy.

As the flood waters rose, thousands of people bought flood insurance at the last minute. At the time, coverage would kick in just five days after purchase. As a result, some people who hadn't paid a dime into the flood insurance pool for years received money for damages after making just a couple of payments. That loophole would later be closed.

Some communities took a hard look at their policies regarding floodplain development and levee construction. Calhoun County, Illinois, banned new residential construction in the hundred-year floodplain, that is, in areas that had a 1 percent chance of flooding in any year. The county restricted new commercial construction in those areas to river-related businesses such as marinas. In early September, residents of Valmeyer, Illinois, voted to move their town out of the floodplain. They would rebuild their city atop the nearby bluffs.

Those places turned out to be the exceptions, though. Many communities doubled down on floodplain development while lobbying for stronger levees. Chesterfield, Missouri, for example, claimed $200 million in damages from their levee failure. Property owners in Chesterfield, who represented a tiny fraction of all affected property owners, collected 5 percent of the total federal insurance payments awarded to flood victims. The city's levee was restored in 1994 to its previous one-hundred--year protection, but local officials lobbied hard for federal funds to raise their levee to protect against a five-hundred-year flood. In 2000, they got their wish. A decade later, $2 billion had been spent on new construction in the Missouri River floodplain at Chesterfield Valley. The area that flooded in 1993 now houses three times as many businesses as it did before the flood.

Midwest farmers recovered quickly, too. In 1994, they bought a record volume of fertilizer and put more acres into production for corn and soybeans than they ever had before. It paid off, as they saw record yields for corn and soybeans.

Everyone was ready to turn the page and get on with life, content knowing that they were unlikely to see the big rivers surge that high again in their lifetimes. When the Mississippi River set record heights again in 2011 and 2019, though, many wondered if we'd ever learn from our mistakes.

Uncomfortably Fragile

Snags and Sinking Steamboats

THE *NEW ORLEANS*, THE FIRST STEAMBOAT TO PLY THE MISSISSIPPI River, worked the lower half of the river from 1812 until July 14, 1814, when an overnight foot-and-a-half drop in the river impaled the boat on a tree stump, destroying it. Its active life of three years was about average for a steamboat, and its death at the hands of a snag, typical.

Even though steamboats proved to be uncomfortably fragile, they ushered in a transportation revolution. Steamboat innovators John Fitch and James Rumsey may not have imagined how radically the boats would transform American life, but Robert Fulton certainly did. Fitch and Rumsey engaged in a bitter struggle to build and operate the first steam-powered boat. They weren't the first to tinker with the idea. On July 15, 1783, Claude-François Dorothée Jouffroy d'Abbans successfully powered a boat with a steam engine on the River Saône at Lyons, France. His boat moved back and forth for fifteen minutes before it shook to pieces.

In the United States, Fitch's boat passed the first tests. On August 22, 1787, his steam-powered boat made a brief run on the Delaware River in front of a crowd that included members of the Continental Convention. Just three months later, Rumsey had his first successful trial run on the Potomac River. Three years later, Fitch's designs had advanced enough to power a ferry that made regular trips between Philadelphia and Trenton, New Jersey.

Still, the timing wasn't right. People were deeply skeptical of the technology, so neither man could line up investors. Their boats ended up in the trash heap of history. When Rumsey died in 1792 (he was forty-nine years old), he didn't have any money left to pass on to his family. Fitch didn't fare any better. He gave up on designing steamboats and moved to Kentucky in late 1795. In the last few months of his life, despondent and alone, he drank himself to the grave. He died in 1798.

THE INNOVATOR

Robert Fulton did not invent steam-powered boats, but he made them work. He combined the best ideas from other inventors and put them together to fashion a stable engine and a profitable business. Engineering wasn't his first career choice. He wanted to be an artist—a painter—and even moved to England in search of a mentor. When painting didn't work out, he shifted his interests to engineering. It was a good choice.

When he lived in Paris, he met Robert Livingstone—the US Ambassador to France at the time—and the two formed a partnership to develop steamboat technology. They were a formidable team. It took a few years to pull off, but their combined resources and expertise culminated in the construction of the first commercially successful boat, the *North River Steamboat*. The boat made its maiden voyage on August 17, 1807, with a trip up the Hudson River from New York City to Albany and back. Just four years later, Nicholas Roosevelt piloted another of their boats, the *New Orleans*, from Pittsburgh to New Orleans, getting steamboat technology to the place Fulton had eyed from the beginning—the Mississippi River.

Steamboats were well-suited to navigate the Mississippi. Their basic design—a powerful engine that turned a paddlewheel and a long, flat hull that didn't sink deep into the water—worked well in the shifting currents and depths of the Mississippi. Decks were stacked one on top of another like layers of a cake. Cargo was stacked on the decks. Even better, the wood needed for construction and for feeding the boilers was plentiful along the Mississippi.

Unfortunately, the primary advantages of steamboats also made them prone to catastrophic failure. Driftwood easily punctured shallow hulls. Wood hulls and decks were kindling for fires. And those powerful boilers that pushed the boats forward could be quite temperamental. A failure on any of these fronts usually ended in tragedy. Before the Civil War, nearly a third of steamboats reached their end because of an accident. Of all the causes that took them down, the most common and perhaps the hardest to avoid was hitting a snag, basically trees and logs floating in the water. Snags caused about half of all steamboat accidents.

Sawyers, Preachers, Planters, and Sleepers

When steamboats first began running the Mississippi, river travelers could be forgiven if they thought that entire trees and limbs were as numerous as fish. Some of that debris floated on the surface, while other bits lodged into a bank or the bottom of the river. Those snags, so dangerous to boats, inspired rivermen to name the more common varieties: sawyers, preachers, planters, and sleepers. Sawyers moved back and forth in the current. Preachers popped up and down in the water. Planters lodged firmly in the river's bottom. Sleepers lurked just beneath the surface.

The pilot had to keep a careful eye on the river, looking for telltale changes in the water's surface that gave away the presence of snags. Still, they were so plentiful that they were virtually impossible to avoid all the time. When a steamboat collided with a snag, the resulting damage could be anything from a small hole that was easily plugged to a death blow.

If a snag fully penetrated the hull, a boat was typically doomed. Most sank in just a couple of minutes. That was the case for the *Glendy Burke*, a steamboat popularized in a nineteenth-century song penned by Stephen Foster that opens with the line, "The Glendy Burke is a mighty fast boat." While it may have been swift, its speed was no help when it collided with one of those mighty snags.

On the afternoon of May 24, 1855, it hit driftwood near Cairo, Illinois, and sunk in about two minutes. The boat settled on a sandbar with its bow in eight feet of water and its stern in eighteen feet. Everyone on board survived, though, and the debris of the *Glendy Burke*, which proved too difficult to remove, became yet another navigation hazard. As late as October 1891, pieces of the *Glendy Burke* poked holes in passing boats.

While hitting a snag was often fatal for a boat, the passengers usually survived, especially if the accident happened in shallow water or near shore, as was the case with the *Glendy Burke*. If, however, the pilot couldn't get the boat close to shore quickly enough, the consequences could be tragic.

In February 1823, the *Tennessee* hit a snag near Natchez, Mississippi, late at night during a heavy storm. The snag—a large tree—ripped a big hole in the hull. As the boat sank, people panicked and jumped into the river. Some pulled off a door or found a piece of debris to use as a raft. Others drowned, though, as the cold water sapped their strength. The accident killed about sixty people, one of the first major snag-related disasters on the Mississippi. Many more followed:

- The *Nick Biddle* went down forty-five miles north of Vicksburg on July 25, 1837; ten deck passengers died.
- The *Eliza* sank near the mouth of the Ohio River on October 8, 1842, killing forty people.
- The *Keokuk* crashed near Sainte Genevieve Island on August 29, 1844, killing one cabin passenger and a dozen deck passengers.
- The *Belle of Hatchie* sank eight miles above Helena, Arkansas, on July 30, 1848; four deckhands slipped overboard and drowned and some panicked passengers jumped in the river and drowned.
- The *De Witt Clinton* sunk near Memphis on January 25, 1852; forty people died, including sixteen enslaved Black people.
- The *General Bent* sunk near Memphis in January 1854; twenty-one deck passengers died.

HARROWING ESCAPES

The suddenness of a snag-related accident, the shock of the impact, disoriented passengers and crew. Many passengers told harrowing stories about how they survived in the harsh conditions. One passenger, remembered only as Mrs. Seymour, was asleep in her cabin on the *John L. Avery* when it struck a large tree on March 9, 1854. Within seconds of the collision, her cabin flooded with river water. One of the boat's waiters, a man named John Anderson, pulled her to safety, but because of the suddenness of the accident, she lost $900 in cash and a completed manuscript she'd stashed in her pillow.

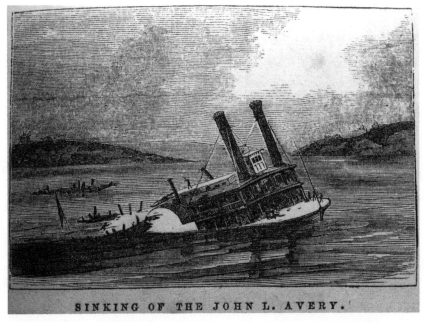

SINKING OF THE JOHN L. AVERY.

Photo 8.1
LLOYD'S STEAMBOAT DIRECTORY, 1856

The *Avery*, only a year old, had apparently been racing the *Sultana* to Louisville. The Mississippi swelled with its late winter rise and drifting trees and limbs clogged the surface; the *Avery* struck one of them. After the collision, the pilot turned the boat toward shore, but his effort was futile. The hull broke off from the cabin and sank in sixty feet of water. Cabin passengers rushed to the hurricane deck, where some of the crew, including the captain, pulled them up through the boat's skylights.

Mrs. Seymour was among those who found safety on the hurricane deck, which gave her a vantage point to witness the tragedy as it unfolded. "The water at first was dotted with human heads, sinking and rising, and then sinking to rise no more," she recalled. At one point, she saw a woman who had just been rescued slip back into the water and disappear. "In a faint but earnest tone, I heard a female voice say, 'Oh, William, do save her!' On directing my gaze to the place from whence the voice came, I saw a woman sinking in the river. At the same time a child's voice exclaimed, 'Oh, mother, he cannot save me!' I saw her fair hair, all wet, fall back from her young face as her little arms loosened their grasp on the neck of her brother, and the mother and her two children sank together."[1]

Heroic Rescues

A few years earlier, on January 3, 1844, the *Shepherdess* was nearing St. Louis when it hit a snag late in the night. Water filled the boat so quickly that even the crew was surprised. "As soon as the shock was felt on board," wrote James Lloyd, "one of the pilots attempted to descend into the hold for the purpose of examining the leak, but he had scarcely entered when the rush of water drove him back."[2] In just a couple of minutes, water had covered the lower deck.

The captain sought to reassure as many passengers as he could, most of whom had been asleep when the boat rammed into the tree. He visited the women's cabins and told them that the boat would be fine. After that, he walked back to his post, then disappeared. The river probably swept him away.

A few passengers got to the yawl and paddled it to shore with a broom. Cabin passengers climbed to the hurricane deck for safety. As the current dragged the boat downriver, it hit another snag, and the boat twisted around. The river then pushed the powerless boat into a bluff, which knocked the cabin off the hull. The hull sank, but the cabin floated further downriver and lodged on a sandbar, where rescuers later found the few survivors.

At least one passenger went to great lengths to save lives. Kentucky native Robert Bullock ran through the cabin and searched the staterooms for survivors, reportedly rescuing several women and children. One person he saved required a little extra help:

"His last effort was to rescue Col. Wood's 'Ohio Fat Girl,' who happened to be on board. Her weight was four hundred and forty pounds, but with the assistance of several persons on the hurricane deck, he succeeded in raising her to that place of security."[3]

Bullock later fell off the boat, probably when it hit that second snag, but swam to shore and saved a couple more lives. When he emerged from the river, he found two shivering survivors. He sat with them and kept them from passing out (and into comas), until they were rescued and taken to nearby Cahokia, Illinois, to warm up.

While Bullock went to great lengths to save lives, people of the day did not value every life lost equally. One account of the disaster noted: "Mr. Muir, of Virginia, and his brother, were on board, with their mother and nine of their slaves. With the exception of seven of the slaves, all of these persons were saved."[4] The deaths of seven enslaved Black people were merely incidental.

A Full Deck

Enslaved Black people were confined to the deck, which was the worst place to be when a steamboat hit a snag. Cargo was stacked everywhere, which sometimes blocked the quickest paths off the boat. The deck was also the cheapest part of the boat to travel on, though. Deck passage got you on the boat but gave you no specific spot, so deck passengers scrambled to claim space among the cargo and deck crew. It was a noisy, loud, uncomfortable, and smelly way to travel, but it was cheap. Boats regularly pushed the limits by cramming the deck with low-fare passengers. It wasn't unusual for a steamboat to carry five times as many people on deck as in the cabins.

Because deck passage was so cheap and much quicker than overland travel, the deck passengers were often immigrants, so when a boat went down, they were overrepresented among the victims:

- Twenty German immigrants died on the *Star Spangled Banner*.
- Forty Germans died when the *Caspian* sank.
- Over a hundred and twenty people died on the *John Adams*, most of them German and Irish immigrants.
- At least one-third of the dead on the *John L. Avery* were "undocumented immigrants—all Irish."[5]

We'll never know how many people actually died in these accidents. The steamboat companies did not always record the names of deck passengers on the ship's manifest. Death tolls for the *John L. Avery*, for example, ranged from thirty to ninety. It was one reality of the day. After exhausting all their money to come to the United States on long, uncomfortable ocean-crossing ships, many died on a Mississippi River steamboat as they made the last leg of their journey to start over.

Burned to the Water's Edge

Steamboat Fires

FIRES WERE A CONSTANT DANGER ON STEAMBOATS, THE THIRD MOST common cause of accidents. It's amazing that more boats didn't burn up considering they were giant wooden boxes powered by a huge furnace that was surrounded by combustible materials (like bales of cotton). What could go wrong with that?

Most steamboats burned wood to fuel their boilers but because they had little extra space to carry it, they'd stop up to twice a day to "wood up," that is, to buy cords of cut wood from shoreline entrepreneurs. Boats typically only burned coal as fuel in areas where it was cheap and easy to buy, such as along parts of the Ohio River or southern Illinois. While trees were abundant in the early days of steamboating, they were a finite resource. Over time, those dense riparian forests disappeared.

After a boat resupplied with wood, the crew stacked it in the engine room near the boilers so it would be easy to feed into the machines. While most engine room crews made sure that those combustible stacks of wood burned inside the boiler only, they weren't always attentive enough. It only took one misplaced pile of wood or random spark to ignite a dangerous fire.

Like many aspects of steamboat travel, there seemed to be a live-and-let-die attitude toward fires and fire prevention. The French economist and political writer Michael Chevalier traveled around North America in the 1830s. He found this attitude rather distressing:

There have been many accidents by fire in the steamers, and many persons have perished in this way, although the river is not very wide. ... The Americans show a singular indifference in regard to fires, not only in the steamboats, but also in their houses; they smoke without the least concern in the midst of the half open cotton-bales, with which a boat is loaded; they ship gunpowder with no more precaution than if it were so much maize or salt pork, and leave objects packed up in straw right in the torrent of sparks that issue from the chimneys.[1]

RACE TO THE BOTTOM

Inattention—and maybe drunkenness—sent the *Ben Sherrod* to the bottom of the Mississippi when cords of wood placed near the boilers ignited. By the time the crew members noticed it—many of them, someone said later, had been drinking liberally from a barrel of whiskey—the fire had grown too large to stop.

BURNING OF THE BEN SHERROD.

Photo 9.1
LLOYD'S STEAMBOAT DIRECTORY, 1856

The *Ben Sherrod* left New Orleans for Louisville, Kentucky, fully loaded with cargo and passengers, and even several horses that were stabled in the boat's forecastle. Even though it was just a year old, it was not among the most luxurious boats on the river. By early May, the peak steamboat season had passed and folks looking for a ride upriver didn't have many choices.

The boat stopped at Fort Adams, Mississippi, then found itself in a race to Natchez with the *Prairie*. Passengers goaded Captain Castleman to show up the *Prairie*, and he obliged. He ordered the engine crew to run at full steam and may have opened a barrel of whiskey to keep the night crew happy. Then he went to bed.

The firemen fed the boilers through the night, adding in pine knots and resin to make it burn hotter. The piles of wood near the boilers occasionally caught a spark, but the crew extinguished them. Early in the morning of May 8, 1837, though, not long after the boat had passed the Homochitto River, a pile of wood ignited and burned beyond the point of no return.

Much of the deck crew panicked and ran for the yawl. The captain, awakened by the ruckus, ordered the men to stop. Still, they kept at it and soon got in the yawl and lowered it. In their haste or inexperience, though, one end of the yawl dropped much faster than the other end and the men fell into the Mississippi, where they drowned.

The fire burned the tiller ropes, so the pilot could no longer steer the boat and the current kept it away from shore. The fire spread so quickly there wasn't time to put on more clothing or grab belongings. Everyone was afraid.

Some passengers, maybe those who had tried to salvage what they could, died in their staterooms. The horses in the forecastle stomped and neighed, but they all perished. Ten women jumped in the river to escape the flames, but only two survived.

A couple of boats—the *Columbus* and the *Statesman*—raced over and pulled people out of the water. The *Prairie*, though, which had been near the *Ben Sherrod* when it erupted in flames, didn't turn back, even though the crew must have seen the boat on fire.

One woman had jumped in the river with her infant child after witnessing her husband being consumed by flames. She hung on to a plank and floated to within forty yards of the *Columbus*. When the crew threw a rope to her, though, she apparently lost all strength and sank into the river with her child.

Another steamer, the *Alton*, entered the disaster zone but didn't slow down. Waves kicked up by the Alton swamped a couple of passengers who had been holding on. One went underwater and didn't resurface. The other regained his bearings and floated fifteen miles downriver, where the *Statesman* rescued him. Many other survivors drowned when the *Alton* passed by. It wasn't clear if the *Alton's* crew hadn't heard the survivors' cries for help or if they just didn't care. Another person who entered the disaster area was far more interested in making money than saving lives. He paddled out from shore in a canoe but refused to help anyone who wouldn't promise to pay him.

As the wreckage of the *Ben Sherrod* floated helplessly downriver, survivors heard several explosions. Barrels of whiskey apparently burst first, followed by the boilers exploding. In a final and dramatic burst, barrels of gunpowder blew up and showered the sky with fireworks. Nothing was left of the *Ben Sherrod* after that.

We'll never know how many people died. The ship's logs burned up, so there were no records of who was on board. One crew member estimated that seventy-eight people had booked passage on the deck, but only six survived. Captain Castleman and his wife survived, but their three children and the captain's father all died. Among the crew, the fire claimed a clerk, a pilot, a mate, all the chambermaids, and all but two of the thirty-five enslaved Black people on board. The best guess is that 120 people died. Even those who survived lost almost everything they had. One man lost $20,000 in cash to the fire, another $38,000.

An unnamed survivor, who lost three siblings but saved a stranger's infant child by swimming with it to shore, later reflected on the experience. "It was more than three weeks after the occurrence before I ever shed a tear. All the fountains of sympathy had been dried up, and my heart was as stone. As I lay on my bed the twenty-fourth day after, tears, salt tears, came to my relief and I felt the loss of my sisters and brother more deeply than ever. Peace be to their spirits! They found a watery grave." He insisted that the tragedy was avoidable: "A little presence of mind, and a set of men unintoxicated, could have saved the boat."[2]

The pilot who died, a man named Davis, had a prescient conversation with another pilot before leaving New Orleans. They were talking about the recent fire on the steamer *St. Martinsville*. Davis said: "If ever I should be on a boat that takes fire, and don't save the passengers, it will be because the tiller ropes burn, or I perish in the flames."[3] He lived up to his words. Those ropes burned, but he stayed at his post and went down with the boat.

THE CONFLAGRATION

Some tragedies become immortalized in song. Such was the case with the story of the *Grand Republic*, which John Hartford turned into a memorable song, "*The Burning of the Grand Republic*." The *Grand Republic* began its life in 1867 as the *Great Republic*. She was a big boat, 335 feet long by 51 feet wide, with fifty-four staterooms in the cabin and ten more on the texas deck. William Wall painted landscapes on the interior walls and the cabin architecture "borrowed from many styles," which some described as "overwhelming," with "fluted columns, wooden flounces, frills, fresco and flubdub, floral-bedecked carpeting, and carved and sculpted furniture."[4] Her inaugural cruise attracted a crowd on the Pittsburg riverfront who braved a snowstorm to watch the showy boat pass by.

She was built to serve the New Orleans to St. Louis trade, but the boat never made enough money to cover the extraordinary debt the owners took on to build it. In less than two years, the owners went bankrupt. As if that wasn't bad enough, the Captain, William Donaldson, was charged with murdering a man on his deck crew, a cabin boy named Henry Anderson. The only witnesses, a porter and another cabin boy who had been chained up with Anderson, fled the country after the boy died, so the case was initially dropped. When the two reappeared a year later, though, Donaldson was charged again. A jury ultimately acquitted him. They determined the captain had fired the deadly shot accidentally. That the captain was tried at all was remarkable given the era: a White steamboat captain was charged for the murder of a Black crew member.

In 1871, William Henry Thorwegan and Thomas Morrison bought the *Great Republic* at a sheriff's sale for $48,500. When Morrison went bankrupt in 1875, Thorwegan became the sole owner. He opted for a fresh start. He put the boat through a major overhaul in 1876 and renamed it the *Grand Republic*. On one of its first trips, the *Grand Republic* transported Brazilian Emperor Don Pedro II and his entourage from St. Louis to New Orleans.

The *Grand Republic* also set a record in December 1876 when she carried 8,210 bales of cotton to the New Orleans levee, beating the old record by 509 bales. The *Grand Republic* pulled into New Orleans on December 6 decked out and ready to celebrate:

> *Blue streamers were floating from her decks and flagstaffs, and across the cotton forward was a large piece of canvas with the following inscription: CHAMPIONSHIP OF THE WORLD, 8210 BALES. Her deck crew wore blue bands on their hats, while from the jackstaff-holder could be observed two large brooms decorated with blue ribbons. We also noted suspended between her derricks a diminutive bale of cotton, also decorated with ribbons.[5]*

Many people in the area were eager to help the boat celebrate. Mrs. Alex DeValcourt of Gaines Landing gave Captain Thorwegan "a plate of butter carved into the shape of a basket of flowers." Memphian E. S. Levy gave the captain a tiny bale of cotton made from silk.

The glorious boat would come to an inglorious end, though. On the night of September 19, 1877, the boat was moored just south of the St. Louis levee, where she'd spent about three months getting touched up. Around 11:30 that night, a fire broke out that lit up the night sky:

> *[T]he river bank at the foot of Lesperance street was brilliantly illuminated by flames. Light fleecy clouds floating in the heavens took on a vermillion hue, and a lurid column of smoke rolling high in air. A man came running at a break-neck pace over the rough fill road that runs past the dog pound, and in breathless accents told a policeman*

who was hurrying toward the scene of the conflagration that the Grand Republic was on fire.[6]

The fire department rushed to the scene, but the boat burned so quickly that there was no way to stop it. "Hardly ten minutes had elapsed, and yet the beautiful boat was a mass of seething, brilliant flame. The light wood, covered with hard, dry inflammable paint, as is usual with boats, offered a food for the flames that was devoured like tinder."[7] A reporter who witnessed the fire along with thousands of other people on the riverfront wrote:

> [T]he shore for a half mile either way on the river was as bright as day, with a brilliant red glare that made the pale moonlight green. The trees on the Illinois shore stood out in bold relief, and the sullen, muddy river was converted into a dancing, sparkling stream of roseate hues. The beautiful boat was a sight for an Angelo or a Dante. From every deck the flames burst forth in glory, and the texas and pilot-house were masses of molten magnificence.[8]

The fire probably started near the boilers, then quickly spread to the cabin before consuming the whole boat. The lone night watchman, Jack Raftus, woke up to the sounds of crackling flames and the smell of burning wood. He got off the boat in time to ring an alarm and to save his own life.

Thorwegan's boat was valued around $175,000, but he only got $50,020 from the insurance settlement, all of which went to creditors. Thorwegan owed $68,000 on the boat. One of his investors, a man named King, was upset that he had lost his entire $12,000 investment, so he sued Thorwegan for misrepresenting the financial status of the boat at the time he agreed to invest in it. The suit worked its way up to the US Supreme Court, which ruled in 1884 that Thorwegan could be held liable for lying about the boat's debts. They ordered a retrial. The suit, *Thorwegan v. King,* is one of the first cases to define fraud in the American legal system.

Primed to Blow

Boiler Explosions

BOILERS—THE HULKING MACHINES THAT DROVE THE STEAMBOATS that revolutionized travel in America—generated power and produced peril. Steamboats needed those huge boilers to create the energy to push a boat against the current of a big river. The high-pressure boilers that eventually became standard on steamboats were not only lighter than the early low-pressure systems but also more powerful, cheaper, and easier to fix on the fly. Those high-pressure boilers, though, came with one unfortunate downside: they sometimes blew up.

Keeping boilers stable was more art than science. Pressure gauges were often unreliable, especially for the first generation of boilers. Still, pilots were encouraged—rewarded, even—to run fast to beat competitors, which required keeping those boilers full of steam. This was not a good combination. Boilers regularly built up too much pressure and exploded in a dramatic and catastrophic burst, which blew through the wooden hull and superstructure and sprayed scalding water everywhere. Boiler explosions accounted for about a third of steamboat accidents, but most of the fatalities. During the golden days of steamboat travel, thousands of people died when boilers exploded, and it didn't matter who you were, how much money you had, or how brilliant you might be.

THE INNOVATOR
A boiler explosion, in fact, nearly put a premature end to the life of one of the early steamboat entrepreneurs. Henry Shreve, the son of a Revolutionary War colonel who served with George Washington, had ambitions

EXPLOSION OF THE WASHINGTON, 1816.

Photo 10.1
LLOYD'S STEAMBOAT DIRECTORY, 1856

to transform river travel with fast, efficient steamboats that could travel with ease on big rivers. In 1814, Shreve piloted the *Enterprise* to New Orleans to bring supplies of weapons and ammunition to General Andrew Jackson's defense against a British attack.

Shreve's trip, though, violated a monopoly granted to Robert Fulton and Robert Livingstone. In 1811, the Governor of Orleans Territory, William Clairborne, had awarded them exclusive rights to operate steam-powered boats on the Mississippi River in Louisiana. Shreve avoided attempts to seize his boat, then piloted the *Enterprise* back up the Mississippi and Ohio. The success of the trip not only showed off his piloting skills but also proved the potential of boiler-powered steamboats to run against the current of big rivers.

Shreve recognized the limitations of the *Enterprise*'s technology, though, so in 1815, when he was twenty-nine, he built the *Washington*.

One of his innovations was to design a hull that floated higher, so the boat could run in shallower water. Shreve built one of the first high-pressure boilers and ditched the heavy condenser that had been standard. He also created a method to draw in water from the river to cool his high-pressure boiler. Shreve had high hopes that the new boat would help him crush Fulton's monopoly on the Mississippi.

Shreve guided the *Washington* on its maiden voyage on June 4, 1816. The boat left from the Ohio River port of Wheeling, West Virginia, with twenty-one passengers. A few lucky guests stayed in one of the three private rooms in the main cabin, where they could socialize in the spacious saloon. The rest slept in one of the twenty berths in the common room.

Five days into the trip, Shreve took the boat out for a test run near Marietta, Ohio. As the boat drifted away from shore, Shreve signaled for the engineer to fire up the boiler. As the engineer fed wood into the furnace, a safety valve failed, and the boiler exploded. Eight people died immediately, while five others were mortally wounded. In a split second, a languid cruise transformed into a scene of grisly horror:

> *The deck was strewn with mangled and writhing human beings, uttering screams and groans of intense suffering. Some, more fortunate than their companions, lay still in the embrace of death. Among the wounded, six or eight, under the influence of their maddening torments, had torn off their clothes, to which the entire skin of their limbs or bodies adhered; the eyes of others had been put out, and their faces were changed to an undistinguishable mass of flesh by the scalding water. But the greatest sufferers, apparently, were those who had been internally injured by inhaling the scalding steam, the effect of which on the lungs is agonizing beyond all the powers of imagination to conceive. The whole scene was too horrible for description, and it made an impression on the minds of those who witnessed it which could never be obliterated.[1]*

The first boiler explosion of the steamboat era killed seventeen of the twenty-one passengers. Shreve survived, but he suffered serious injuries. The explosion damaged the *Washington* but did not destroy it, so Shreve had it towed back to port for repairs. In early fall, he relaunched it, then successfully navigated the Ohio and Mississippi Rivers. He arrived in New Orleans on October 7 with his boat intact. The monopoly tried unsuccessfully to seize the boat in New Orleans, allowing Shreve to make a triumphant return upriver. A short time later, the courts invalidated the monopoly, and Shreve would go on to great success as one of the most esteemed rivermen of the era. Shreveport, Louisiana, was named in his honor.

THE EXPERIENCE OF A BLOWN-UP MAN

Hundreds of steamboat boilers exploded in the nineteenth century, but few people survived to describe the experience. One who did was H. A. Kidd, who was the editor of the *New Orleans Crescent* when he had a brush with death. Kidd had been on board the *Anglo Norman* when its boilers exploded on December 14, 1850. The boat was returning to New Orleans on its inaugural cruise with 210 passengers when the accident

EXPLOSION OF THE ANGLO-NORMAN.

Photo 10.2
LLOYD'S STEAMBOAT DIRECTORY, 1856

happened. Kidd wrote a rather detached and breezy account of the event called "The Experience of a Blown-Up Man":

Mr. Bigny, one of the editors of the Delta, and myself, took the only two chairs remaining unoccupied on the deck; his chair having the back towards the pilot-house, and mine with its back to the chimney. It will be seen at once that we had seated ourselves immediately over the monster boilers of the boat.

We had been engaged in conversation but a very few moments, when a jet of hot water, accompanied with steam, was forced out of the main pipe just aft the chimney, and fell near us in a considerable shower. I had never noticed anything of the kind before, and thought the occurrence very extraordinary. Just as I was about remarking this to Mr. Bigny, I was suddenly lifted high in the air, how high it is impossible for me to say. I have a distinct recollection of passing rather irregularly through the air, enveloped, as it seemed to me, in a dense cloud, through which no object was discernible. There was a sufficient lapse of time for me to have a distinct impression on my mind that I must inevitably be lost. In what position I went into the water, and to what depth I went, I have not the slightest idea. When I arose to the surface, I wiped the water from my face, and attempted to obtain a view of things around me, but this I was prevented from doing by the vapor of steam, which enveloped everything as a cloud. This obscuration, however, lasted but for a short time, and when it had passed away, I had a clear conception of my situation. I found myself in possession of my senses, and my limbs in good working order. I looked around in every direction, and discovered that I was not far from the centre of the river, and in the neighborhood of some twenty or thirty people, who seemed to have been thrown into the water somewhat in a heap. They were sustaining themselves on the surface as best they could, many of them endeavoring to get possession of floating pieces of the wreck. I could see nothing of the exploded boat, and was fully satisfied in my mind that she was blown all to pieces, and that all my fellow passengers were lost, except those who, like myself, were struggling in the water. I will do myself the simple justice to say that, from the time at which I had risen to the surface, I had no apprehensions of drowning, though to a more disinterested spectator the chances might have appeared to be against me. I never felt more buoyant, nor swam with greater ease. Still I thought it well enough to appropriate whatever aid was within my reach; so, like others, I began a race, which proved to be a tedious one, after a shattered piece of plank. I finally reached it, and putting my hands rather rudely upon it, I got a sousing for my pains. The piece was too small to render me any material service. I abandoned it, and turned in the direction of a steamboat, which I perceived advancing, and which I afterwards discovered to be the Naniopa. To keep my face towards the approaching steamer, I found that I had to oppose the strong current of the river. This, together with the coldness of the water, so exhausted my physical energies, that, for a brief space, I felt that I should not be able to keep afloat until the boat should reach me. As the steamer came near, there was a cry from my unfortunate neighbors in the water, "Stop the boat! Stop the boat!"

There was, indeed, great danger of our being run over by it. I however had no fears on this point, and made no effort to get out of its way. Fortunately for myself, I was one of the first which the boat approached. A sailor threw out to me a large rope, which I succeeded in grasping at the first effort. I was drawn to the boat's guards, which were several feet above the water. While drawing me up, the kindhearted sailor cried, "Hold on, partner! hold on!" But I could not, my strength being exhausted; the rope was slipping through my hands, and I should certainly have fallen back into the water, and been irrecoverably lost under the boat's guards, had not another sailor quickly reached down and seized hold of my arms. I was drawn on board as nearly lifeless as any one could be without being actually dead. Two stout men assisted me to reach the cabin. My chest, as I discovered from its soreness and my spitting blood, had been somewhat bruised, but a little bathing with whiskey soon gave me relief. My friend Bigny was one of the first I met on board.[2]

The explosion killed nearly a hundred passengers and crew from the *Anglo Norman*. Mr. Kidd was listed among the dead, but, as with Mark Twain, reports of his death were greatly exaggerated.

Another firsthand account came from an anonymous survivor of the *Clipper* disaster in 1843. The boat was making a run between the Louisiana river towns of Bayou Sara (near present-day St. Francisville) and Tunica. Just after midnight on September 19, the boiler exploded and ripped the boat apart. The unnamed but articulate survivor wrote in vivid and gruesome detail about the experience, writing that the boiler

blew up with a report that shook earth, air, and heaven, as though the walls of the world were tumbling to pieces about our ears. All the boilers bursted simultaneously; vast fragments of the machinery, huge beams of timber, articles of furniture, and human bodies, were shot up perpendicularly, as it seemed, hundreds of fathoms in the air, and fell like the jets of a fountain in various directions; some dropping on the neighboring shore, some on the roofs of the houses, some into the river, and some on the deck of the boat. Some large fragments of the boilers, &c, were blown at least two hundred and fifty yards from the scene of destruction. The hapless victims were scalded, crushed, torn, mangled, and scattered in every possible direction; some were thrown into the streets of the neighboring town (Bayou Sara), some on the other side of the bayou, three hundred yards distant, and some into the river. Several of these unfortunates were torn in pieces by coming in contact with pickets or posts, and I myself, saw pieces of human bodies which had been shot like cannon balls through the solid walls of houses at a considerable distance from the boat.[3]

Boiler explosions were a great equalizer. When the boiler blew up, you were just as dead, whether you were luxuriating in a first-class cabin or sleeping on a cotton bale on deck. Rosanna Dyer Osterman was among the well-known victims of a steamboat disaster. Her family had been among the first settlers—and the first Jewish settlers—of Galveston, Texas, when they arrived in the late 1830s. When a yellow fever epidemic swept through Galveston in 1853, she built a temporary hospital on the grounds of her family home. During the Civil War, she converted her house in Galveston into a hospital where she nursed both Union and Confederate soldiers.

In 1866, she booked passage on the steamer *W. R. Carter*. When the boiler exploded on February 2 near Vicksburg, Mississippi, she was one of 125 dead. The proceeds from her estate, some $200,000, went to hospitals and charitable organizations and helped to fund construction of synagogues in Galveston and Houston. The *Carter* explosion was the third major steamboat disaster in six days. Nearly four hundred people died in those accidents. The shock of those disasters finally pushed the US Congress into passing a few modest safety mandates for steamboat boilers.

MOURNING A BROTHER

Even the most famous riverman of the nineteenth century, Mark Twain, suffered a crippling loss from a boiler explosion. In 1858, when the twenty-two-year-old was still going by his birth name, Samuel Clemens, he lost his younger brother Henry to a boiler explosion on the steamboat *Pennsylvania*. The disaster might have taken both of their lives, if young Samuel hadn't had a short fuse.

Samuel and Henry had been working on the *Pennsylvania* just a few days before the boat went down. Samuel had a gig as steersman for the trip from St. Louis to New Orleans, part of the lengthy apprenticeship he completed to become a full-fledged river pilot. Henry was a mud clerk, a job that didn't come with a salary, but one that could, maybe someday, lead to a promotion to a position that paid. En route to New Orleans, Henry relayed a message to the pilot, William Brown, that the *Pennsylvania* would need to make an unplanned stop at an approaching landing. Twain, in his typically subtle manner, described Brown as a "horse-faced, ignorant, stingy, malicious, snarling, fault-hunting, mote-magnifying tyrant."[4]

According to Twain, Brown was also hard of hearing. When the boat floated past the landing, Captain Klinefelter went to the pilothouse to talk to the pilot. Brown feigned ignorance about the stop, but Samuel, who had been in the pilothouse when Henry passed on the instructions, backed up his brother's story.

Siding with a mud clerk over a pilot broke a professional code of conduct, though, so Brown was angry with the Clemens brothers. As Henry left the pilothouse, Brown chased after him while carrying a sizeable chunk of coal. Samuel assumed Brown was going to crush Henry's head with the coal, so he got in between them to protect his brother, then flattened Brown by smacking him with a stool. At that moment, the long and tortuous history that Samuel had endured with Brown overwhelmed his conscious thought. With Brown dazed from the chair strike, Samuel punched Brown repeatedly. "I do not know how long," Twain wrote, "the pleasure of it probably made it seem longer than it really was."[5]

Striking a superior was even less consistent with the professional code of conduct than siding with a mud clerk, so Captain Klinefelter wasn't pleased. He wasn't fond of Brown, either, though, so when Brown issued an ultimatum—to either keep him or Samuel Clemens—Klinefelter chose Clemens. Unfortunately, when the *Pennsylvania* reached New Orleans, the captain wasn't able to find a pilot to replace Brown, so Samuel had to leave the boat. Captain Klinefelter needed Brown to pilot the boat on its return trip upriver, but he promised to get Samuel back on board in St. Louis. The captain arranged for Samuel to ride back to St. Louis on the *A. T. Lacey*, which left New Orleans two days after the *Pennsylvania*. Henry remained on the *Pennsylvania*.

When the *Lacey* pulled into Greenville, Mississippi, a few days later, Samuel got word that something terrible had happened to the *Pennsylvania*. At each subsequent stop, Samuel learned more about the accident, but the stories sometimes conflicted. At one port, for example, Samuel heard that his brother Henry was near death, while in another he was told that Henry was fine. He wouldn't learn the full story until the *Lacey* reached Memphis.

Early on the morning of June 13, as the *Pennsylvania* passed near Ship Island (sixty miles south of Memphis) four of the boat's eight boilers exploded. The front third of the boat blew apart, and the stacks fell forward and crashed into the river. Debris shot up and landed on the back end of the boat.

Many of the 450 crew and passengers were asleep when the boilers blew, including the ship's carpenter, who landed 75 feet from the boat—still on his mattress. Brown vanished in the explosion. Captain Klinefelter, who had been sitting in the barber's chair when the boilers exploded, was unharmed, as was the barber.

Within moments of the explosion, flames engulfed the entire boat. Walls collapsed and trapped deck passengers behind debris. Many people burned to death when they couldn't break free. Some survivors escaped onto a barge that the *Pennsylvania* had been towing and floated to Ship Island, where they waited for rescue. Boats transported forty survivors, including Henry, to the Exchange Building in Memphis, where doctors attended to their wounds. Some of the wounded, though, just waited to die.

When the *Lacey* finally reached Memphis—two days after the accident—Henry was still alive. But he was gravely wounded. A Memphis newspaper reported that Samuel "hurried to the Exchange to see his brother, and on approaching the bedside of the wounded man, his feelings so much overcame him, at the scalded and emaciated form before him, that he sunk to the floor overpowered. There was scarcely a dry eye in the house; the poor sufferers shed tears at the sight. This brother had been pilot on the *Pennsylvania*, but fortunately for him, had remained in New Orleans when the boat started up."[6] Samuel stayed by his brother's side for the next six days, until Henry died, one of the two hundred passengers and crew killed in the disaster.

Twain believed an overly liberal use of morphine probably caused Henry's death rather than the injuries he suffered in the accident. Henry had been improving, but the attending doctor worried that moans from other victims might disturb Henry and set back his recovery. He left instructions for the next shift of doctors to give him a very small dose of morphine. Those doctors didn't have a reliable way to measure the dose, though, and Samuel believed they ultimately gave him too much. Remarkably, Twain didn't hold any grudges. "The physicians on watch were young fellows hardly out of the medical college, and they made a mistake."[7]

Years later, in his autobiography, Twain described a dream he'd had a few weeks before that fateful trip. In the dream, Samuel had seen Henry laid out in a coffin that rested upon two chairs. Certain details in the dream stood out: the casket was made of metal; Henry was dressed in one of Twain's suits; there was a bouquet of white roses on his chest, with one red rose in the center of the bouquet. The details of the dream had been so clear, the sense of loss so strong, that Samuel Clemens awoke convinced that his brother had died. It wasn't until after he had exited the boarding house where he had been sleeping that he realized the scene of Henry's death he had witnessed had only been a dream. He felt elated, but admitted that his sense of relief felt precarious.

After Henry died in Memphis, Samuel left the Exchange Building for a while to get some sleep. When he returned, he scanned each of the simple pine coffins looking for Henry. Samuel was startled, though, to find Henry in a metallic coffin instead. Several women had raised money for Henry's burial, which made the upgrade possible. It also surprised Samuel to see Henry dressed in a suit that Henry had borrowed from Samuel a while back. The scene felt all too eerily familiar. Then the last detail fell in place. As Samuel looked down upon his brother's corpse, a woman walked up to Henry's casket and placed a bouquet of white roses on his chest. In the center of the bouquet lay a single red rose.

Going Home

The Sultana

WARS ARE MESSY. SO IS THE END OF A WAR. THE LAST DAYS OF THE Civil War were no exception. Fears ran deep on each side. Trust was in short supply. And everyone was in a hurry to get home.

Robert E. Lee surrendered his army to Ulysses S. Grant on April 9, 1865. Both sides began to release soldiers held in prison camps. Hosea Aldrich and William Boor joined other Union soldiers as they left the overcrowded camp at Cahaba, Alabama. The Confederacy also released

Photo 11.1. The *Sultana* at Helena, Arkansas, April 26, 1865
LIBRARY OF CONGRESS; PHOTO BY THOMAS W. BANKES.

men from the infamous Andersonville prison camp. Of the 41,000 men held at Andersonville during the war years, about a third died. Chester Berry and James Brady were among the lucky two-thirds who survived.

The Confederacy shipped prisoners from Cahaba and Andersonville to a temporary location just outside of Vicksburg, Mississippi, known as Camp Fisk. When the soldiers arrived at the camp, they were wounded or suffering from disease and malnutrition. All were weakened. James Brady weighed just ninety-six pounds, sixty pounds below his prewar weight. Most had also suffered terrible trauma. Getting men out of the camp and back home took time, though, because the rules at the time required the release of one Confederate soldier for each Union prisoner released. As the number of men in Camp Fisk swelled—to five thousand men by April 1865—managing them all became untenable.

On April 22, the *Henry Ames* took 1,300 soldiers toward home. The next day, the *Olive Branch* transported 600 more men away from the war. When another boat, the *Sultana*, arrived at Vicksburg in late April, military commanders were eager to keep the momentum going.

A Troubled Past

The *Sultana* that docked in Vicksburg in April 1865 was the fifth boat with that name. In 1862, Preston Lodwick spent $60,000 to build the boat at the John Litherbury Boatyard in Fulton, Ohio. It would enter service the following year. The *Sultana* stretched 260 feet from bow to stern and rose four decks high. It could accommodate seventy-six passengers in the cabins and another three hundred on deck.

The boat's paddlewheels were on the side. Four tubular boilers, an innovation of the day that produced a more powerful machine, turned the giant wheels. Each of the *Sultana's* boilers had a system of twenty-four flues that connected the firebox to the chimney. Coal burned in the fireboxes under the boilers, which generated hot gasses that filled the flues and heated the river water that was pumped into the boilers, which turned to steam that powered the boat. Even with all that weight, the *Sultana* could run in water as shallow as seven feet deep.

Captain Lodwick earned his investment back quickly, helped in part by contracts to transport goods and soldiers for the Union Army. In

March 1864, he sold the boat to a group of investors. One of the new owners was Cass Mason, a man in his early thirties who had already gained a reputation for poor judgment, except when it came to choosing whom to marry.

Mason's wife was Mary Rowena Dozier. Her father, James Dozier, was river royalty, the owner of several steamboats and a lot of land. Dozier gave Mason command of one of his steamboats, the *Rowena* (named after his daughter). Mason landed in trouble in February 1863 when Union soldiers seized the boat's cargo. Mason had been secretly—and illegally—trying to run supplies (uniforms and quinine) to the Confederate Army. The army impounded the *Rowena*. Dozier wasn't impressed and cut Mason out of the family business. Mason had frequent money problems after that and would later sell most of his ownership share in the *Sultana* to cover his debts.

On April 15, 1865, the day after President Lincoln died, the *Sultana* left Cairo, Illinois, bound for New Orleans. Its flag flew at half-mast. Telegraph lines were down throughout the Mississippi Valley, so steamboats often carried the news of the day. On this trip, the *Sultana* carried news of Lincoln's death.

When the *Sultana* reached Vicksburg, Captain Mason learned the Union was eager to send hundreds of soldiers home from Camp Fisk. The Union would pay five dollars for each enlisted man transported and ten dollars for each officer. Mason recognized the financial opportunity. Before they left Vicksburg for New Orleans, he met with Union officers to lobby for a load of passengers on the *Sultana's* return trip. The *Sultana* continued on to New Orleans, where it loaded up with cargo that included seventy mules and horses and three hundred thousand pounds of sugar. It also took on forty passengers, including the Chicago Opera Troupe bound for Memphis for their next round of performances.

When the *Sultana* returned to Vicksburg, though, one boiler had developed a leak. Chief engineer Nathan Wintringer raced into town to find someone to fix it, while Captain Mason did his best to keep news of the boiler leak quiet. The boiler expert Wintringer spoke to recommended a time-consuming and costly fix. Wintringer—aware of Mason's desire to get going as quickly as possible—insisted that a metal patch over the leak would be sufficient. Reluctantly, the repairman complied.

Meanwhile, Union officers were busy organizing men to board the *Sultana* from Camp Fisk. The process was more rushed than usual and communications were poor, so they undercounted the number of men who had boarded. They packed so many men onto the ship's hurricane deck that it visibly sagged and had to be temporarily reinforced.

Hosea Aldrich boarded the *Sultana* with Berry, Boor, Brady, and the masses. "I went on board the boiler deck of the steamer 'Sultana' with the other prisoners, like a flock of sheep," he wrote.[1] When William Boor boarded, he heard noises from the engine room (the repair work, probably), so he went to look at the boilers. Unimpressed with what he saw, he and a few others moved from the hurricane deck to a more protected part of the lower deck, in case the worst happened.

UNDER WAY

The *Sultana* left Vicksburg on the night of April 24. Most of the soldiers barely had space to sit, much less lie down to sleep. There weren't enough blankets to go around, and the rations weren't as good as they had hoped. Still, the men adapted. After all the pain they had survived as prisoners of war, many felt they could stand a few more days of discomfort to get back home.

On the way to Memphis, the boat stopped in Helena, Arkansas. A local photographer showed up to take a picture of the boat. When word got around the boat about the photographer, a lot of men moved to the port side to get in the picture, which caused the boat to lean and induced a momentary fear that the boat might capsize.

The *Sultana* stayed upright, though, and steamed into Memphis about twelve hours later. Some of the cabin passengers exited, as did the opera troupe. Many of the soldiers took advantage of the extended layover and went into town to stretch their legs and look for something to eat.

Around midnight, the *Sultana* pulled out of Memphis and made a quick stop across the river to stock up on coal. George Kayton steered the boat back upriver, guiding it through an island complex known as

Paddy's Hen and Chickens. First mate William Rowberry stood next to him. Down below, assistant engineer Wes Clemens managed the boilers. Around two in the morning, life would change for all of them.

The Explosion

Joseph Bringman fell asleep soon after the *Sultana* left Memphis. He dreamt he was walking up a hill to a ledge that overlooked a river. When he stepped on the ledge "the rock seemed to burst with a report like the shot of a distant cannon. I felt pieces of rock striking my face and head and I seemed to be hurled out into the river."[2] The shock of the rocks hitting him in the face woke him. He was stunned when he realized he was no longer on the *Sultana* but in the Mississippi River.

Around two in the morning on April 27, one of the *Sultana*'s boilers exploded, then two more exploded in quick succession. The sound of the explosions carried all the way to Memphis, some seven miles downriver. The burst created a hole in the middle of the boat that swallowed passengers. As the boat sagged toward the middle, one smokestack fell forward, while the other fell backward.

Kayton fell from the pilothouse down toward the engine room. After freeing himself from debris, he looked for buckets of sand to put out the fires, but he didn't find any. Some soldiers had emptied the buckets and then filled them with water from the river to drink. Kayton grabbed a piece of wood and jumped into the river. The fires raged on.

First Mate William Rowberry recalled seeing a flash, then falling into the river with the remains of the pilothouse. When he surfaced, he saw "a sea of heads for hundreds of yards around."[3]

The explosion killed many people instantly. Flying pieces of metal pierced bodies. Steam scalded others. Burning wood trapped some passengers, while others fell in the river. Chief Engineer Wintringer later recalled that the chaos after the explosion was "as fresh in my memory today as it was twenty-one years ago. . . . I stood bewildered for a moment, and then saw the river perfectly alive with human beings struggling in the water."[4] He pulled off a shutter and jumped in the river as the fire approached him.

When Murray Baker woke up, "Men who were scalded and bruised were crawling over one another to get out of the fire." The sound of a terrible crash and a feeling that everything was falling startled Hosea Aldrich. "The things I had under my head, my shoes, and some other articles and specimens that I had gathered up and had them tied up in an old pair of drawers, they all went down through the floor. . . . Brave men rushed to and fro in the agony of fear, some uttering the most profane language and recommending their spirits to the Great Ruler of the Universe."[5] In the middle of the chaos, Aldrich got pushed into the river. He couldn't swim.

Pieces of flying wood struck Chester Berry on the head. Steam from the explosion scalded to death the man he had been bunking next to. Berry, a good swimmer, looked around and saw the chaotic scene in the water and waited before going in. As he made his way along the deck, he encountered a man who was crying. The man kept repeating that he couldn't swim and was sure he was going to drown. Berry tried to help him but, frustrated and fighting for his own life, he panicked and pushed the man overboard, where he almost certainly drowned. Berry then jumped into the river equipped with a board he had salvaged. He tried to paddle toward a bank of willows, but the current was too strong. He felt hope slipping away.

James Brady woke to find himself on fire and his friend, David Ettleman, putting it out. Most of the hair on his head had burned off by that time. They ran to the front of the hurricane deck, then found a rope they used to lower themselves down. "O, what a sight met our gaze!" he recalled. "There were some killed in the explosion, lying in the bottom of the boat, being trampled upon, while some were crying and praying, many were cursing while others were singing. That sight I shall never forget; I often see it in my sleep, and wake with a start."[6] They figured fate had doomed them at that point, but a group of men showed up dragging part of the gangplank. They tossed it into the water and right after that, forty to fifty men followed it into the Mississippi.

STRUGGLING TO SURVIVE

As fire spread throughout the boat, hundreds of people sought shelter at the bow, where they were upwind of the flames. When the paddlewheels quit churning, though, the boat rotated around, and they found themselves in the direct path of the fire. Some jumped in the water, but many others couldn't escape.

The survivors in the river could only hold on for so long. The waters of the Mississippi River are still cold in April, even down around Memphis, typically in the mid-fifties (Fahrenheit). When the water is that cold, muscles cramp, and dexterity declines within fifteen minutes. Within an hour or two, a person gets drowsy and teeters on the verge of consciousness. With the help of a flotation device, a person could survive for maybe five hours, but that's the upper limit. The people in the river, therefore, had to get out or the cold water would kill them.

Hosea Aldrich clung to debris to stay afloat, but he had to fight off other passengers who tried to grab hold of him. He yielded some scraps to other men in the water, and eventually supported himself on one end of a ladder before he passed out from the cold.

Joseph Bringman also held on desperately to debris to stay afloat. It was too dark to see anyone around him, but he could hear people screaming and begging for help. As he floated downstream with the current, he encountered a group of men hanging onto part of a floor. They invited him to join them, but when he tried, the wood sank below the water, so he gave up and went back to his board. Not long after that, those other men collided with debris. Some shook loose and drowned. Bringman yelled for help as he floated past Memphis, but he was too far away from shore for anyone to hear him.

After the boilers exploded, William Boor figured that his best chance for survival was in the river. He prepped a bundle of clothes and a blanket and picked up a piece of wood to float on, then leapt off the boat. A short time later, he got sucked into a whirlpool and struggled to stay afloat. Fighting the circling current tired him out, though. He gave up fighting and dove into it. Just as he was nearly out of breath, he popped back up. He resurfaced safely away from the whirlpool and near his board. He grabbed another piece of wood to add more stability. When another man floated by begging for help, Boor initially refused to help, telling him that "we had got where every one must be for himself, and that I could not swim and had to depend on that board to bring me to safety."[7] The other man couldn't swim, either, and continued to plea for help. Boor changed his mind and helped him onto the makeshift platform, and it held steady. They floated together until they landed on the Arkansas shore.

James Brady and his friend, David Ettleman, followed the gangway into the water. As Brady struggled to get a secure grip on it, he felt someone grab his right foot. He shook his leg to free himself until he felt his sock slip off and saw the person sink away. Later that night, Ettleman directed the other men around the gangway to climb on top while he held it steady. It worked, and they used their hands to paddle toward a building in the distance. It turned out to be a stable where they sheltered overnight. In the morning, Brady counted twenty-three other men with them "and as far as the eye could see, upon every old snag and every little piece of drift big enough, you would see a man. That sight I never will forget."[8]

Even as passengers struggled and sometimes fought to survive, there were remarkable stories of selflessness. Chester Berry recalled one incident in particular:

Among the passengers on board were twelve ladies, most of them belonging to the Christian commission, an association akin to that of the sanitary commission of the Army of the Potomac. One of these ladies, with more than ordinary courage, when the flames at last drove all the men from the boat, seeing them fighting like demons in the water in the mad endeavor to save their lives, actually destroying each other and themselves by their wild actions, talked to them, urging them to be men, and finally succeeded in getting them quieted down, clinging to the ropes and chains that hung over the bow of the boat. The flames now began to lap around her with their fiery tongues. The men pleaded and urged her to jump into the water and thus save herself, but she refused, saying: "I might lose my presence of mind and be the means of the death of some of you." And so, rather than run the risk of becoming the cause of the death of a single person, she folded her arms quietly over her bosom and burned, a voluntary martyr to the men she had so lately quieted.[9]

RESCUES

The Mississippi was running high, so the survivors struggled to find a dry bank, especially in the dark. For a short time, the fire from the boat lit up the night and made it easier to spot treetops or a shoreline. Some passengers, like Otto Bardon, lodged themselves in one of those trees. While it got him out of the cold water, he later wrote that "It seemed as if the gnats and mosquitoes would eat us alive."[10]

People did whatever they could to survive. William Barnes floated to shore on a bale of hay. Hiram Allison found a horse trough floating in the river and grabbed the middle of it. There were men at either end who were praying continuously, even when he tried to talk to them. The next morning, they were both gone. Barnes rode the trough into shoreline brush, where he was later rescued.

William Lugenbeal found an even more unusual way of staying alive. He survived the boiler explosion, even though flying debris had pierced the man next to him. During the panic, he remembered that someone had brought a pet alligator on the boat. He raced to the closet where it had been stored, opened the box, and ran a bayonet through the gator's head. He then dumped the gator out, tossed the box into the river, and jumped in behind it. It took him three tries before he got inside, and then he had to fight off other men who were trying to hang onto the box. He spotted the outline of trees on a bank while he had light from the fire, but they disappeared when the flames went out. Still, his box stayed afloat, and the crew of the gunboat *Essex later rescued him.*

For Chester Berry, his prospects seemed increasingly bleak as he floated alone, at least until his mind flashed back to his hometown and he heard his mother's voice: "God save my boy!" she said. The experience renewed his hope. After an unsuccessful attempt to climb into a tree—and after fighting off a man trying to take his board—he found a cluster of ash tree branches he used to stabilize his board. It got him out of the cold water, and he slept through the night.

In the middle of the night, people who lived along the river raced out to rescue as many people as they could. John Fogleman and his sons built a makeshift raft. They completed multiple trips in which they rescued passengers who were stranded on the *Sultana's* bow as it burned. They rescued perhaps a hundred men—carrying only six at a time!—all of whom they took to the Fogleman home, which became a temporary hospital.

Franklin Barton, recently discharged from the Confederate Army, paddled a canoe from his home on the Arkansas shore. He later told a reporter that "he did not care if they were Federal soldiers, humanity demanded that they should have help, and that he would do all in his power to help them."[11] William Boor was one of the men rescued by Barton. He had nearly passed out from hypothermia when Barton pulled him out of the river.

Locals in small boats made the first rescue attempts, but steamboats got involved quickly, too, including the *Bostona II*, which saved upwards of 250 people. The crew of the gunboat *Essex* pulled sixty men and one woman from the river. One man on the *Essex*, Thomas Love, recalled a gruesome encounter during the rescue efforts. He found a man "so badly scalded that when I took hold of his arms to help him into the boat, the skin and flesh came off his arms like a cooked beet." He got the man on the boat and to a hospital in Memphis, and the man, remarkably, survived. Years later, Love reunited with that man and shook his hand, "with a grip that did not slip as when I went to pull him into the boat."[12]

Joseph Bringman eventually succumbed to the cold and passed out after he floated past Memphis. When he came to, he lay on a mattress on the Memphis riverfront. He had a broken arm and three broken ribs, his face was scalded, and he had plenty of bruises, but he was alive.

Hosea Aldrich also survived. After floating nearly six miles downriver, the crew of the *Pocahontas* rescued him. "They poured whiskey down me, rolled and rubbed me, and finally brought me back to life," he said.[13] People from the *Pocahontas* also rescued Chester Berry, although he would later find his name listed among the dead. (His mother even received a death notice from the army.) James Brady and David Ettleman hung on long enough to be rescued by the *Jenny Lind*. Brady's muscles had stiffened so tightly that he couldn't move, so Ettleman and others helped him onto the rescue boat. Among the crew, pilot Kayton survived, as did First Mate Rowberry and Chief Engineer Wintringer.

Rescuers took some survivors to Fort Pickering where men from the Third US Colored Artillery tended to them. Most, though, went to Memphis to recover. Some victims even found sanctuary in the home of the mayor of Memphis, who volunteered his residence as a temporary hospital. About three hundred victims died in Memphis from their injuries.

Search teams scoured the river for bodies into the second week of May, but victims kept turning up for a while after that. Phineas Parks, an engineer on the USS *Vindicator*, recalled that the boat's paddlewheel had a habit of collecting driftwood, so the crew had to clear it daily. "When clearing the wheels after the *Sultana* disaster we would find them clogged with dead bodies from the *Sultana*."[14]

Many victims were buried on the riverbank where they were found. Others were buried in a couple of mass graves near the site of the wreck. Hundreds more were buried in Elmwood Cemetery, then later removed to the Memphis National Cemetery. The bodies of many of the victims were never recovered, though, including the *Sultana's* captain, Cass Mason.

WHAT HAPPENED?

No less than three military commissions investigated the disaster, but none took a deep dive. Some of the top officers involved had resigned by then and were no longer subject to military law. The investigations were critical of the officers who let the *Sultana* become so overcrowded, and rightly so.

Captain Frederick Speed believed he had boarded no more than 1,700 men. In fact, it was closer to 2,100. Two other steamboats left Vicksburg without taking any soldiers, and there were accusations that bribes may have been to blame, although it wasn't clear who was supposed to have bribed whom.

Still, it wasn't unusual for the military to cram soldiers onto steamboats, and none of the reports reached any conclusions about the cause of the explosion. In the end, the military charged only Captain Speed. He was convicted of neglect of duty for overcrowding the *Sultana*, but his conviction was later overturned.

Contemporary researchers have estimated that the *Sultana* was carrying nearly 2,300 people at the time of the explosion: 2,100 soldiers, 100 paying passengers, and a crew of 80. Fewer than 800 people survived, including only a dozen of the paying passengers and crew. The *Sultana* disaster killed upwards of 1,600 people, which is 100 more than perished on the *Titanic*.

There's never been a definitive answer about the cause of the disaster, though. Sabotage was proposed at one time. In 1903, a St. Louis newspaper even published a story claiming that a farmer had hidden explosives inside cordwood he had sold to the *Sultana*. Every theory touting a conspiracy or sabotage has been debunked, though.

A lot of suspicion has centered on the boiler repair in Vicksburg, that metal patch that was applied to cover a leak. Second engineer Sam Clemens was on duty at the time of the explosion. Before he died from the injuries he suffered in the explosion, Clemens told investigators that the boilers had been full of water and running fine before the explosion. If he was right, then the patch wasn't the trigger.

The consensus today is that the *Sultana*'s tubular boilers were fundamentally flawed. In fact, in the year after the *Sultana* disaster, two other steamboats with tubular boilers suffered explosions: the *Walter R. Carter* and the *Missouri*. By 1866, tubular boilers were largely out of use. The *Sultana*'s chief engineer, Nathan Wintringer, later wrote that tubular boilers had been "used with some success on the Upper Mississippi, where the water at all times is clear and not liable to make much sediment or scale."[15] The sediment was thick in the Lower Mississippi's waters and was prone to accumulate in the flues of tubular boilers. It wasn't easy to remove. When it got too dense inside, it could cause an explosion.

TOO EASILY FORGOTTEN

The lucky passengers who survived the *Sultana* disaster still had to find a way home. For most, that meant getting on another steamboat. There just weren't many other options. James Brady was among those who continued upriver. When his boat reached Cairo, Illinois, he headed directly to the soldier's home, where he got his first good meal in three years and a comfortable bed to sleep in. The next day, he boarded a train for Mattoon, Illinois, which had prepared a big welcome. "O, what a sight we witnessed! The platform at the depot was crowded, from one end to the other, with the citizens of Mattoon and surrounding country, with baskets filled to over-flowing with every thing you could think of to eat."[16] When he got home to Ohio a short time later, though, he felt shocked. Everyone he had known, it seemed, had left town or was dead.

The sorrow ran deep. Maybe A. C. Brown put it best: "After my comrades had faced the leaden hail, had fallen into the hands of the enemy, passed through all the harrowing experiences of prison life, that they should meet such a fate when almost in the embrace of friends at home seemed doubly sad."[17]

Some survivors formed groups to stay in touch and share their memories. Many of them met once a year. Chester Berry contacted survivors and invited them to write about their experiences. He compiled their essays into a memorial book.

The *Sultana* disappeared into the Mississippi River near Fogelman's Landing, just upriver from Mound City, Arkansas. Since that time, the river's channel has shifted, so the remains of the *Sultana* are now buried deep under layers of silt.

Stories of the *Sultana* disaster nearly disappeared in the layers of time, too. The disaster got lost in a rapid series of events, from the last decisive battles of the Civil War, to President Lincoln's assassination, to the killing of Lincoln's assassin, John Wilkes Booth on the day before the *Sultana* went down.

A couple of generations of Americans grew up knowing nothing of the worst maritime disaster in American history. In recent years, a few books and articles have brought renewed attention to the disaster. Still, there are shockingly few public tributes. A group of survivors paid for a memorial in Knoxville, Tennessee's Mount Olive Cemetery. There's a small museum in Marion, Arkansas, preserving the memory of the tragedy. That's about it.

For A. C. Brown, that tragic day provided a lesson in perspective that he never forgot: "Now, when I hear persons talking about being hard up, I think of my condition at that time—up in a tree in the middle of the Mississippi river, a thousand miles from home, not one cent to my name, nor a pocket to put it in."[18]

Let Us All Die Together

The Monmouth

AMERICAN INDIAN COMMUNITIES THRIVED IN THE SOUTHEASTERN United States for centuries before Europeans first set foot in the Americas. The invasion led by Hernando de Soto set in motion a series of events that altered that world forever and triggered massive political and social upheaval.

Europeans brought diseases that Indigenous Americans had no immunity to. They also brought social and economic systems, including the slave trade, that further decimated Native American communities. Christopher Columbus's first money-making venture was the capture of five hundred Indigenous people, who he shipped to Europe to be sold into slavery. From 1492 to the late 1800s, Europeans enslaved over twelve million Africans in the Americas. What is less well known, though, is that another two to five million Native Americans were also enslaved during that same period, which wiped out many Indigenous communities.

By the eighteenth century, only scattered remnants of the former southeastern communities remained. Many of the surviving people merged into new groups. The confederacy that became known as the Muscogee (Creek) Nation was one of them.

Muscogee communities grew in Alabama, Georgia, and parts of Florida, roughly divided geographically into upper and lower units, and often built along rivers. These communities were multiethnic and multilingual, but all were equal in Muscogee society.

Muscogee towns—the heart of the confederacy—governed themselves and controlled specific sections of land. Many Muscogee farmed, and some of the wealthier Muscogee adopted the American practice of buying enslaved Blacks to work their farms.

White Americans gradually moved into Muscogee territory. Many terrorized Muscogee communities by stealing livestock, burning down houses, and sometimes murdering residents. Some White Americans also tried to steal land by squatting in Muscogee territory. A series of treaties with the US government gradually reduced Muscogee possessions. After the US Congress passed the Indian Removal Act in 1832, the Muscogee reluctantly agreed to sell their remaining lands in the Southeast and relocate to Indian Territory (what is now Oklahoma).

Many Muscogee moved west in 1834 as part of the Trail of Tears, but thousands stayed behind. The 1832 treaty had dissolved communal (tribal) ownership of land, but individual Muscogee could own their own parcels and stick around. Land speculators and squatters who used deceptive (or illegal) practices to take ownership victimized many of those who stayed. A small group of Muscogee who were fed up with that state of affairs raided an illegal White settlement in 1836 (the so-called Second Creek War). The US government used the outbreak of violence as an excuse to remove the remaining Muscogee from the Southeast. The military rounded up several thousand people and held them in stockades until officials worked out plans to move them west.

The US Army hired contractors such as the Alabama Emigrating Company to manage the logistics of relocating thousands of Muscogee people. The Alabama Emigrating Company moved Muscogee from Mobile Point, Alabama, to Pass Christian, Mississippi, then to the Mississippi River near New Orleans. They traveled in large groups, often by steamboat but sometimes on foot. One large contingent of several thousand reached New Orleans in the fall of 1836, then made temporary camp about fifteen miles north of the city to avoid exposure to yellow fever. A short time later, they were herded onto several steamboats that would take them up the Mississippi River to Arkansas: the *John Nelson*, *Yazoo*, *Monmouth*, *Farmer*, *Black Hawk*, and *Far West*. Dave Barnett described the scene when he boarded the *Monmouth*:

When we boarded the ship, it was at night time and it was raining, cloudy and dark. There were dangerous waves of water. The people aboard the ship did not want the ship to start on the journey at night but to wait until the next day. The men in command of the ship disregarded all suggestions and said, "the ship is going tonight."[1]

The *Monmouth* was an old, two-deck boat near the end of its service. It probably would have been scrapped if the company hadn't pressed it into service to transport the Muscogee. Instead, over six hundred Muscogee boarded it for the trip to Arkansas, where they were to disembark and then walk to Fort Gibson.

Besides hundreds of Muscogee, the *Monmouth* carried boxes of whiskey that were stacked high. "The officers in charge of the ship became intoxicated and even induced some of the Indians to drink," Barnett recalled. "Timbochee Barnett, who was my father, and I begged the officers to stop the ship until morning as the men in charge of the steering of the ship could not control the ship and keep it on its course but was causing it to go around and around."[2]

Officers ignored their pleas, and the boat continued on its course upriver. Deep in the night of October 31, as a cold rain fell, the *Monmouth* reached Phophet's Island (Profit Island today), where the river channel splits. Pilots expected upriver boats to stay right and follow a chute around the east side of the island and downriver boats to follow the main channel down the other side of the island. The *Monmouth*, though, stayed to the left.

A few minutes later, the *Monmouth* crashed into another boat, the *Trenton* (it was being towed by the *Warren*). The force of the collision knocked the cabin off of the *Monmouth*'s hull and split the lower deck. Hundreds of people were thrown into the river. Those who were still on the floating wreckage ran to the upper deck.

As the remains of the cabin floated downriver, with about two hundred people still on board, some of the crew from the *Yazoo* and *Warren* rushed out in small rescue boats. The cabin, though, split and sank before most of the remaining passengers got off, dumping more people into the river. Some of the Muscogee in the river were rescued, and some swam to shore. Many drowned.

For three days, the *Yazoo* ran along the shore looking for survivors and bodies. Surviving Muscogee did their best to identify their lost friends and relatives. "The dead was gathered and buried and some were lost forever in the waters," Barnett recalled.[3] Many of the victims were buried in a mass grave by the Mississippi River.

Nearly half of the Muscogee on the *Monmouth*—over three hundred men, women, and children—died in the accident, but only two *Monmouth* crew members died, a fireman and a bartender. In addition, thirty-four enslaved Black people owned by a few of the wealthier Muscogee also died.

When word of the disaster reached the steamboats upriver of the *Monmouth*, they stopped at the mouth of the White River. An agent on one of those boats went to help. A few days after the wreck, the *Monmouth* survivors boarded the *Yazoo* and the *John Nelson* and resumed their trip. The boats traveled up the White River to Rock Row in Arkansas, then the Muscogee walked the remaining distance to Fort Gibson and their new home.

News of the accident took a while to get around. There were no telegraphs. Information got around by steamboat, stagecoach, or on horseback. When word of the accident reached a group of Chickasaws at Memphis, who were also being forced west, most of them chose to walk rather than risk death on a steamboat.

The *Monmouth*'s owner took some heat for the accident. He had been on board the *Monmouth* when it crashed and was eager to share his version of events with the public. "The steamer came in contact with a ship with such violence as to break in the bows of the *Monmouth* and causing her immediately to be filled with water," he told a newspaper. He defended his boat and crew. "The boat was but little over 12 months old, was well manned, all of her officers were of experience, and knowing their duty, did not neglect it, and in fine, she ranked among the best boats on the river."

Mostly, though, few people bought his defense. One newspaper wrote:

[T]he fearful responsibility for this vast sacrifice of human life, rests on the contractors for emigrating the Muscogee Indians. The avaricious disposition to increase the profits on the speculation, first induced the chartering of rotten, old, and unseaworthy boats because they were of a class to be procured cheaply; and then to make those increased profits still larger, the Indians were packed upon these crazy vessels in such crowds, that not the slightest regard seems to have been paid to their safety, comfort, or even decency. The crammed condition of the decks and cabins, was offensive to every sense and feeling, and kept the poor creatures in a state unfit for human beings.[4]

Twenty years later, memory of the wreck had already faded, although criticism of the boat's owner hadn't. "It is not without some feeling of indignation," wrote James Lloyd, "that we mention the circumstance that the drowning of four hundred Indians, the largest number of human beings ever sacrificed in a steamboat disaster, attracted but little attention. . . . Even the journalists and news-collectors of that region, on the waters of which this horrible affair took place, appear to have regarded the event as of too little importance to deserve any particular detail; and accordingly the best accounts we have of the matter merely state the outlines of the story, with scarcely a word of commiseration for the sufferers, or a single expression of rebuke for the heartless villains who wantonly exposed the lives of so many artless and confiding people to imminent peril, or almost certain destruction."[5]

For the Muscogee survivors, the *Monmouth* disaster was just one more traumatic experience in a series of traumas. After they had boarded the steamboats that were taking them to an uncertain future, a song went around, credited to a woman named Sin-e-cha, that captured the feelings of many Muscogee in that moment:

I have no more land,
I am driving away from home,
Driven up the red waters,

Let us all go,
Let us all die together and,
Somewhere on the banks we will be there.[6]

Shattered Reminders of Our Weakness

The Sea Wing

BY THE END OF THE NINETEENTH CENTURY, DAY TRIPS ON STEAMBOATS known as excursions had replaced long-distance river travel. Excursions on the Mississippi were a popular pastime from Minneapolis to New Orleans. When Captain David Wethern and his business partner Marion (Mel) Sparks scheduled an excursion of their own for a summer Sunday, they expected a big crowd. They also expected the trip to be the swan song for their boat, the *Sea Wing*, which they had already agreed to sell.

Wethern and Sparks had the *Sea Wing* built in 1888 so they could move lumber rafts on the Mississippi, a profitable business. The boat rested on a flat hull 135 feet long, with a cabin and pilothouse that rose 22 feet from the base but stretched only 16 feet wide. The *Sea Wing* looked rather precarious, but the design worked well in the Mississippi's shallow waters. Unfortunately, a top-heavy boat just doesn't fare well when the wind blows hard, as Wethern would learn all too well on a summer day in 1890.

THE EXCURSION
Wethern and Sparks scheduled the trip for July 13. For fifty cents, passengers would cruise down Lake Pepin—a natural widening in the Mississippi's main channel—to Lake City, Minnesota, then return home in the late afternoon. This excursion had the added attraction of taking folks to visit a National Guard encampment. Watching men run through military drills was a popular leisure activity in the days before people could share memes on social media. Expecting a full boat, they lashed a

barge, the *Jim Grant*, to one side of the *Sea Wing* to provide space for a band and dancing.

Not everyone was enthusiastic about the cruise, however. An itinerant preacher known only as Georgas had been telling anyone who would listen about visions he'd been having of an impending disaster. For a week, he had been warning people in Diamond Bluff, Wisconsin, the *Sea Wing*'s home port, that the excursion was going to end in tragedy. He swayed a few people, just not Wethern or the crew.

Captain Wethern guided the boat out of Diamond Bluff at 8:40 a.m., with eleven passengers and ten crew members. He also brought along his wife, Nellie, and their two sons, ten-year-old Roy and eight-year-old Perley. Georgas packed up and left town. He said that he wouldn't be able to bear their grief after the coming storm sank the boat.

Twenty minutes after leaving Diamond Bluff, the *Sea Wing* docked at Trenton, Wisconsin, and loaded twenty-two more passengers, then Wethern guided the boat across the river to Red Wing, Minnesota, where the bulk of the passengers got on. Peter and Maria Gerken boarded with their five children, who ranged in age from five to fifteen. Eighteen-year-old Mary Leach traveled with several friends. The crowd skewed young, with many of the passengers single men and women.

One of the last people to get on was ten-year-old Lenus Lillyblad. He and a friend were watching the boat fill up when a crew member offered them a free ride if they would help load ice. They accepted, but didn't have time to tell their parents they were going on the trip. At least a hundred people boarded in Red Wing, but no one knew the exact number because the crew wasn't required to keep a complete list for an excursion.

The passengers were primed for a special day. Women were decked out in their best dresses. Mary Leach wore a new white lace dress accented with a black satin bodice, and she carried a black satin parasol to shield herself from the sun. Men dressed in their finest suits. The mood was festive and maybe a little flirtatious.

As the *Sea Wing* cruised down the river, Henry Rehder's band entertained passengers on the *Jim Grant*. The air was humid and temperatures were warmer than normal, but a cooling breeze blew off the river. When the *Sea Wing* docked at Lake City at 11:30 a.m., passengers found its citizens in a celebratory mood. Lake City residents had set up stands selling ice cream, popcorn, and lemonade.

Passengers made their way to the National Guard encampment south of the city, where soldiers, many of them from Red Wing, gave guided tours. At four in the afternoon, the passengers enjoyed a band concert. Captain Wethern was ready to head back upriver after that, but most of the passengers wanted to stick around for the dress parade at seven. The captain went along, reluctantly.

Around 4:45 p.m., a violent storm ravaged the communities of Little Canada and Lake Gervais just north of the Twin Cities. No one on the excursion knew about the storm, though, so when the skies darkened around Lake City a short while later, no one understood what was coming. The skies opened up around seven, interrupting the dress parade. Mary Leach and a few friends ducked into a tent for shelter.

After the rain had let up, Captain Wethern blew the whistle alerting passengers that the boat would leave soon. He was eager to get going, as were many of the passengers by then. Most believed the worst of the storm had passed. A few people encouraged the captain to wait a little longer, but they were in the minority. At eight o'clock, Wethern guided the boat away from Lake City for the seventeen-mile trip back to Red Wing. Mary Leach and her friends raced back to the dock, but they were too late. The *Sea Wing* had already left.

As the boat navigated around a peninsula known as Central Point, passengers caught sight of a bank of ominous clouds rolling in. Passenger Charlie Sewall didn't like what he saw. He yelled goodbye to his friends, then jumped off the boat and swam to shore.

The storm erupted over Lake City. As windows shattered, Mary Leach and her friends ran for cover again. When they emerged from shelter after the storm had passed, they saw a destroyed Collins' Brothers mill, a music academy missing its roof, and entire blocks of damaged buildings. Down at the National Guard camp, soldiers reported seeing "the angry waves of Lake Pepin . . . rolling mountain high."[1] The storm blew down sixty of the sixty-five tents in camp.

Mary Leach walked into a hotel to gather herself. Before she could settle in, someone ran inside and yelled that *Sea Wing* was in danger and needed help.

A FATEFUL DECISION

When Captain Wethern guided the *Sea Wing* away from Lake City, he had to veer toward the middle of the river to maneuver around Central Point. A strong, steady wind was blowing from the west. Those powerful gusts were making the passengers increasingly nervous. Most of the women had moved inside the cabin for shelter. As the winds grew even stronger, the boat rocked violently and chairs blew off the upper deck. A few passengers put on life preservers. Captain Wethern struggled to maintain control of the boat. His wife Nellie sent Perley to bed in the captain's stateroom, then she sat in a rocking chair just outside the door. She projected calm.

Five miles into the return trip, Wethern spotted a squall over the river. He turned the boat to run directly into its headwinds. The *Sea Wing* bounced over giant waves, sometimes rising so high that the rudder lifted completely out of the water. Water splashed into the cabin. The waves knocked engineers Mel and William Sparks off their feet. Wethern was losing control of the *Sea Wing*.

Out on the *Jim Grant*, passengers held on tight as their barge rolled and twisted. The ropes securing the *Jim Grant* to the *Sea Wing* repeatedly tightened and went slack. Some men on the barge debated cutting the barge loose. They weren't sure if the barge was keeping the *Sea Wing* stable or making matters worse. Winds pummeled the boat from multiple directions. Before the people on the *Jim Grant* could decide about the ropes, they watched in horror as the *Sea Wing* tilted forty-five degrees, froze in place for a moment, then flipped over completely. The *Jim Grant* then broke free.

Engineer Mel Sparks escaped from the flooded boat and swam to the surface. He hung onto the keel for a moment, then found a piece of debris that he rode to shore. His brother William also got out, but he lost consciousness as he floated toward shore. Captain Wethern was trapped upside down in the pilothouse. He braced himself against the wheel and pushed the window. It didn't budge on the first try, but the second push worked, and he swam out and under the overturned boat. When he surfaced, he swam to the keel, then looked around for his wife and children. He didn't see them anywhere.

About a hundred passengers, most of them on the *Jim Grant*, struggled to survive. Passengers in the water tried to hang onto the hull, but it was too slick for many and they slipped away. Some hung onto debris to stay afloat. The passengers in the cabin never had a chance. They were quickly trapped inside as the boat filled with water.

The *Sea Wing* rolled on its side again, tossing everyone who had been hanging onto the hull back into the water, including Captain Wethern. He swam to shore, hoping to get a skiff so he could return and rescue people. When he reached shore, though, he was exhausted. A local farmer led him to his farmhouse to recover. Assistant engineer William Sparks washed ashore unconscious but alive.

The storm raged on and the sky lit up—"In half an hour the whole heavens were converted into a complete canopy of lightning,"[2] the *Minneapolis Tribune* reported. Those flashes of lightning gave survivors on the *Jim Grant* horrific glimpses of the faces of women and children who had died inside the cabin.

Frank Lampman and Ed Stevens tried desperately to keep their girlfriends Annie and Francis Staiger floating, but their dresses were waterlogged and just too heavy. The men eventually lost strength and had to let go, then watched helplessly as the women disappeared into the river.

The storm tossed teenagers George Seavers and Robert Adams into the water, too. They found a piece of wood to cling to, then eagerly grabbed a couple of life preservers when they floated by. They put them on and attached themselves together.

The *Jim Grant* drifted close to Central Point, close enough that some passengers jumped off and made it to shore before the barge drifted back into open water. Harry Mabey was one of those who jumped off. Once he was on land, he covered his head with a life jacket to shield himself from hail as large as eggs. He ran the two miles into Lake City, where he rang a fire bell for help. He and Theed Minder, who had also jumped off the barge, then returned to the river in a rowboat. They rescued eighteen people in three trips. Corporal B. L. Perry and Wesley Hills also rowed out and brought several people back to shore safely.

Rescue to Recovery

The *Jim Grant* washed ashore before midnight with sixty survivors. After that, the rescuers lost hope that they would find any remaining passengers alive, so the focus shifted to recovering the dead. By four in the morning, they had recovered fifty-two bodies. Most showed no signs of struggle or injury. Death had come swiftly.

There was some good news, though. Around five in the morning, teenagers Seavers and Adams were spotted walking down the shoreline. They had washed ashore two hours earlier near the village of Frontenac, Minnesota, after spending six hours in the water. They had survived by riding with the wind and current instead of fighting them.

Friends and relatives filled a train from Red Wing to Lake City. Others traveled on horseback or just walked. Many more waited at the train station for news about their loved ones. The *Ethel Howard* steamed into Red Wing just after six on Tuesday morning carrying the first load of victims. The first round of funerals took place Monday evening.

Recovery efforts turned up few bodies on Tuesday. National Guard troops fired cannons over the lake and dropped dynamite into its waters. They hoped the shock waves would raise the dead, but neither worked. As bodies of the victims decomposed, they became more buoyant and floated to the surface. Thirty-two victims were recovered on Wednesday, including ten-year-old Lenus Lillyblad.

Rosa Rehder was the last victim recovered. Her father, Henry, was the bandleader. Her brother, Henry, was also among the dead. The Rehder children had been traveling with their uncle and aunt, Peter and Maria Gerken, and their cousins, the five Gerken children, all of whom perished in the accident.

Gazing out over the wreckage, one writer observed, "The barge lay quietly on the water just above town and the steamer, toppled over on the port side, had drifted against her tow, and together they lay, the shattered reminders of the storm's power and man's weakness."[3]

Assessing Blame

It didn't take long for the blame game to begin. Captain Wethern was the natural target. "Strong words and bitter thoughts are on the lips and in the hearts of almost every one that is to be met with around the town [Red Wing]," one newspaper wrote. "Capt. Wetheren [sic] and his crew are denounced vigorously, and if all that is said were true they would surely DESERVE SPEEDY JUSTICE."[4]

Sometimes Wethern didn't help his own cause, such as when he complained about the way the boat was being torn up to remove bodies. It's hard to imagine that he was thinking clearly at that point. While Andrew Scriber had rescued his son, Perley, Wethern's wife Nellie and their other son, Ron, did not survive.

An official investigation into the wreck began on Wednesday. The committee quickly debunked rumors that the crew had been drinking. Some survivors testified that Captain Wethern did all he could to avoid the tragedy. There were conflicting accounts as to whether anyone had cut the *Jim Grant* free before the *Sea Wing* tipped over and if it even mattered.

Still, investigators questioned Wethern's decisions. They determined that the boat was carrying 205 passengers, not the 175 that Wethern had estimated, which was 30 more than the boat was licensed to carry. They confirmed 98 deaths.

The final report labeled Wethern "unskillful" for leaving port when a storm was approaching and for failing to keep the boat close to the Minnesota shore, where it may have been possible to pull up quickly in the face of trouble. The investigators also determined that Wethern did not have the proper license to operate the boat. They suspended his existing license and referred the case to the US district attorney to consider criminal prosecution.

Living with the Loss

Wethern, though, was never charged with a crime, and he would later get his pilot's license restored. Maybe the people making those decisions felt that Wethern had suffered enough with the loss of his wife and son and the weight of ninety-eight deaths on his conscience.

He remained in Diamond Bluff after the wreck and continued to run his store. He kept his status as a valued member of the community, later getting elected to terms as town board chair and treasurer. Once the recovery operations were over, he got the damaged *Sea Wing* towed back to Diamond Bluff. In 1893, he built a new superstructure on top of the old hull. He made a token effort to change the name—it was unsuccessful—so the *Sea Wing* returned to the waters of the Mississippi. It ran the river for another six years.

Wethern died in 1929 at seventy-five. His son, Roy, became a highly respected boat pilot on the Mississippi, despite his near-death experience on the river. Later in life, when a reporter asked Roy about the effect of the wreck on his father, he noted that he went back to piloting river boats but added that "it was years before I saw him smile again."[5]

The reality of the death toll hit Red Wing hard. Of the ninety-eight dead, seventy-seven were from the city. Even more shockingly, fifty of the fifty-seven women on board died. Black sheets were draped over the fronts of many buildings and black crepe paper hung from doorknobs. A steady procession of funeral trains filled the city's streets. Mary Leach mourned the loss of her friend, Minnie Fisher. The stress of dealing with so much death overwhelmed undertaker Arland Allen, who needed help from furniture maker Mathias Kayser to finish preparing bodies for burial.

Red Wing held a citywide memorial service on Friday. Businesses shut down at noon. Five thousand people attended, including many dignitaries. The city placed flowers throughout the park, some sculpted into tall archways. Photographer James Kellogg put together a poster with photographs of most of the victims; all but nine were represented.

At the service, Wesley Kinney, the Red Wing city attorney, summed up the feelings of many:

> [W]hen a sorrow has fallen upon us, when the mind has become weary with reflection, and the eyes dim with weeping, a word of sympathy, however homely or crudely spoken, a tear, while it cannot

remove the burden, may, so far as human sympathy can aid those who have been bereft of friends, soften the pangs of sorrow, and assist in preparing the heart to bear the burden.[6]

Sporting Girls

Brothels on the River

WHEN ELIZA HAYCRAFT DIED IN 1871, ST. LOUISANS TURNED OUT BY the thousands for her funeral procession. She had been a generous philanthropist in the city who built a fortune from scratch and used her money to help Black and White St. Louisans who were down on their luck. She left an estate valued at a quarter of a million dollars (the equivalent of several million dollars today), but despite her wealth and charity, the city's elites shunned her.

When she asked to buy a burial plot in the well-tended necropolis that is Bellefontaine Cemetery, she was initially turned away. The Methodist church she belonged to wouldn't host her funeral, so the service was held at her home, the large house she had purchased from the Chouteau family, descendants of the city's founders. Bellefontaine Cemetery eventually agreed to sell her a plot, but she reputedly had to agree to a burial with no marker. Haycraft may have been wealthy and generous, but the respectable classes turned their backs on her because she had earned her fortune by running houses of prostitution.

When Haycraft was twenty years old, her parents kicked her out after they discovered that she—an unmarried woman—had been sexually active. She canoed down the Missouri River from Callaway County to St. Louis and settled in the city with absolutely nothing. In 1840, single women had few ways to make money legitimately, especially if they were illiterate, like Haycraft, so she got a job in a brothel. She eventually became the boss and oversaw a steady increase in business as the city's population grew exponentially. In the thirty years she lived in St. Louis, the population exploded from 36,000 to 350,000. Many of those new residents were single men with money to spend. By the end of the Civil War, she owned five brothels.

She invested her profits in real estate around the city and donated money generously to people in need. Most of her estate was divided among her surviving family members. She gave two of her sisters a hundred dollars each, but the rest of her estate was split equally among her other four sisters. She stipulated in her will that her sisters' husbands had to keep their hands off of the inherited money.

Haycraft's success was unusual for a woman of that era, but many women worked in the same profession, and the brothels in towns along the Mississippi River were as busy as any in other places. Like their counterparts in other communities and times, authorities in Mississippi River towns have tried many ways to tolerate, regulate, or suppress prostitution. Some red-light districts were eventually forced to close around World War I when the US Army and Navy banned prostitution within five miles of military bases. That forced the closure of brothels in the Bucktown district of Davenport, Iowa, and in Storyville in New Orleans. Despite the bans and attempts at regulation, though, people continue to find ways to buy and sell sex.

CONTROLLING SOCIAL EVILS

St. Louisans were no strangers to prostitution. In the nineteenth century, men who wanted to buy sex could go to a brothel and choose from among the women who lived there, or they could bring a woman to a house of assignation where they could rent a room. Both types of places ranged in quality from high-class to lowbrow. In St. Louis, brothels concentrated near the riverfront in the blocks of Poplar, Christy, and Morgan Streets.

Arrests were common, but most resulted in a small fine, although sometimes the penalty was harsher. Mary Ann Frost, for example, was convicted of running a brothel in January 1870 and fined $1,000. When she couldn't pay, the judge threw her in jail and ordered her eight-year-old son into the custody of a city institution. Police rarely arrested men who paid for sex.

In the latter half of the nineteenth century, reformers in the United States pushed to register and regulate prostitution like some European countries were doing. Meanwhile, anti-prostitution activists made moral arguments for the continued legal sanctions. Both sides recognized the threat that sexually transmitted diseases posed to public health. They just didn't agree on ways to reduce the risks.

Reformers got an opening in 1870 when the State of Missouri passed a revised charter for the City of St. Louis. The new charter included a provision allowing the city to regulate "bawdy and disorderly houses, houses of ill-fame or assignation."[1] Shortly after that, St. Louis passed the Social Evil Ordinance, a measure that created a system of legalized prostitution.

Under the new law, working women had to register with the city, pay a fee, and pass regular health exams. If a woman failed the health exam, she was required to stay at a hospital until cured. The city used some of the revenue from the fees to build a hospital at the edge of town to treat prostitutes. They named it the Social Evil Hospital.

Police had the authority to close any brothel or order it to relocate. No new brothels could open without permission from the Board of Police Commissioners. The new law also banned women from openly soliciting their services, whether on a city street or in the window of a brothel.

Over seven hundred women registered in the first few months, as did nearly a hundred brothels. Six medical examiners checked registered prostitutes every week. The new system reduced but didn't stop arrests of prostitutes. Police sometimes charged women with public drunkenness, vagrancy, using profane language, or disturbing the peace instead of sex offenses.

Still, the law probably increased the visibility of prostitutes and may have given the profession a new sense of legitimacy. That displeased many people. When leadership proposed a new city charter in 1872, it included a provision to make legalization permanent. Opponents organized.

One of those opponents was William Greenleaf Eliot, a Unitarian minister and one founder of prestigious Washington University. His allies included religious and women's groups, many of whom had been vocal abolitionists. Eliot began a relentless public campaign against the social evil ordinance that included writing editorials for local papers. In 1873, for example, he wrote:

> *Consider what it is that we are doing . . . we register their houses at a stipulated price, we enter their names on the city record, we cause them to be "inspected" every week by physicians . . . we take payment for this from the wages of sin. . . . Can Christian women who respect their own sex quietly look on while their sisters, for whom Christ died, are by law recognized and upheld in a pollution so deep?*[2]

Opponents attacked the law from multiple angles. Families might suffer from diseases because of a husband's misdeeds. Husbands could stray without facing consequences. The law fostered "a class of women who are to be permanently held as the instruments of the legalized lust of habitually profligate men,"[3] Eliot wrote.

Those tactics failed, though, as did challenges to the law's constitutionality, but support for legalization waned as the social evil law appeared to undermine enforcement of other city ordinances aimed at keeping undesirable people under control. The city had a vagrancy law that gave it wide discretion to arrest people who associated with lawbreakers. Because prostitution was legal, one court ruled that the vagrancy law could not be used to punish people who associated with prostitutes.

By 1874, the public had turned against the law. Stories of police using the law as a pretext to harass respectable women troubled people. There were rumors of inappropriate behaviors by the medical examiners. In the middle of all this, a corruption scandal embroiled the city administration. Newspapers jumped on the bandwagon and lobbied for repeal of legalization.

In March 1874, the State of Missouri did what the city hadn't yet done and repealed the city's authority to regulate prostitution. They also passed a companion bill that banned police raids of brothels, except under very limited circumstances, which was an attempt to prevent retribution against women who had registered under the law. The legislature once again relegated prostitution to the underbelly of society, with half-hearted enforcement against women and officials willing to look the other way for certain favors.

The Worst Sort of Dancing

Other cities along the Mississippi, including La Crosse, Wisconsin, stuck to a look-the-other-way approach. Prostitution had a long history in La Crosse. In 1876—just twenty years after the city incorporated—police arrested Kate Champion for running a brothel. A police officer gathered evidence by standing outside a window of her house and observing a rendezvous, and neighbors tattled on her. Champion was convicted and sentenced to six months of hard labor at the state prison in Waupun.

On September 22, 1897, police arrested Carrie Scott in Olson's Saloon while she was talking to a man at the bar. They weren't doing anything sexual, but La Crosse, like other cities, had an ordinance that banned women from bars unless their husbands or fathers accompanied them. A police officer had seen Scott chatting up men on the street, then following them into a saloon. That was enough to prompt the arrest. She was fined twenty dollars and ordered to pay another twenty-four dollars in court costs.

The Mississippi House did a steady business in the latter half of the nineteenth century. It was a rough place, basically a hotel near the river that connected rivermen—their primary customers—with temporary company. It operated for over thirty years, changing locations a few times but always staying close to the river.

La Crosse officials tolerated a red-light district in the 100 block of Pearl Street for many years, but in 1908, Mayor Wendell Anderson ordered the brothels closed. The policy change wasn't universally embraced. Many police officers preferred to keep the district open, because the regulars often tipped off the police about suspicious new people in town.

Mayor Anderson had kept the district open during a previous term as mayor, but he changed his mind because each brothel was paying a fifty-dollar fine every quarter. For Mayor Anderson, that seemed like a licensing fee and suggested that the city was profiting from prostitution. He was also uncomfortable with the fact that police didn't permit women in the brothels to walk the streets together and had to be back in their houses by six in the evening. Other women in the city did not have to worry about those restrictions.

The closure didn't last, though. The next mayor, Ori Sorensen, reopened the district in 1909. He believed it was better to keep the brothels operating in the open but restricted to a specific part of the city rather than driving prostitution underground. The rollercoaster ride continued from there. Anderson lost reelection and his replacement, John Dengler, closed the district again.

When Sorensen campaigned to get his old job back, he changed his position and pledged to keep the brothels closed. "During my first administration," he said, "I was of the opinion that the tenderloin was a necessary evil." He believed that a forced closure would just scatter the problem around the city, but after careful study, he found that conditions "have grown better instead of worse since the resort keepers and inmates were driven out."[4] He won in 1913 and did not let the brothels reopen.

Sorensen's return to office coincided with an investigation into prostitution led by Wisconsin State Senator Howard Teasdale. In the spring of 1913, Teasdale convened a committee to take a hard look at the "white slave traffic and kindred subjects."[5] Investigators traveled around the state determined to uncover the widespread damage caused by prostitution.

In La Crosse, the investigators found a high concentration of brothels along Third Street between Pearl and State Streets. In any of those establishments, a man could hire a prostitute for two dollars or rent a room for one dollar and bring his own companion. Most of the women were in their twenties, but some were considerably older.

Investigators also found evidence of prostitution on the city's north side. One investigator at a tavern on French Island observed: "As soon as a man enters these women take him by the arm and lead him to the bar and keep him there as long as he will treat them. . . . The worst sort of dancing, ragging, and tango, are allowed."[6]

The final report accused the La Crosse police department of enabling prostitution:

There are 21 members of the department, all included except the Chief. Many of them are bad; hand in glove with vice and on the most intimate terms with sporting girls. Prominent among them is Officer Wermuth, a brother of a saloonkeeper of the same name, on North Third St. It is common talk among the girls and generally talked about town that after closing hours of the saloon this officer having a key to the rear entrance of the WET GOODS Saloon, takes girls in there, spending considerable time with them. Viola Friday, or Atchinson, a well-known prostitute, boasts of his friendship with her, and other[s] say Sophie Zak, a young Polish girl . . . was also his paramour.[7]

The committee recommended several changes to existing laws to reduce prostitution, including banning women from saloons and eliminating back and side entrances. Mayor Sorenson and Police Captain Lawrence Dugan expressed support for those ideas. The committee also recommended raising the age of consent from fourteen to eighteen, writing:

We must take into consideration that no possession of a woman is of as value to her as her honor; yet existing laws permit her to yield this in childhood at a period when in her innocence and lack of knowledge she does not comprehend what she is doing nor the frightful consequences of her act, thus permitting her to sacrifice that which is of far more value to her than her property.[8]

Mostly, though, nothing changed.

In 1925, Anna Bennett, better known as Ma, opened the European Hotel on Second Street. "Ma's was a classy place. She wouldn't let any bums in," recalled an anonymous former customer. For twenty years, a steady stream of men—top business managers and city officials—patronized the brothel, entering through the back door for privacy. "Those places were just another incidental spot where a guy went," said another former customer.[9]

From the outside, the building was nothing special, just a two-story brick structure with few architectural frills. Inside, though, it looked like a palace. An elegant chandelier hung in the front room; tapestries draped the walls; ritzy carpeting covered the floors. The brothel even had a nickelodeon for musical entertainment. Men paid a base rate of two dollars, and Ma kept half of it.

The women worked in one of the seven upstairs rooms. She employed up to twenty women at a time, most of them between eighteen and twenty-five years old. All dressed immaculately. Eight of the women lived in the European Hotel, the rest in apartments nearby. Most didn't stay long, maybe three months at the most. "Ma was on a pipeline," a friend of Ma Bennett remembered. "Whenever she needed a new girl, all she'd have to do was make a call to New York, Chicago, Cleveland, or Minneapolis. They'd send her a picture of the girl. She never turned one down."[10]

Many people in town didn't seem to mind the presence of the brothel. "If I had a teen-age son," one anonymous woman said, "I'd rather send him to a place like Ma's. Then I'd know he wouldn't be picking up any diseases."[11]

After Ma's husband, Jack, died in 1932, she would visit his grave at Oak Grove Cemetery on Saturdays in a chauffeur-driven car, maybe the Packard or Cadillac she owned, and often accompanied by women who worked for her. She also picked up a hobby: collecting racehorses. She traveled around the country to watch them compete.

She lost nearly $200,000 when a bank failed in 1933, but she still seemed to have plenty of money left. She built a new house in town and helped several families get through the tough years of the Depression.

She ran another brothel in town that was raided regularly, but she was always alerted in advance, so the police found nothing illegal going on when they arrived. Her fortunes changed in 1946, though, when police raided the European Hotel. Police arrested Ma, and the court fined her $200 and sentenced her to six months in jail. She didn't serve a day, though. She retired from the business and moved to California, where she died around 1963, probably in her eighties or nineties. The European Hotel was torn down in the early 1970s.

Known Far and Wide

Winona, Minnesota, just thirty river miles upriver of La Crosse, has its own lengthy history of tolerating brothels. The city banned prostitution in 1857, which led to occasional raids. In 1866, police arrested two women at a suspected brothel, but enforcement was infrequent. Mayor Toye ordered a raid of brothels in 1891, but someone tipped off the women—either the police chief or a judge—so police arrested just a few women.

Brothels were scattered around the city initially, but over time they clustered along Second Street near the Chicago & Northwestern rail station and the Mississippi River. People called them sporting houses, and the women were sometimes called "2 Streeters."[12]

By 1920, Winona's red-light district was attracting men who worked on riverboats and railroads, as well as soldiers from Wisconsin's Camp McCoy, who arrived by the trainload for a night on the town. Police raided some places in 1920, but someone tipped them off again, except for the National Hotel run by Jane Bailey, who must have angered the wrong person. From 1923 to 1939, though, the police didn't arrest anyone for vice offenses. For a while, the city licensed brothels, even though prostitution was illegal under state law. Women got regular medical checks, and some police received complimentary services. The city even considered legalizing brothels outright at one point.

Winona was known throughout the United States for its brothels, probably because the soldiers from Camp McCoy helped spread the word. Mostly, Winonans didn't seem terribly bothered by it all. Taxi drivers said the women were generous tippers. And sometimes the locals got cheap entertainment. One brothel had holes in the floor of a third-story room. Voyeurs could pay a small fee to peek through those holes and watch the action below them.

Claude Weber began a four-year stint running errands for brothels when he was fourteen years old. The women treated him well, and he made decent money. One of his regular assignments was picking up and delivering dresses the women had ordered from downtown stores. He also ran errands for brothel madam Queenie LeVaque. Weber recalled that she always wore a robe with two pockets: paper money in one pocket, coins in the other. When he finished a job for her, she'd reach into the coin pocket and hand him change without counting it. In an interview later in life, Weber extolled the virtues of young people in his day. "There wasn't so much chasing around and looseness,"[13] he said, presumably without irony.

The brothels' popularity with soldiers from Camp McCoy would eventually lead to the downfall of the district. In the early years of World War II, US Army officials grew increasingly concerned about the frequency with which soldiers contracted sexually transmitted diseases. Some soldiers were getting infections that were taking them out of duty before they could be sent overseas to fight. The Army pressured cities to close red-light districts that were close to its bases.

The final blow came on Christmas Eve 1942, when a fight broke out between soldiers from Camp McCoy. A group of White men fought with Japanese American soldiers from Hawaii. While on base, Army officers kept a lid on open conflict, but fights sometimes broke out when soldiers crossed paths on the streets of Winona. On Christmas Eve, a melee erupted that resulted in multiple arrests. The police later released all the soldiers, though, and they returned to base.

Two days later, twenty-eight agents from the Minnesota Bureau of Criminal Apprehension descended on Winona just after midnight. Local law enforcement didn't know they were coming. Minnesota Governor Harold Stassen, responding to pressure from Army officials, closed Winona's red-light district. Agents raided five brothels and arrested eleven women. Minnesota was in no mood to play around, so the state charged the women with felonies, padlocked the buildings, and seized their contents. The women who ran the brothels eventually pleaded guilty to running "a house offensive to public decency,"[14] a misdemeanor. The courts fined each madam one hundred dollars, and each prostitute twenty-five dollars. But the buildings stayed closed. Officials auctioned off the contents of the buildings and padlocked them for a year.

And that was that, of course. Just kidding. Creative entrepreneurs found new ways to keep the industry alive. A brothel called El Cid's operated as an open secret in Winona well into the 1990s.

The River Never Ran Dry

Moonshiners

PROHIBITION, THAT PERIOD WHEN THE UNITED STATES BANNED THE manufacture and sale of alcoholic beverages across the entire country, didn't come out of the blue. Americans had been debating it for decades. Maine first banned the production and sales of alcohol in 1846 (then repealed it a few years later). Late in the nineteenth century, some states

Photo 15.1. Isleño trappers camp in a narrow channel near Delacroix, Louisiana.
LIBRARY OF CONGRESS

passed their own versions of prohibition. Bans on alcohol spread through the South, the Midwest, and the West.

Many states had also passed laws allowing individual counties to go dry, which created some tricky situations. In Minnesota, for example, folks who lived in Eden Valley could drink in the part of town that was part of Stearns County, but if they carried a drink across the street into Meeker County, they could be arrested.

By the time the Eighteenth Amendment to the US Constitution passed banning the manufacture and sale of alcohol, much of the country was already dry. With the ratification of the Eighteenth Amendment and the passage of the Volstead Act defining the terms of the ban and penalties for violating it, the United States began a massive social experiment. Ultimately, Prohibition was perhaps the most widely ignored law in US history, except, maybe, for automobile speed limits.

No PLACE FOR PROHIBITION

Many people along the Mississippi River resisted the new federal law. River towns had a history of a live-and-let-live mentality that lingered well into the twentieth century. The thicket of islands and marshes along the Mississippi were ideal places to conduct activities without getting noticed. The backwater channels took time to learn, so federal agents relied on local guides to help them out, but many locals weren't enthusiastic about helping a federal agent arrest their neighbors. In many Mississippi River cities, finding an alcoholic beverage remained as easy as hopping on a streetcar.

In East Dubuque, Illinois, folks expressed their displeasure at the end of legal drinking by rioting on the eve of the ban on alcohol. Crowds damaged city hall and the fire station and freed inmates from the city jail.

In St. Louis, a few hundred people marked the transition to Prohibition by staging a mock funeral. The city's Riverview Club filled a coffin with alcohol and wrapped a suit around it, then buried it in the ground at midnight. Attendees, including some city officials, sang songs that included "Pickle My Bones in Alcohol."

New Orleans police prepared for a large crowd of "mourners" on June 30, 1919, when people filled the city's hotels to stage a "wake for John

Barleycorn."[1] In the spirit of mourning, though, folks behaved themselves just fine, and the mood was melancholic. An article in the *Times-Picayune* lamented that "Gloom, Deep Dark And Dismal, Descends As Drought Comes . . . dig out the sackcloth and ashes, get on the wagon, welcome Old Man Gloom and pretend you like it."[2]

Folks regrouped and adapted, though. The hills and islands of the Mississippi River filled with stills. Liquor flowed again in speakeasies, more so in some places than in others. East Dubuque became known as "Sin City" because of the abundance of speakeasies and gambling halls. Al Capone probably had a hand in many of those businesses.

The lax enforcement and abundance of hiding places sometimes attracted crime bosses looking for a break from the stresses of city life. There were rumors, for example, that Al Capone owned a house near St. Paul, Minnesota, a city that offered a safe space to bootleggers and other criminals as long as they didn't cause any trouble in St. Paul. Capone was also reputedly fond of the small resorts and duck hunting around Oquawka, Illinois, especially on Benton Island, and liked to slip away to Quincy, Illinois, for personal retreats.

COMING OUT OF RETIREMENT

Prohibition created opportunities for entrepreneurs accustomed to working on the margins of society. One person who benefited right away was John Looney. Officials in Rock Island, Illinois, had driven him out of his stronghold in the Tri-Cities of Iowa and Illinois (Davenport, Rock Island, and Moline) a few years earlier, but Prohibition opened a door for him to come out of hiding and reestablish his criminal empire.

Looney was born in Ottawa, Illinois, in 1866, the third of eight children but the first son. His parents had moved to Illinois after emigrating from Ireland and had settled into a comfortable middle-class life. Looney was fifteen years old when his powerful uncle got him a job as a telegrapher with Western Union. Just three years later, Western Union put Looney in charge of their office in Rock Island, Illinois. Three years after that he ruled a criminal empire.

In Rock Island, Looney became a lawyer, which introduced him to a network of criminals and gave him an insider's view of the legal system.

His legal practice was not a financial success, but he found better ways to get rich: graft, extortion, and prostitution. While Al Capone was busy irritating the nuns at his grade school, Looney was building one of the first national crime syndicates.

Looney's tactics created some powerful enemies, though, including Rock Island's mayor, Harry Schriver, which eventually caught up to him. After a riot in the streets in 1912 stoked by Looney and his allies, authorities forced Looney out of town. He hid out on a ranch in New Mexico until 1919, just as prohibition fever swept the United States.

Looney returned to Rock Island and quickly consolidated control of the vice trade. Former allies had become enemies, but some powerful enemies from the past had joined Looney's criminal syndicate, including Mayor Schriver and Police Chief Tom Cox.

The second time around, Looney added alcohol to his revenue streams. He dominated the production and distribution of booze in the area and owned a few bars, too. His drinking establishments never closed. The doors didn't even have locks on them.

Looney relied on Helen Van Dale to run the prostitution trade. She was good at her job. Under her leadership, it grew it into what was probably the largest employer of call girls in the country. She even supplied prostitutes to clubs run by Chicago's Johnny Torrio, who would later mentor Capone.

Once again, though, Looney couldn't keep his syndicate together. William Gabel, a former Rock Island cop turned bar owner, thought that Looney was charging him too much for whiskey. They eventually negotiated a deal, but Gabel had had enough and turned informant. When Looney discovered Gabel had been talking to federal agents, he had him killed.

Gabel's murder triggered retaliation from Looney's enemies. On October 6, 1922, gunmen ambushed Looney's entourage outside the Sherman Hotel in Rock Island. They ran into the hotel for cover, all except for Looney's twenty-one-year-old son Connor. He died in the initial flurry of bullets.

The battles triggered an especially violent period in Rock Island that forced Mayor Schriver's hand. He ordered the bars and brothels in the red-light district closed. Shortly after that, the Illinois attorney general opened an investigation into the murder of Gabel and, on October 10, two dozen agents raided Looney's businesses. Looney buried his son, then skipped town again.

A grand jury soon indicted Looney for automobile theft and more charges followed. The mayor and police chief were arrested, and Looney's protection network crumbled. It would take two years for authorities in Illinois to get their hands on Looney, but when they did, they finished him off.

Looney was transported from his ranch in New Mexico back to Illinois for trial. When the Illinois attorney general announced that the state didn't have the money to conduct the trial, Rock Islanders raised the money themselves. On July 31, 1925, a jury convicted Looney of conspiracy charges related to gambling, prostitution, and alcohol trafficking. Helen Van Dale, his former business partner, testified against him.

Five months later, another jury convicted Looney of murdering William Gabel. State officials booked a room for Looney at the prison in Joliet, where he served just under nine years. When he was paroled, his daughter, Ursula, picked him up and took him to her home in southern Texas, where he quietly lived out the rest of his days. He died at seventy-five in a sanitarium in El Paso, Texas.

LOUISIANA BOOTLEGGERS

Louisianans were split on Prohibition. The idea was popular in the northern parishes but reviled in and around New Orleans. When the state passed a local option law in 1902, many parishes quickly banned alcohol. Seven years later, the Louisiana legislature passed the Gay-Shattuck law, which banned the sale of alcohol within three hundred feet of a school or church. It also banned gambling in saloons and mandated racial segregation in bars. Temperance forces were winning.

By the time Prohibition passed at the federal level, 82 percent of Louisiana was already dry, and more than half of the state's residents didn't have access to legal alcohol. New Orleans, of course, was not one of those places. Anyone who wanted to go out for a drink in the city could head to one of the city's five thousand bars. Opponents of Prohibition, including most New Orleanians, had expected the dry movement to lose momentum after World War I. They were wrong.

After Prohibition was the law of the land, it took a few months for bootlegging networks to organize and scale up, but New Orleans would eventually become one of the easiest places in the United States to get a drink. Boats smuggled booze into the city through Lake Pontchartrain, then through the parishes below New Orleans, where the Mississippi River split into thousands of small channels.

Much of that booze came up from St. Bernard or Plaquemines Parishes, and many of the best smugglers were *Isleños*, people descended from immigrants from the Canary Islands who had settled in the area in the eighteenth century when Spain governed Louisiana. Many of the smugglers lived on Delacroix Island, an Isleño village thirty-five miles southeast of New Orleans where the road ended.

Because it wasn't an easy place to reach, the community had remained isolated for generations. One historian who visited Delacroix Island in 1891 wrote that the people lived in "palmetto huts" and were still "children of nature,"[3] which was a polite way of saying that they were poor by contemporary standards and lived off the land. Spanish was still their first language, and they didn't trust outsiders, not even their Isleño cousins who lived around English Turn. Delacroix Islanders earned a living by fishing and trapping in the dense network of marshes below Bayou Terre aux Boeufs. They shipped their haul on railcars to markets in New Orleans.

Prohibition ushered in new business opportunities. That dense network of channels in the Mississippi River Delta was ideal for transporting items covertly. They were navigable all year, and few people—mostly just the trappers and fishers—knew them well enough to navigate without getting lost.

Ships carried alcohol across the Gulf of Mexico from Cuba, British Honduras, and other countries. The boats parked in international waters near the mouth of the Mississippi, then couriers, many of them Isleños, sped out in so-called "mosquito" boats to meet the ships. They carried the cargo—up to a thousand cases of booze per boat—through the marshes, then handed it off to trucks or trains.

Some of that booze supplied the drinking establishments of New Orleans, but much of it was destined for markets in Texas or communities up the Mississippi River. Bootleggers could be quite creative. In one case, they hid liquor in paint cans and shipped them by barge to St. Louis. Federal law enforcement disrupted the Gulf-based network in 1925 when the Coast Guard brought in bigger, faster boats of their own, but smugglers often found ways around them.

Some people in the lower parishes also got into the production of alcohol. In May 1922, a raid by law enforcement netted ten people who had been operating stills. Courts fined some moonshiners up to $1,500, and sentenced others to six months in jail. Deputy Sheriff Morgan told the papers, "We're bone-dry here now."[4] They weren't, of course.

Around the time Prohibition began, residents of the lower parishes were voting out the old political guard. In 1920, Leander Perez won a judicial seat in Plaquemines Parish (winning by just three votes). Four years later, he won election as district attorney for Plaquemines and St. Bernard Parishes and became the dominant power in the area.

An early ally of his was a country doctor named Louis Meraux, who moved into law enforcement by winning election as St. Bernard County sheriff. Sheriff Meraux was a big man—three hundred pounds and six feet four inches tall. He was also volatile. One minute he comported himself as a sophisticated gentleman, the next he could scream like a foul-mouthed gutter snipe.

Perez and Meraux weren't the only power brokers. Isleño Manuel Molero grew into one of the biggest bootleggers in the South. Molero bought property in the marshes, a grocery store in Delacroix, and a fleet of delivery trucks that helped him move merchandise, but mostly it was to transport bootlegged booze. Meraux and Molero hated each other, but they kept the booze moving.

The folks in St. Bernard and Plaquemines Parishes enjoyed boom times for a while. Sheriff Meraux supplemented his official salary by charging a toll on booze that moved through his parish. Bootlegging had become so normalized that, for some, stealing from bootleggers was the real crime. Officials hauled a few people who stole illegal booze from a bootlegger into a parish criminal court and charged them with theft.

Meanwhile, the partying was on again in New Orleans. Soft drink stands sold bargain booze on the sly, while speakeasies catered to the better off. In many restaurants, waiters served alcohol from flasks they kept on their hips.

In 1923, Izzy Einstein, one of the country's most famous federal agents, went to New Orleans to find out how long it would take him to buy illegal booze. He hopped in a cab to begin his search and asked the driver where he should go. The driver pulled out a bottle from under his seat and offered to sell it to him right then. Einstein's search took all of thirty-five seconds.

Local police did little to enforce the alcohol ban, so federal agents arranged a major sting operation in 1925. Two hundred agents descended on the city and seized ten thousand cases of alcohol. The raid barely made a dent in consumer prices, though, as there was still plenty of booze available. By the end of 1926, federal agents had padlocked eighty-six establishments, more than in any other city. New Orleanians just shifted their drinking to private homes.

As federal agents interrupted the flow of booze imported from other countries, local moonshiners filled in the gap. It wasn't a great trade for drinkers. Foreign booze was reliably safe and tasty. Locals sometimes produced moonshine with lye, iodine, acetone, or even kerosene. Moonshiners hid those smells by adding vanilla, lemon, or other substances that made the color and smell of the liquid seem acceptable. Local moonshine made quite a few people sick.

On the day that beer became legal again in Louisiana—April 13, 1933—three hundred truck drivers rumbled through the streets of New Orleans to deliver it to thirsty customers, imbibing as they drove around the city. New Orleanians were jubilant. They honked their car horns. Whistles blew from boats on the Mississippi. The city's sirens roared in celebration. It was business as usual again in New Orleans, or maybe business as usual without the fear of being raided.

MINNESOTA 13

In Stearns County, Minnesota, many folks also refused to go along with Prohibition. The Mississippi River runs along the county's eastern border. The county's largest city, St. Cloud, straddles the Mississippi in the northeast part of the county. Much of the county west of the river was originally prairie, which was converted to agricultural land in the nineteenth century by German and Polish immigrants.

Many of those farmers grew up in households with long traditions of making beer and wine for home consumption. Similar traditions persisted among the county's many Catholic clergy. "At lunch," recalled Father Valerian, a priest at St. John's Abbey, "we'd get a quart of beer and two pieces of black bread."[5] Alcohol was far too integrated into people's lives for them to give it up overnight.

Voters in Stearns County rejected the Prohibition amendment in 1919 with nearly 70 percent against it, even though the measure passed statewide. The man who sponsored the legislation that defined the rules for Prohibition, Congressman Andrew Volstead, lived in a district that included parts of Stearns County. His legislation passed Congress in 1919, but he lost his bid for reelection in 1922 (and lost badly). Two years later, though, he got the top job at the National Prohibition Enforcement Bureau, a position he held until the end of Prohibition in 1933.

Federal prohibition coincided with a terrible crisis in the farm economy. During World War I, American farmers supplied food to much of Europe. Land appreciated quickly, and profits soared. As Europeans returned to growing their own crops, prices tumbled. Many farmers went bankrupt and lost their land.

Farmers in Stearns County soon realized that moonshining offered a way to stay afloat. "I had a family of five kids, and no crop, no money and then my cousin told me . . . he was cooking," Matthew Schreifels said. "He told me he'd buy it from me and peddle it."[6]

Prices were good, especially compared to agricultural products. When the first batches of moonshine hit the market, they fetched twenty dollars a gallon. As the supply increased, prices stabilized around five dollars a gallon. One large still could produce at least one hundred gallons of 110-proof liquor, which would then be cut with distilled water to yield a final proof of 90. Even at five thousand a gallon, one batch could bring in a lot of money. In contrast, a single calf sold for about four dollars.

The moonshine coming from Stearns County was no ordinary liquor, as it turned out. It became famous throughout the United States and was sold at speakeasies from coast to coast under the name Minnesota 13, which was derived from a breed of corn developed specifically for northern farmers. That breed of corn typically matured in 87 days, rather than the 100 to 120 that was standard for the varieties of the day, so it was perfect for the shorter growing season of central Minnesota.

A Stearns County farmer from Holdingford was the first to call his moonshine Minnesota 13. He made his own labels and signed each one. Eventually, all moonshine from the area came to be known as Minnesota 13, and there was a lot of it. And a lot of demand for it, too. Al Capone reportedly drank it regularly.

By some estimates, 80 percent of county residents had some skin in the moonshining game. At least a third of farm households distilled it, and the monks at St. John's Abbey continued brewing beer. Hardware stores sold the equipment to build the stills. Car dealers sold vehicles to people who moved the moonshine from producers to markets. Some bankers gave out loans in which they accepted a still as collateral.

Many religious leaders told their congregations that even though making alcohol was illegal, it wasn't a sin. Many of those ministers and priests understood how important the income from moonshine was to struggling families. Some Catholic priests even alerted parishioners when federal agents were in town.

The swamps and weedy creeks in the rural areas gave suitable cover to the distilling equipment, as well as access to clean water. Some farmers built secret rooms in barns or underground. This didn't always go well, as a few barns burned down because of distilling-related accidents.

Resourceful Nick Thielen built his first still in the middle of a cornfield, a second one near a pond in the woods, and then another under a chicken coop. Putting the still into action required two people: one who crawled into the space to operate the still and the other to stay outside to replace the camouflage and keep an eye out for intruders. Like many Stearns County moonshiners, Thielen was a small operator who handled much of the work himself. He sold his product by going to saloons and selling directly to them. Federal officials eventually caught him.

Local police in the county—and around the state—had little enthusiasm for enforcing Prohibition, so enforcement fell to federal agents. In 1929, local police in Minnesota made 70 arrests for Prohibition-related offenses, while federal agents made nearly 2,300. Federal agents liked to pit people against each other and encouraged friends to rat on friends. "There was a lot of very bad neighboring at that time," Michael Schneider remembered. "My brother-in-law claims that it was a very good friend of his that gave him away."[7]

Folks found creative ways to move their products. Drivers sometimes dressed like priests to avoid getting pulled over. One farm family ran coded classified ads. When they announced, for example, that they had rutabagas for sale, local folks understood they had moonshine available for purchase. There were also rumors that a certain milk truck carried more moonshine than dairy products.

Whiskey was plentiful throughout the county, not just in St. Cloud, but in the small towns, too. Speakeasies developed clever ways to frustrate federal agents. Some bars, for example, kept a bottle of booze hidden in the bar near a hole in the floor. If a liquor agent showed up, the bartender would kick the bottle over and into a hole which had a rock in it. When the bottle hit the rock, it would crack open, and the evidence would leak away. This strategy failed soft drink proprietor W. J. Kopp, though. When an agent entered his business, he kicked the bottle, but the glass was so strong that it didn't break when it hit the rock. He was fined a hundred dollars.

One of the best customers in the area was a judge. He "used to bring his car into the old Ford garage," Harold Servatius said. "This was at night. I'd drive my car right along side the other one [the judge's]. The keys were under the mat in his car. I'd open the trunk and load it up, put the keys back. I'd drive out. That's the way business was done. There were no witnesses, ever."[8]

Stearns County's assortment of small producers didn't have the influence of a gangster-affiliated organization, so law enforcement raided them regularly. At least the local judge, who was a satisfied customer, did all he could to hand out the lightest possible sentences. One family survived multiple raids and a fire in their house, but they refused to shut down their still. At one point, the father was arrested and sentenced to a year in jail. "We knew it was illegal and we just got caught," his wife said later. They weren't bitter or angry. But, as soon as he got home, they started distilling again. They needed the money. While their cows produced enough milk to meet the family's needs, selling moonshine was their primary source of income. "We traded moonshine for groceries, syrup and flour," his son recalled.[9]

On rare occasions, local law enforcement got the pleasure of a little reprisal against the federal agents who moved through their communities. An agent named C. P. Nolander drove a car full of agents through Richmond. When he made a U-turn in the middle of a block, he violated a local ordinance. The local cop arrested Nolander, who had to pay a $10 fine and $3.50 in court costs. Still, those agents arrested sixteen people that day.

Eighty percent of Stearns County residents voted to repeal Prohibition in 1933. That time, they were on the winning side. St. Cloud had approved licenses for sixty-one drinking establishments in time for the first day of legal drinking. Nine counties in western Minnesota opted to stay dry and didn't allow liquor sales for another thirty years.

Most of the bootleggers in Stearns County went back to regular farming. It's not entirely clear why they didn't want to make whiskey legally. After all, most already had the equipment and experience to keep it going, and they had a reputation for producing top-notch liquor. Maybe the years of constant stress and worries about being caught played a role. The farm economy bounced back, too, so that helped.

While people in the area today prefer not to dwell on the moonshining activities of their ancestors, many reaped substantial benefits from those years. The profits paid off mortgages and allowed some farmers to buy more land. Some businesses that are still going strong got their start with profits from moonshine.

A few years ago, Eleven Wells Spirits brought back a legal version of Minnesota 13. It's a white whiskey made from a Prohibition-era recipe. Best of all, we can now sample it in area restaurants and liquor stores without speaking a secret code word.

In the Mississippi River

A Double Murder

THE MEN

It was May 2, 1964, and the air already felt Mississippi muggy. In the United States, the Beatles' latest single—"Can't Buy Me Love"—rose to the top of the music charts. *From Russia with Love* and *The Carpetbaggers* drew crowds to movie theaters.

In Meadville, Mississippi, Henry Dee and Charles Moore, both nineteen years old and with their eyes on the future, needed a ride. Dee was outgoing and personable, with a reputation for being a snappy dresser, a flair he may have picked up during one of the trips he took to Chicago to visit an aunt. Dee's grandmother had raised him. She took him in after his mother was institutionalized for mental illness.

Moore was a student at Alcorn A&M College. He was bright and curious and dreamed big. His father died when he was very young, so his mother had raised him and his brother Thomas by herself. She pieced together a living by working in the home of a White family and from public assistance. "We was three people that loved each other, cared about each other," Thomas Moore told journalist David Ridgen. "You never thought about not spending your life with these people."[1]

Dee was trying to get to the nearby town of Roxie, Mississippi, to pick up his paycheck from the Haltom Lumber Company. Moore just wanted to go home. They stopped in a store where they each bought a honeybun and a large soda and bumped into a friend, Joe Lee Rollins. They asked him for a lift, but Rollins's father didn't allow him to drive out of town, so Dee and Moore did what they had always done: they hitchhiked.

A HEINOUS CRIME

Moore and Dee exited the store and stood near Meadville's ice cream shop. A white Volkswagen pulled over, and the driver offered them a ride. Dee and Moore turned him down, but the driver insisted they get in. He said he worked for the Internal Revenue Service and was investigating bootleggers in the area. They got in.

The driver, James Ford Seale, drove them deep into the nearby Homochitto National Forest. Four men followed close behind in a pickup truck: Charles Marcus Edwards, Clyde Seale, Archie Prather, and Curtis Dunn. None of them were federal agents. They were part of the Ku Klux Klan, and an especially violent wing that was based around Franklin County.

The Klan men had a mission. Outsiders were increasingly coming into Mississippi to dismantle the structures of White supremacy. Activists traveled around the region organizing Black people to vote and challenging the status quo. African Americans were making demands for equal treatment. Some Klan members feared that African Americans were stockpiling weapons in preparation for a war to end White dominance.

One of the Klan men, Edwards, had singled out Dee as someone who might be bringing guns into Franklin County. His frequent trips to Chicago made him suspicious to the Klan, and he sometimes wore a black bandana, which the Klan associated with radical Black activists. The Klan wanted Dee. Moore was simply in the wrong place at the wrong time.

In the forest, the Klan men tied Dee and Moore to a tree and beat them savagely. They asked them repeatedly to reveal the locations where "Blacks had been storing guns." The Klan men beat Dee and Moore until they bled and were nearly unconscious. Under duress, Dee and Moore told the Klan men that the Reverend Clyde Briggs had stored guns in the basement of Roxie Baptist Church.

Edwards and two others left the forest and went right to local law enforcement with the "confession" they had obtained. Sheriff Wayne Hutto and Patrolman Bernice Beasley went to the Roxie Baptist Church and searched it. They didn't bother to get a warrant. They searched the entire building but didn't find any weapons. Afterwards, they kept quiet about the search, so folks wouldn't know that they had been working with the Klan.

After Edwards and the others went to the sheriff, the other Klan men took Dee and Moore to Seale's farm, where they called for more help. Two men answered: Ernest Parker and Seale's brother Jack. Parker was part of a wealthy family in Natchez that was heavily invested in segregation. The Parkers had funded private, Whites-only schools and supported Americans for the Preservation of the White Race, a White nationalist group.

The Klan men tied up Dee and Moore and taped their mouths shut, then tossed them into the trunk of a car that they had covered with a plastic tarp. For ninety minutes they drove, traveling from Seale's farm to Natchez, crossing the Mississippi River, then heading north to an isolated backwater slough near Davis Island, the place where Jefferson Davis, the president of the Confederate States of America, once lived on a big plantation.

Ernest Parker and his brother Robert Lee Parker III owned thousands of acres on the island, so some locals called it Parkers Island. The Parkers raised cattle on the island, but they also spent a lot of time hunting and fishing there. They had built a boat landing on the Louisiana side to make it easier to ferry supplies across.

When the Klan men reached the landing, they stopped, opened the trunk, and got Dee and Moore out. They were surprised to discover that both men were still alive, but it didn't change their plans. They strapped Dee to an engine block from a 1944 Jeep, then put Dee into a boat. James and Jack Seale rowed the boat into the Mississippi River, then threw Dee overboard. Moore almost certainly watched as his friend disappeared into the Mississippi River. The Klan men rowed back to shore, then tied Moore to train rails. James Seale and Earnest Parker rowed the boat with Moore back into the middle of the channel and threw Moore into the water.

A QUICK INVESTIGATION

When Thomas Moore went home on leave in June 1964 after completing basic training, his brother was missing. No one, though, was searching for him. A story went around that Dee and Moore had gone to Louisiana to look for work.

Moore and Dee might have disappeared into history as anonymous victims of Klan violence if not for one big event. On June 21, six weeks after the Klan men killed Dee and Moore, three young men who had been working to register African American voters—James Chaney, Andrew Goodman, and Michael Schwerner—vanished. Their disappearance made national news and triggered a massive search led by the FBI.

On July 12, a fisherman spotted human remains—the lower half of a body—on a piece of driftwood near Tallulah, Louisiana. The next day, another set of partial remains surfaced nearby. The bodies got the attention of the FBI. One of the dead men was wearing a bronze belt buckle with an M on it, so there was speculation that it could be the body of Michael Schwerner.

It wasn't, though. Officials tentatively identified the dead men as Dee and Moore. Thomas Moore was playing ping pong on base when he was told that his brother's remains had been found. He went back home, where he made the heartbreaking confirmation that one of the men was his brother Charles. It was Thomas, after all, who had given the brass belt buckle to him. Charles's death would haunt Thomas for decades.

Divers returned to Davis Island in October and recovered the rest of the two men's remains, as well as the Jeep engine and rails. The next month, on November 6, the Mississippi Highway Safety Patrol arrested James Ford Seale and Charles Marcus Edwards for the murders of Dee and Moore. Edwards confessed to picking up the men and beating them, but denied doing anything else. Seale didn't admit to anything. They were released on bail the next day.

Two months later, in early January 1965, the local district attorney, Lenox Forman, dropped the charges against Seale and Edwards. Forman said that the cases had become too difficult to prosecute, because Seale and Edwards had alleged that law enforcement had mistreated them after being arrested.

Forman probably also understood that he had no chance of convincing an all-White jury in Mississippi to convict the two men. He was an elected official, so pursuing a case like that would have jeopardized his political career. Forman was also afraid of the Klan and had cause to be. Klan members sometimes snuck onto his property at night and shot his cattle. Sometimes when he traveled to court hearings, he requested a police escort.

Unknown to Forman, by September 1964, the FBI had gathered a lot of details about the Dee and Moore murders, thanks to an informant within the Klan. The FBI, though, didn't share any of that information with Forman or other local law enforcement, mainly because the FBI didn't trust local law enforcement in Franklin County; too many of them were affiliated with or sympathetic to the Klan. The FBI, consumed with solving the murders of the three civil rights workers, assumed that Forman had accumulated enough evidence on his own to prosecute. The FBI also had a valuable informant and, given the ongoing threats, they didn't want to jeopardize that information pipeline.

After Forman gave up on pursuing the case, the FBI followed suit. By May 1966, no one at any level of law enforcement was investigating the murders of Henry Dee and Charles Moore.

COLD CASES REOPENED

For the next thirty years, no one bothered to investigate the murders of Dee and Moore. By the mid-1990s, momentum was building to reopen unsolved murder cases from the civil rights era. In 1994, a jury convicted Byron De La Beckwith of killing Medgar Evers thirty years earlier. Five years after that, journalist Connie Chung and producer Harry Phillips investigated a couple of civil rights–era murders for the ABC News program *20/20*. One case was the Dee and Moore murders. Still, the FBI decided not to pursue charges against anyone, and in June 2003, they closed the case again.

In 2005, Canadian journalist David Ridgen took an interest in the case. He reached out to Thomas Moore, who brushed Ridgen aside for weeks before finally talking to him. By that time, Thomas had retired after a thirty-year career in the military, which included a tour in Vietnam as a gunner in a Huey helicopter. Thomas carried a heavy burden from his brother's death, a mixture of grief and rage and self-blame. He had always been there to look out for Charles and couldn't help but feel that he had let down his brother by not being there to protect him. It deeply troubled Thomas that no one had been held to account for killing him. He had sometimes fantasized about getting revenge against the men who killed Charles, but his mother had talked him down.

When he retired from the military, he settled in Colorado. He had no intention of going back to Mississippi. He didn't feel safe there. When Ridgen contacted him, he was living in Colorado. He had no reason to trust a journalist, so he took his time responding.

The two hit it off, though, and Thomas agreed to travel with Ridgen back to Mississippi to look into the case and to take part in a documentary that Ridgen was filming, *Mississippi Cold Case*. They soon learned that there were only two men still living who were involved in the murder: Charles Marcus Edwards and James Ford Seale.

THE TRIAL

By the time Thomas Moore and Ridgen started piecing together the evidence, prosecutors had tried several other men for civil rights–era murders. Juries convicted each one. They revisited the sites associated with the murders of Dee and Moore, consulted with the federal attorney, Dunn Lampton, who had jurisdiction over the case, and poured through long-forgotten FBI files. They even dropped in—unannounced—on Edwards and Seale, neither of whom welcomed their visit.

Federal officials were soon able to convince Edwards to testify against Seale. The combination of immunity from prosecution and Edwards's troubled conscience were enough to convince Edwards to break the oath of secrecy he had taken when he had joined the Klan decades earlier. Had he broken that oath much earlier, the Klan would have killed him.

On January 24, 2007, a federal grand jury returned an indictment against Seale for two counts of kidnapping and one count of conspiracy to kidnap. Police arrested Seale and put him in jail. Four months later, his trial began. Thomas Moore sat near the front of the courtroom to watch the proceedings, as did Thelma Collins, Henry Dee's sister. Dee's mother was still alive but institutionalized, and the family had never told her that her son had been murdered.

Seale, who was sickly enough that some (including his attorney Kathy Nester) wondered if he'd survive the trial; he did not take the stand in his own defense. In one of the more dramatic moments of the trial, Edwards—from the witness chair—apologized to the Dee and Moore families and asked for forgiveness for his role in the murders.

On June 14, the jury returned a quick verdict: Seale was guilty on all counts. Two months later, the judge sentenced the seventy-one-year-old Seale to life in prison. A year later, while Seale was confined at the federal penitentiary in Terre Haute, Indiana, an appeals court threw out his conviction, determining that the statute of limitations had expired. The full appeals court then reviewed the case but split nine to nine. As a result, Seale's conviction stood. On August 2, 2011, Seale died in prison.

Thomas Moore and Thelma Collins accepted Edwards's apology. They each shook his hand and forgave him. It didn't make up for what Edwards and the other Klan men had done, but for Moore, anyway, it was an act that God demanded of him. Unlike Edwards, Seale never publicly owned up to his actions, and he never asked for anyone's forgiveness.

SEARCHING FOR JUSTICE
The bodies of Moore and Dee weren't the only ones found in the Mississippi River. Most of the dead pulled from the river were African American. A student working on the Mississippi Summer Freedom Project observed in a letter: "Mississippi is the only state where you can drag a river any time and find bodies you were not expecting. Things are really much better for rabbits—there's a closed season on rabbits."[2]

Justice was incomplete and slow for the killers of Charles Moore and Henry Dee, but at least it was served, partially. After the verdict came down, Thomas Moore said he felt like a tremendous burden had been lifted from him.

In 2011, Thomas Moore went back to Meadville, Mississippi, to talk with Edwards. They walked among the fruit trees Edwards tended and talked over coffee. They revisited the murders, their feelings about what happened, about what God expected of them, and about reconciliation.

The following Sunday, Thomas Moore joined Edwards for services at the Bunkley Baptist Church, a congregation that had once been exclusively White. Moore and Edwards sat together near the front.

The trial in 2007 and Edwards's apology couldn't bring Charles Moore and Henry Dee back to life, of course, and it certainly didn't make up for the centuries-long reign of terror against African Americans. But the long-sought conviction gave the family some closure. Thomas Moore felt a burden lifted. Justice was served to Seale. These were small steps, but at least they went forward.

In 2008, President Bush signed the Emmett Till Unsolved Civil Rights Crime Act. The legislation directed the FBI to reopen unsolved murders of African Americans committed before December 31, 1969. The FBI identified 113 cold cases with 126 murder victims, which was almost certainly just a portion of the actual murders. Eight years later, the FBI had closed 105 of those cases. Only one case had resulted in a conviction, though. Prosecuting perpetrators 40-plus years after a murder is extraordinarily difficult, as many of the people involved had died. Double jeopardy also came into play at times, as some perpetrators had been tried once before and acquitted by all-White juries.

Righting past wrongs is a monumental task, but as Thomas Moore said, "When you get an opportunity to correct some wrong, then you take that opportunity."[3] And sometimes the present catches up with us, anyway. In 2015, voters in Natchez and Adams County—the area that had once been an epicenter of Klan activity and where law enforcement often worked hand-in-hand with the Klan—elected a Black man, Travis Patten, as sheriff.

Hot Coals Rained Down from the Sky

The St. Louis Fire of 1849

IN THE LATE 1840S, ST. LOUIS WAS A BOOMING CITY THAT ATTRACTED people from all walks of life. Native Americans, free and enslaved Black

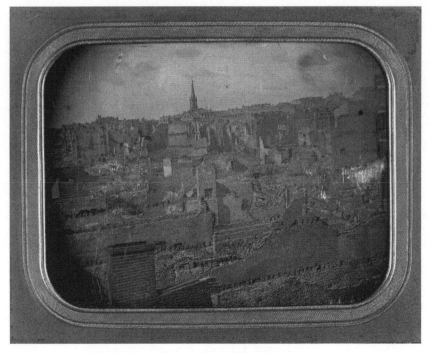

Photo 17.1. St. Louis in ruins after the Great Fire of 1849.
MISSOURI HISTORICAL SOCIETY, PHOTO BY THOMAS EASTERLY.

people, and Irish immigrants rubbed shoulders with descendants of the city's founding French families and with the thousands of German immigrants who found St. Louis a good place to call home. Jobs were plentiful in the city's expanding factories, but many new St. Louisans found it more profitable to start their own businesses. The city also had its share of "ruffians, robbers, swearers, and swindlers,"[1] according to former mayor John F. Darby. (He knew how to sell his city!)

St. Louis was a hub in a river transportation network that connected it to other cities (such as Cincinnati, Louisville, and New Orleans), so naturally the heart of the city was the Mississippi riverfront. Boats came and went along a mile-long stretch of riverbank, an area that was sometimes so jam-packed with boats that a person could make their way along the riverfront by jumping from one to another. Boats didn't dock in St. Louis, they landed, which meant they ran right up onto the bank and then tied up. The city paved the middle portion of the riverfront with cobblestones in 1844, but most of the bank was a sloppy, muddy mess.

Roustabouts moved cargo between the boats and the riverfront, items such as cotton, lumber, fruit, whiskey, salted pork, fine china—all of life's necessities plus a few luxuries. Warehouses, three or four stories tall, faced the river, most of them built from brick and stone. A steady procession of wagons carried goods into the city's busy neighborhoods.

The riverfront could also be dangerous. Criminals slid in and out of the crowds, sometimes lifting items from a distracted person's pocket or maybe robbing them at knifepoint in a back alley. Con artists had well-rehearsed stories aimed at separating naïve travelers from their cash. Now and then, someone would fall off a steamboat and drown. And in the middle of all that, St. Louis faced the ever-present threat of fire.

Steamboat fires were very hard to put out. The wood the steamboats were built from dried out over time, so a fire on board could rapidly consume an entire boat. On May 2, 1849, the steamer *Highland Mary* ignited, and the flames spread so quickly that the captain's clothes caught on fire. He jumped into the river before he burned to death, but the *Highland Mary* burned to the waterline. Fortunately, nearby boats got out of the way before the fire could spread to them. Two weeks later, St. Louisans wouldn't be so lucky.

The Night Sky Lights Up

St. Louis didn't create a municipal fire department until 1857, but the city wasn't defenseless against fires. Private citizens, like William Belcher, sometimes created their own systems for fighting fires. Belcher wrote to his brother that "we have made large expenditures for water cisterns in order to have a supply of water to guard against fire."[2]

Ten volunteer fire organizations also served the city by the end of the 1840s. While their stated purpose was keeping the city from burning into oblivion, they were also fraternal clubs. Each organized with a hierarchical structure, and the clubs sometimes competed to see which organization could put out a fire the quickest.

Thomas Targee served as the president of one of those groups, the Missouri Fire Company #5, at the end of the 1840s. He and his family had moved to St. Louis in 1836. Soon after arriving, he joined the Union Fire Company #2, then three years later he was part of the group that founded Missouri Fire Company #5. Targee worked as an auctioneer, but he also held a lucrative job in city government. He was the city weigher, a position in which he assessed fees on most goods coming into and leaving the city.

On the evening of May 17, 1849, a Thursday, men from Targee's old company held one of their regular meetings. The evening sky was bright and clear and the air pleasantly cool. A steady breeze blew from the northeast. The men probably talked about the city's ongoing cholera epidemic, which posed an increasingly grave threat. As the meeting broke up and the men exited the building, "their attention was suddenly attracted by a brilliant light appearing in the direction of the Northern portion of the Levee, immediately followed by the violent ringing of Steamboat bells."[3]

Sally Smith Flagg heard the alarms, too, but thought little of it. "Fire bells rang before I went to bed, last night. It being a common affair, I paid no attention to it."[4] Panic would later sweep away that complacency when flames approached her home.

Down on the levee, a night watchman had been making his rounds. Around nine o'clock he encountered a man leaving the steamer *White Cloud*, a regular boat on the New Orleans–St. Louis route. The man claimed he had been looking for a friend, and the watchman didn't think much of it as he left. Still, the watchman inspected the boat and found nothing obviously wrong.

Half an hour later, though, the watchman smelled smoke. He boarded the *White Cloud* again and headed straight for the ladies' cabins, where a fire had recently broken out. Flames were sweeping through the cabins. He rang the boat's fire bell, and the tolling echoed throughout the city. Targee heard the call from his home on Fourteenth Street, and he and the Missouri Fire Company #5 got there quickly, as did the men of Liberty Fire Company #6.

John Beggs, who volunteered with the Franklin Company, heard the alarm bell ringing from the north levee. He was near a Liberty company, so he raced down to the levee with them. When they arrived, they saw the *White Cloud* aflame.

They hooked up a hose to one of the city's fire hydrants and dragged it on board the boat just south of the *White Cloud*, the *Edward Bates*, from which they had a good vantage point to direct water from their hose. The fire had already gotten too big to extinguish, though, so they cut the *White Cloud* loose to drift away from the other boats.

As the *White Cloud* slipped away from the levee, fire spread onto the *Edward Bates*. What happened next isn't clear. Some witnesses claimed that the firemen and crew cut the *Edward Bates* loose, while others thought that the fire burned through the mooring ropes. Regardless, the *Edward Bates* drifted away from the levee, too. As the current carried the boat downriver, it bumped into other boats on the levee and spread fire to them, first the *Belle Isle* and then the *Julia*, eventually setting at least nineteen more boats ablaze before it settled on a sandbar at Duncan's Island.

A VAST SHEET OF FLAME

The speed with which the fire spread must have shocked and disoriented the firefighters. Fredrick Colburn recalled, "Looking to the South, the whole front of St. Louis seemed one vast sheet of flame. Whilst our eyes were transfixed with this grand, but fearful sight, a heavy smoke bursting from one of the large Levee stores gave notice of increasing danger to the City."[5]

Those steady northeast winds blew coals from the boats onto the levee. Cargo on the levee ignited. Packages of hemp and stacks of lumber burned first, which ignited barrels of lard and bacon. The fire quickly intensified and spread to the warehouses and offices that lined the levee. Wood frames held the brick buildings together, and all that wood added still more fuel to the fire. A wall of fire engulfed the entire riverfront, with smoke so thick that it became increasingly hard to see a person a few paces away.

As the fire spread, it overwhelmed the volunteer firefighters. A call went out for any able-bodied person to help. A thousand people engaged in the battle against the fires at one point. They prevented fire from spreading any farther north, but winds blew flames into the central part of the riverfront. Some fire companies focused their efforts on spraying water onto the rooftops of riverfront buildings, but it ultimately wasn't enough. The advancing flames forced the fire companies into a steady retreat.

The Union Company shifted southwest to protect buildings around Olive and Main Streets, then moved again to the ferry landing at Market Street, where they pulled water from the Mississippi River to help protect the South Market building, an important landmark in part because City Hall occupied the upper floor, which housed the city's most important documents. The flames were intense. "Large planks were placed in front of the pipemen to shield them from the fearful heat."[6] Even though fires raged around it, firefighters saved the building.

A short distance away, fire surrounded the stone building that St. Louisans now call the Old Cathedral—it was just fifteen years old in 1849. The men from the Union Company were losing the battle to save the cathedral, at least until the Liberty Company showed up. Their combined efforts kept the flames at bay and saved the building.

A City in Panic

The news from the rest of the city was less encouraging. Hot coals rained down from the sky and spread the fire beyond the levee. Frances Sublette recalled "Never did I see anything so awful in my life the flames, seemed as if, they would come over Mother's house and coals of fire larger than both of my hands fell over all the yard and the house. . . . I never felt so much alarmed in my life."[7]

Panic spread around the city. Businesses tried desperately to move their inventory somewhere safe, but a lot of the city's wagons were busy transporting the bodies of cholera victims. Some wagon drivers also took advantage of the chaos by jacking up their rates. Goods piled up in streets, which proved to be a tempting target for some of those ruffians that Mayor Darby alluded to. Police arrested seventy people for looting during the time the fire raged.

As the fires raced toward her house, Sally Smith Flagg could no longer brush aside the alarms. She and her family packed up what they could. "We first filled all the trunks, & then too took pillow-cases, stuffed them full and tied them up." They found wagons to carry away what they had packed up, then waited. She didn't feel optimistic. "Everything almost seemed to conspire against putting it out."[8]

There was cause for pessimism. As the volunteers fought to contain the flames, a massive explosion ripped apart the steamboat *Martha*—the boat had been carrying gunpowder. The shock wave lifted firefighters on the levee off their feet and tossed them backwards. The firefighting efforts overloaded the city's primitive water system and it gave out. Fire companies pumped water from the Mississippi when the fire didn't block access to it. St. Louisans grew more desperate. People climbed on rooftops where they tried to extinguish fires by dumping washbasins of water. Others tried to smother flames with wet blankets.

A DARING ACT

As the firefighters grew increasingly worried, they concocted a bold plan. Several men suggested creating a firebreak to deprive the flames of fuel. In order to do that, firefighters would have to destroy a row of buildings on the edge of the fire zone. Captain Targee was among the volunteers who quickly embraced the idea.

They sent a wagon to collect kegs of gunpowder from a storehouse at the St. Louis Arsenal, and Targee ran home to visit his family. When the wagon came back, they piled the kegs of gunpowder up at the southwest corner of Third and Market Streets, then covered them with a tarp to protect them from flying embers.

They targeted six buildings for demolition. They didn't have a method to control the timing of the explosions, though, so each had to be started individually, and then the men would have to get the hell out as quickly as they could. One by one, the buildings went down. Targee carried kegs into three of them. As he carried gunpowder into the building that housed the Phillips music store—the final one—he passed Isaac Sturgeon, who thought Targee looked "smoke-begrimed and haggard."[9]

As Targee entered the building, a keg exploded. He never had a chance. Two other men in a nearby building, lawyers Wells Colton and Russell Prentiss, were badly burned and died a few days later. The blast scattered Targee's remains around the immediate area; a portion of one of his legs landed next to Sturgeon's horse. The fire break seemed to have helped though, that and the nonstop efforts of the volunteers. By seven in the morning, the fire was mostly extinguished.

A CITY DEVASTATED

The fire devastated the commercial heart of the city, though. Hulls of burned-out steamers lined the riverfront. "Steamers which were to be seen at any hour thronging at the wharf, from North to South, are now visible only in black and rotten timbers, thrusting their jagged ends a few feet above the waters edge, as if in mockery of mans ingenious handi-work, which should be so defaced in a few minutes."[10]

The conflagration destroyed over four hundred buildings, including the offices of three English-language newspapers and the telegraph office. Nearly three hundred businesses were ruined, including two-thirds of the wholesale dry goods merchants and half of the grocery stores. A writer at the *People's Organ*, one of the newspapers destroyed by the fire, lamented that "those streets which a few days since exhibited all the glorious signs of bustling prosperous mercantile community, are now but a bricky maze paved with fallen walls and calcined timbers, bordered with ruins threatening at every slightest wind to topple down."[11]

For Fredrick Colburn, the walk home was "a sad return in full view of the heaps of smoking ruins. Sad faces appeared wherever you might turn, but there was a determination not to surrender, and the magnificent St. Louis of today, is the result of that spirit."[12] The fire spared the Flagg household. They spent a day retrieving the furnishings that had shipped out by wagon, but they didn't have to abandon their home. Hamilton Gamble, who had also survived a bout of cholera, wrote that he had lost "every one of most valuable books and all my papers," plus $250 in cash.[13] He was relatively lucky, though. The disaster left many people with only the clothes on their backs.

Some people initially suspected that the *White Cloud* had been set afire intentionally, but no evidence of arson ever surfaced. A fire had, after all, broken out before on the boat and in nearly the same spot.

Within a week of the Great Fire, the city's levee was bustling again. The city passed new building regulations aimed at preventing future fires. The city also upgraded its water and sewage systems. And less than a decade after the fire, the city created one of the first municipal fire departments in the United States.

The city suffered an estimated loss of between $3.5 million and $6 million. Insurance covered much of it. Three of the big banks had fire-proof vaults that proved their worth. They reopened quickly. Within two years, the burned-out district was completely rebuilt.

Remarkably, just three people died in the fire, including Targee. His remains were faithfully collected and placed in a casket, then taken to Christ Church, where he had served as choir director. Bishop Cicero Stephens Hawks conducted the funeral. Because of the ongoing cholera epidemic, only a few people could attend. After the service, he was buried in an unmarked grave at Christ Church Cemetery. His bravery lived on, however. To this day, firefighters revere him for his bravery and the sacrifice he made to protect his fellow St. Louisans.

When the Walls Caved In

The Milford Mine Disaster

The day was overcast, like so many February days in northern Minnesota. Snow covered the ground. The Mississippi River and the lakes and marshes that emptied into it had frozen over. Outside, the air was frigid and dry, but when Frank Hrvatin Junior descended into the depths of the Milford Mine on that day in 1924, he wouldn't need a

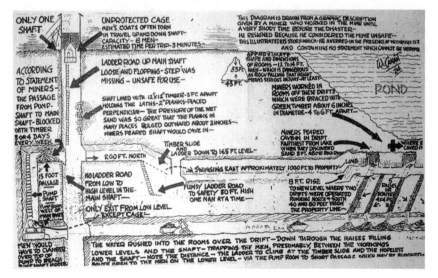

Photo 18.1. Layout of the Milford Mine
CUYUNA IRON RANGE HERITAGE NETWORK

parka. The air was damp, but temperatures inside the mine held steady in the fifties.

Frank Junior, just two weeks from his fifteenth birthday, got to work shoveling dirt between mining cars and a chute. In another part of the mine, his father, Frank Senior, worked with a crew that loosened rocks by blasting and then chipping away at them with shovels.

Frank Junior was already no stranger to hard work. When he dropped out of school, his father had told him, "If you don't go to school you gonna have to go to work."[1] So he went to work. He left the family home in Crosby, Minnesota, and got a job a hundred miles away in Chisholm at the Glen Mine, where he drilled twenty-foot holes with a hand crank. Mining companies weren't supposed to hire anyone under eighteen years of age, but Frank was big—over six feet tall—and strong, so no one asked to see his birth certificate.

He worked six days a week and got paid $3.80 for each eight-hour workday. He lived with another mining family in Chisholm and saved $300 from the summer work. In the fall, he moved back to Crosby, and his father got him the job at the Milford Mine. It was supposed to be short term. Some miners were concerned that the Milford's mine shafts were getting too close to a lake and jeopardizing their safety.

Iron ore mining was booming in northern Minnesota's three ranges: the Vermillion, the Mesabi, and the Cuyuna. The Milford Mine was in the Cuyuna Range. Ore in the Cuyuna Range was deeper than in the other ranges, most of it buried under as much as two hundred feet of glacial drift. When companies got serious about removing the ore from the Cuyuna Range, they needed thousands of men willing to perform physically demanding work underground for low pay.

The companies found the labor they desired among the waves of immigrants arriving in the United States. Many had little formal education, and few spoke English. They came from across Europe: Croatia, Serbia, Bosnia, Romania, Bulgaria, Ukraine, Sweden, Finland, Norway, Italy, Great Britain, and Germany. Some immigrants saved enough money to buy land to farm in northern Minnesota, but the growing season was short and the fertile soil shallow, so many farmers worked in the mines in winter.

Cuyuna ore had a higher concentration of manganese than the ore in other Minnesota ranges. Manganese makes steel stronger and longer-lasting, so demand for Cuyuna ore was high, especially during World War I, when foreign supplies were cut off. During the war years, there were sixteen mines removing manganiferous iron ore in the Cuyuna Range. But most of the ore deposits were small, so by 1923, only the Milford Mine was still operating.

George Crosby's Whitmarsh Mining Company owned the land around the Milford Mine, but they leased it out to E. T. Merritt's Cuyuna-Minneapolis Iron Company, which conducted the first explorations of the site in 1912. They named the mine the Ida Mae after Merritt's wife. Merritt's company couldn't make the mine work, though, so it closed. Whitmarsh took over in 1921 and began mining it again the next year. They renamed it the Milford Mine in honor of the Connecticut city where Crosby's mother was from.

Miners sunk the mine shaft—the only one—between Island Lake and smaller Foley Pond, which was surrounded by wetlands that connected it to another lake. The Mississippi River snaked around the lakes and wetlands just to the north. The ground was perpetually saturated, so pumps had to run continuously to keep water out of the mine tunnels.

By 1924, the mine employed a hundred men. They worked two shifts around the clock. Some men and their families lived in one of the dozen shacks at the mine. Single miners lived in boarding houses nearby. A few lucky families lived in a nice two-story bungalow in town. The mining company owned all the housing and charged anywhere from five dollars a month for a shack to twenty dollars a month for a bungalow. Despite the language differences, miners and their families formed tight-knit communities, which they would lean heavily on in the days after February 5.

THE ACCIDENT

At 3:45 in the afternoon of February 5, 1924, near the end of a shift, the unthinkable happened.

"I was working not near anybody," Matt Kangas recalled. "Then the wind hit me. I fell down and my lamp went out. I lit it, it went out again. It was dark and cold. The wind hit me again. I knew what it was. . . . I knew if we lost a minute, it was too late. I yelled. Then I ran like hell. We can't save our life no more if we don't run, I know. So I run. No time for gates, no time for the cage. No time for anything. I just run and fall down, and run some more."[2]

Kangas heard a noise that sounded like a car getting tuned up. Other survivors described hearing a waterfall. As Kangas ran toward the ladder in the shaft—175 feet below the surface—he heard Frank Junior warning: "For God's sake, run faster! The whole lake has come in."[3]

When Kangas made it to the ladder, "I reach for it. I miss it. I grab it and start up. I am all in. But I'm damned if I stop!" He felt winded and struggled to climb up. Frank Junior got underneath him. He put Kangas's legs on his shoulders, then pushed him up to the top. "The men were just struggling their very very best to move," Frank Junior remembered.[4]

Once they had reached the surface, "I took my partner out of the mud—he was in mud up to his hips!" Frank Junior said. "That's how fast the water was coming in and the mud—but we made it! When we got to the top we just laid down on the surface—everybody came running to see what the hell was the matter! Well, that took about fifteen minutes and the whole thing was over! I knew then I would never see my dad no more. They were all dead."[5]

Forty-eight men were working in the mine when the ground between a tunnel and Foley Pond collapsed. Ice cracked on the lake's surface as the water level dropped. Only seven men made it out. Once on the surface, the survivors lowered the cage, hoping to save a few more men. It came back up empty and covered in mud.

Frank Junior sat next to the shaft for three hours after escaping, "shaking like a leaf. My nerves wouldn't stop shaking until I quieted down."[6] Aboveground, reality was sinking in.

"As we passed the four small houses on the mine location, we heard a woman scream and saw her tearing her hair," Arnold Gustafson, an engineer at the Milford Mine, recalled:

It was Mrs. Crellin, the mine captain's wife, running out of the miners' change house. We stopped, stunned. In the dry (change house) sat seven dejected men, those who had been close to the bottom of the

200-foot deep shaft, when they saw water gushing down the main drift. They had scrambled up the series of ladders in the manway, the last with water at their knees.

Frank and I ran to the shaft to measure how close the water was to the surface. By then others had gathered; as we looked at the forty-foot mark on the tape, we all realized that our forty-one coworkers had drowned. . . . Some of the women rolled in the snow as they moaned in their grief.

As I talked to one of these who arrived with the small son of a miner who had worked on the day shift, I experienced the saddest moment of this occasion. The little boy, sensing that things of importance had occurred and that his father was involved, looked up at me and said proudly, "My daddy is down there too." Tears again come to my eyes as I write of this experience.[7]

Calls for help overwhelmed the Aitkin-Deerwood Telephone Company, where Jennie Myhres and her sister, Maybelle, worked the switchboard. For several hours, they made calls to organize emergency assistance. They handled hundreds of calls an hour, all while wondering about the fate of their brother Arthur, who worked at the Milford Mine.

In the nearby towns, meanwhile, whistles sounded the alarm. "For almost an hour that afternoon of February 5th, 1924, the steam whistles all over the Cuyuna Range—the mine whistles at the Milford and every surrounding underground mine, the whistles on the locomotives of the ore trains, each with its distinctive unblending tone—continued to wail like a thousand banshees."[8]

Frank Junior, exhausted, changed clothes and got a ride into town. "I had to go home and tell my mother my father was dead."[9]

RECOVERING THE DEAD

As the country mourned the recent death of former President Woodrow Wilson, mining communities in northern Minnesota struggled to come to terms with their own shocking losses. People flocked to the mine site, but there wasn't much to see when they got there. All they could do was wait for the bodies to be recovered.

Mines throughout the area sent pumps to help recover the dead. It was a slow process, as the water had to be drained not only from the mine, but also from Foley Pond. As they pumped water out, mud flowed in. Pumps were continually getting clogged.

Officials told the press that they were pumping the water and mud into nearby Island Lake, but Frank Junior knew otherwise. "I think they pumped the water from the lake into the Mississippi River. They don't say that in the paper but that's where it went."[10]

The pumps ran continuously. Within two weeks, Foley Pond was only 4 feet deep, and water in the mine had dropped 123 feet. Emptying Foley Pond stranded fish, turtles, and other animals. Recovery teams collected them and gave them to grieving families so that they had a little extra to eat.

By mid-March, the lake was dry. Recovery operations began in earnest at the end of the month. It was an arduous process. Three teams of men each worked eight hours a day slogging through shafts clogged with mud, roots, and plants. The work was demanding and gut-wrenching and sometimes the rescue workers could only stand it for fifteen or twenty minutes before they needed fresh air.

"The air underground had the smell of death," Arnold Gustafson said, "not only of bodies yet to be found, but also of the rotting fish and frogs. We could always tell when we were getting close to a body, and then we would start spraying with the formaldehyde that the undertakers furnished us. As the water from the hose washed away the mud, often the first evidence of a man was the grotesque white face, swelled to look like a rag doll, peering out of the black muck. The body would be placed on a wire stretcher, carried to the shaft, and hoisted to the surface."[11]

Crews recovered the first two miners seven weeks after the accident: Valentine Cole and Minor Graves. They were just fifty feet from the shaft and were found embracing each other. "The mud and water trapped them so they couldn't move their legs, so what could they do?" Frank Junior said. "They grabbed each other and said a prayer, I guess. It's not no time to swear, nothing like that. You start praying to your maker. It's the end."[12]

Frank Junior worked with the recovery operation. He was on-site four months after the collapse when a crew found his father's body, the sixteenth body removed. The family buried Frank Senior two days later at Lakewood Cemetery in Crosby. He was forty-three years old and left behind a wife, Frances, and eight children, the youngest just six months old.

The recovery operation continued for nine months. Arthur Myhres, the brother of telephone operators Jennie and Maybelle, was among the dead. The last miner recovered was thirty-one-year-old Arvid Lehti.

The immediate families of the dead miners received some financial assistance, thanks to a worker's compensation program that Minnesota approved in 1913. A widow with no children was eligible for 40 percent of her husband's wages. Widows with at least 4 children could claim up to two-thirds of their husband's salary. Beatrice Bedard, the widow of twenty-three-year-old Earl, received $14.56 a week; they had only been married for six weeks. Frank Junior's mother received the maximum of $20 a week.

Mourning

Just two days after the greatest loss of life in a Minnesota mining disaster, officials declared it an "Act of God." A panel appointed by Governor Jacob Preus reached a similar conclusion:

> *The commission finds that the accident at the Milford mine was not the result of negligence on the part of the Whitmarsh Mining Company; that it was not foreseen, and that engineers for the company had used the usual diligence and care in caving the top sub-level rooms under the swamp, the first of which was brought down several months before the accident without the slightest evidence of mud or water following the cave.[13]*

The panel made several recommendations for improvements, including providing more money for inspections and more training for inspectors, strengthening some safety rules, draining bodies of water near a mine, improving ventilation, and providing rescue stations.

Many families were not impressed with the outcome of the investigations, though. Depositions to the governor's commission were public, so many miners were afraid they would lose their jobs if they were openly critical. One man who had planned on giving critical testimony later said that two men had approached him the night before and threatened to harm his family if he talked. He kept quiet.

The Milford mine had a reputation for being unsafe. Some miners had expressed concerns about seepage before the accident. In a letter to the *Minnesota Daily Star*, A. C. Bacel wrote that "Several miners had quit their jobs at this same mine for the reason that they refused to work in the dangerous drift when the operators made no provision for safety. Just a week before the disaster one man protested to the captain about the very condition and the result was he was fired and told he was an agitator and a bolshevik."[14]

Deerwood resident F. L. Pitt expressed a common reaction to the official report: "[S]everal times we have heard it remarked by mining men that the same thing might have happened in many of the mines around here, had the mine operators depended on God, instead of timbers to hold back the overburden."[15]

As for Frank Junior, he too was unimpressed with the official conclusion. "And how is it that a small person without any funds gonna fight a guy with a lot of money, or a group with a lot of money. How you gonna do that? It's absolutely impossible. So they made it stick."[16]

Frank worked wherever he could after the accident. He moved around the country and even worked for a while at an underground mine in Montana. "I was with my kind of people—miners," he said.[17]

After the last body was recovered, the company cleared the mine and reinforced its tunnels. Whitemarsh formed a partnership with Bethlehem Steel to create Amherst Mining Company, which then reopened the mine. It operated until 1932. In fifteen years of operation, the company removed 1,266,172 tons of ore and forty-one bodies.

Today, Milford Mine Memorial Park occupies the former mine site. Foley Pond is now Milford Lake. A boardwalk etched with the names of the victims stretches over peaceful wetlands where white and yellow lotus flowers bloom and ducks swim. A light wind rustles the leaves on the trees around the lake. No buildings remain, but the path leads to the old mining shaft and to a walkway where visitors can read about and pay homage to the men who died on that horrible day.

Tragedy at Rush Hour

The I-35W Bridge Collapse

IT WAS JUST ANOTHER WEDNESDAY EVENING IN MINNEAPOLIS. THE AIR was typically warm for August, with temperatures topping out in the lower nineties. Commuters raced to get home, many of them along I-35W, part of the 1,568-mile-long highway that spans the middle of the United States from Laredo, Texas, to Duluth, Minnesota. In Minnesota's

Photo 19.1. Vehicles and wreckage from the I-35W bridge collapse.
WIKIMEDIA COMMONS, PHOTO BY KEVIN ROFIDAL.

Twin Cities, I-35 splits, with one branch that runs through Minneapolis (I-35W) and another that passes through Saint Paul (I-35E).

When commuters on I-35W reached the bridge over the Mississippi River on August 1, 2007, they found half of the lanes closed for construction. Traffic slowed to a crawl. Jeff Ringate and seventeen other construction workers were on the bridge getting ready to pour concrete that evening. Bobcat driver Greg Jolstad was driving a Bobcat to position materials for the evening's work.

Alicia Babatz was on the way to pick up her two-year-old daughter. Near Babatz, children and staff from the Waite House Community Center, including twenty-year-old Jeremy Hernandez, sang in a school bus after a fun day at a water park.

Marcelo Cruz also slowed down when he approached the bridge. Paralyzed several years before, he was driving a van that had been adapted to meet his needs. Sherry Lou Engebretsen was on her way home to join her family for a celebratory dinner. Caroline Yankelevich slowed down, too, as did Gary Babineau in his pickup truck. His mind was preoccupied with thoughts about his child that was due in two weeks. Angela Wong and her twelve-year-old son waited patiently for traffic to open back up.

Commuters who glanced down at the river probably glimpsed the *Minneapolis Queen* on one of its scenic tours of the Mississippi. Around six in the evening, *Minneapolis Queen* Captain Charlie Leekley was guiding the boat and its forty-eight sightseers near the I-35W bridge.

Then everything changed. The I-35W bridge creaked, rolled, and collapsed without warning. Everyone on the bridge plunged a hundred feet down to the Mississippi River, and a frantic scramble for survival began.

Swaying and Rolling

Jay Danz had just passed under the bridge on West River Parkway on his way to watch the Minnesota Twins play a game in the Metrodome. He heard the bridge "creaking and making all sorts of noises it shouldn't make. And then the bridge just started to fall apart."[1]

A large sign fell down in front of Angela Wong. "The next thing I knew," she said, "the road was in a wave. I heard people screaming."[2]

Berndt Toivonen was on his way home from work when the bridge "went up and came down. I thought I was going to die."[3]

Marcelo Cruz felt the roadway sway. He steered toward the bridge's rails and slammed on the brakes to avoid falling into the river. After he stopped, his van perched precariously on the sloping roadway. He watched several vehicles fall over the edge. Drivers behind him had managed to stop their vehicles from falling into the river. A couple of them ran up to Cruz's van and helped him to safety.

Peter Siddons was one of the unlucky drivers whose car fell over the edge. "I saw this rolling of the bridge," he said. "It kept collapsing, down, down, down, until it got to me."[4] His car fell to the bottom of the gorge, but it landed on a big slab of the roadway lodged up against another car. He got out and climbed to safety.

THE RACE TO RESCUE

Around the Twin Cities, family and friends called to check on loved ones who may have been on the bridge, but all that activity overloaded the cellular networks. At the Metrodome, the announcer informed the crowd about the disaster, but the baseball game went on as planned. Ending the game early would have sent thousands of vehicles back out on the roads just as emergency crews were rescuing victims of the collapse.

People nearby leapt into action to help before the first responders arrived, including twenty-four-year-old Noah Kunin, who lived near the bridge. When he felt the ground shake, he looked out his window just in time to see the last seconds of the collapse. He immediately ran to the site to help.

The Mississippi is about four hundred feet wide and anywhere from three to eleven feet deep under the I-35W bridge. The US Army Corps of Engineers used one of its nearby dams to lower the level of the river a couple of feet to help the rescue workers, but then had to raise it back up a foot because the lower level created turbulence that was hard on the rescue workers.

Caroline Yankelevich was among those who needed rescue. "I could kind of feel the bridge shake a little—it did a little shimmy. Then the bridge started falling, cars were flying everywhere and I saw the water coming up."[5] Her car landed in the Mississippi River. As the inside filled with water, she rolled down a window and crawled out. Kristin West landed in the river, too. After she swam out through a window, a rescue team in a boat pulled her to safety. She wasn't injured.

Alicia Babatz was sure she was going to die as her car fell. After landing on a collapsed portion of the road deck, her vehicle rolled into the river. She pushed herself out of the car after it filled with water, even though she felt sharp pains around her hips. The swim to shore was a struggle, but she made it. She later learned that her tailbone had broken when she landed.

Ringate, one of the construction workers, crashed down on concrete, but he wasn't seriously hurt. As the cloud of dust and black smoke around him thinned out, he picked up a long pole that he used to pull a coworker and other victims from the river. Three construction workers went to hospitals with serious injuries. Greg Jolstad, though, was still unaccounted for three hours after the collapse.

Alerts sounded throughout the city's emergency networks. Dr. John Hick, the head of disaster planning at Hennepin County Medical Center and an experienced emergency room physician, raced to the scene and quickly got busy assessing and treating the injured. There was constant worry that the remnants of the bridge would give way, so rescuers moved quickly and improvised. Pieces of plywood served as stretchers. Ripped shirts bandaged wounds.

Shanna Hanson, a captain at a Minneapolis Fire Station, also heard the alerts. She was off duty at the time but went to help anyway. She was among a handful of people who waded into the river to search vehicles for survivors.

After Captain Charlie Leekley realized that the bridge had collapsed, he offered to steer his boat to the site of the disaster to help with rescues, but the waters around the wreck were too dangerous. He took his passengers back to port.

Meanwhile, folks scrambled to help other survivors. The school bus had fallen with the other vehicles. The fifty-two children and nine adults on board had screamed and grabbed their seats as it fell and crash-landed on its wheels. Everyone sat in stunned silence as a cloud of dust filled the bus. As the air cleared, many felt afraid that the bus was going to slide into the river.

Jeremy Hernandez felt the roadway shaking and jumped into action. He forced open the back door, then guided the kids off the bus. A couple of people who were standing on the collapsed road deck near the back door guided the kids to safe ground. "If it would have been a second later," Hernandez said, "we would have been in the water or under the pavement."[6]

Gary Babineau was one of the people who helped escort the kids to safety. His truck fell with the bridge and broke in half when it landed. "We hit bottom and I couldn't believe that I could open my eyes," he said. "I couldn't believe that I could move." His back was injured, but he still had the presence of mind to help the kids on the bus. "It [the bus] was leaning. It looked like it might fall and I knew we had to get those kids off of that bridge."[7] Amazingly, the kids were fine; most only suffered bumps and bruises. Two staff members and the bus driver spent a night in the hospital, but their injuries weren't life-threatening.

Ambulances carried several dozen wounded to area hospitals. Many more people got to a medical facility on their own. By nightfall, the first responders had shifted their focus from rescuing potential survivors to recovering the dead. The body of Sherry Engebretsen was among the first group removed, along with that of Artemio Trinidad-Mena, who had been running an errand for the grocery store he worked for. Trinidad-Mena left behind a wife and four children.

Donations poured into the Red Cross and other relief organizations. People lined up to donate blood. A local coffee shop near the bridge gave free drinks to first responders. A sales representative for a food company set up a grill near the disaster site and cooked brats until all the first responders who wanted to eat had eaten, which turned out to be about five hundred brats. A grocery store donated the buns.

As the days dragged on, crews found the bodies of Julia Blackhawk, a thirty-two-year-old mother of two and a member of the Winnebago Tribe of Nebraska, and twenty-three-year-old Sadiya Sahal and her two-year-old daughter. It was tedious work. Divers only had about six inches of visibility in the murky waters of the Mississippi River.

Crews recovered the last victim from the wreckage on August 20. It was Greg Jolstad, the missing construction worker. His wife, Lisa, struggled to adjust to the loss. "I sit home every night, and I just can't believe he's not coming home. I look out the back door window and it's weird not to see his truck out there. I look out the bathroom window at the sky and know he's up there, and I say, you know, why did you have to leave, Greg?"[8]

Bridge Autopsy

Federal and state investigators moved quickly to reconstruct a timeline for the disaster and to identify the cause of the bridge collapse. The bridge gave way around 6:05 p.m., at which time, they concluded, there were 111 vehicles on it. One thousand feet of road deck gave way and fell one hundred feet to the Mississippi River. Only a few vehicles ended up in the water. Most landed on pieces of the collapsed roadway.

A police car reached the scene just five minutes after the collapse; a fire truck arrived just one minute after that. When the first responders arrived, construction workers, students and staff from the University of Minnesota, passersby, and even some medical professionals who had been attending training at a nearby Red Cross office had jumped into action to help survivors.

Investigators determined that 190 people had been on the bridge when it collapsed. Thirty-four suffered serious injuries and 111 had minor injuries. Thirteen people died. More people might have died if not for a combination of factors that included the safety features of modern vehicles (such as air bags) and the prompt response of rescuers. The way the bridge collapsed probably helped, too. The roadway sloped as it fell, which reduced the intensity of the impact for many vehicles.

The official report from the National Transportation Safety Board concluded that failed gusset plates were the likely cause of the collapse. A gusset plate is a flat sheet of steel that connects beams and columns. The report concluded that some of the bridge's gusset plates were thinner than they should have been and that they gave out when they carried more weight than they were meant to handle. On the day of the collapse, a particular set of conditions came together that stressed those plates beyond their capacity: the extra weight of construction equipment and vehicles from rush hour, plus an increased load on the original structure after multiple renovations in the bridge's forty-year history.

While their conclusion wasn't universally accepted, it triggered a series of inspections of similar bridges, as well as big lawsuits. Since the disaster, Minnesota has replaced or overhauled more than a hundred bridges in the state. State officials added weight restrictions to some bridges and closed five. The state provided some immediate financial relief to victims of the collapse. Some of the engineering firms responsible for bridge construction and inspection eventually agreed to multimillion-dollar settlements.

On the day after the collapse, infrastructure stocks rose. Three days after the disaster, the US Congress authorized $250 million to build a replacement bridge. Ten weeks after the collapse, Minnesota had chosen a contractor to start construction. The replacement, known as the St. Anthony Falls Bridge, opened on September 18, 2008. Construction finished in eleven months, which was three months ahead of schedule. The new structure has sensors buried in it that measure in real time all the movements that bridges normally make—every shake from a passing car, the sag from accumulating snow, a bend from the wind, and contraction or expansion as temperatures fall and rise.

On the four-year anniversary of the collapse, Minneapolis unveiled a memorial garden for the victims. The centerpiece is a series of thirteen steel beams, one for each of the dead. It's in a quiet location on West River Parkway near the new I-35W bridge. At night, it's a magnificent spot to watch the play of colorful lights that illuminate the St. Anthony Falls Bridge, and to reflect on the preciousness of life.

Death Is Wielding His Scythe

The Cholera Pandemic

EUROPEANS IMPORTED MANY THINGS TO NORTH AMERICA—HONEY-bees and apples, for example. They also brought disease, a lot of it: small-pox, measles, influenza, typhoid. Those diseases had a devastating impact on Indigenous people in the Americas, killing entire communities in some outbreaks. Europeans also imported diseases that brought death and terror to burgeoning European and American communities: cholera, malaria, and yellow fever. And many of the worst outbreaks of those dis-eases were in cities and communities along the Mississippi River. Travel on the big river proved to be an efficient way to spread them around.

Nineteenth-century American cities were messy, smelly, and noisy. People were just beginning to understand how sanitation affected health, but few cities spent money to build sewers or water systems. Residents dumped their waste in the streets. Horses and oxen tromped through the streets, and pigs and other livestock often roamed freely, too. They all left behind large piles of feces in the streets. Much of the human and animal waste flowed right into the wells, ponds, and rivers that residents drank from. When the bacteria *Vibrio cholerae* found its way to North America in the 1830s, it would thrive in these conditions. Cholera would kill tens of thousands of people and terrify nearly everyone else.

Cholera first showed up in 1832 in Canada and New York City. It arrived on ships packed with immigrants from Europe, where a full-blown cholera pandemic had been raging across the continent from Russia to England. The disease eventually spread to North American cities along major waterways, including the Mississippi River. Cholera reached the Lower Mississippi River by the end of the year, where it killed upwards of four thousand people in New Orleans.

People who contracted cholera were in for a rough time. They suffered bouts of watery diarrhea, vomiting, and severe leg cramps. It could take a couple of days for symptoms to show up, but some infected people got sick within a few hours. Most people, fortunately, only experienced mild symptoms. Fatalities were usually the result of the dehydration caused by the constant vomiting and diarrhea.

Today, we understand that the best treatment for most cholera victims is hydration—drinking plenty of clean water. In the nineteenth century, however, doctors treated victims by bloodletting, purging, or opium. One drug treatment of choice was Perry Davis' Pain Killer, a concoction of whiskey, opium, and capsicum. Doctors also sometimes prescribed a drug called calomel, a powder comprised of chlorine and mercury. If cholera didn't kill you, the cure might.

People of the day also didn't really understand how cholera was transmitted. It was common to blame miasma, which was basically air fouled by rotting organic matter. The idea that foul air caused disease goes back at least to the Greek physician Hippocrates, who proposed the theory in the fourth century BCE. When people weren't blaming foul air, they often blamed poor immigrants (Irish, especially) and Black people for epidemics, people who often lived in rundown housing in overcrowded neighborhoods.

It was also common for some people to blame disease outbreaks on immorality. In 1835, a religious newspaper proclaimed:

We regard cholera as the judgment of God upon a sinful nation, an intemperate, ungrateful Sabbath-breaking nation . . . a nation which has robbed and spoiled the Indian and withheld that which is just and right from the enslaved African. Cholera will go where it is sent. Best advice: Be ready for death. Death stands at your door. Repent of your sins.[1]

CHOLERA REACHES THE MISSISSIPPI VALLEY

After its initial spread in 1832, subsequent outbreaks of cholera were smaller and geographically isolated. In December 1848, though, cholera roared back to life and spread across the United States from its points of origin in New York City and New Orleans. Waterways again played a major role in spreading the disease, but people in wagon trains also carried the disease west. One of the hardest-hit places in the United States was St. Louis, then a city of about 77,000 residents and growing rapidly.

St. Louis didn't escape the initial cholera outbreaks—some five hundred people died from it from 1832 to 1835—but the city did little after that to prepare for any future outbreaks. City streets were a mess. People regularly tossed their waste in the streets. There were those mounds of manure all over the place. Factories also did their part to foul the city. Tallow plants—the businesses that rendered animal fat for candles and for cooking oils—and slaughterhouses dumped their waste into adjacent bodies of water. Waste routinely overflowed or leaked into the rivers, lakes, and shallow wells that provided drinking water.

One of the most affected water sources was a place known as Chouteau's Pond, an artificial lake that was located close to today's Union Station. In the early nineteenth century, St. Louisans flocked to the pond for picnics or a refreshing dip on a hot summer day. Over time, though, pollution from the city's factories and all the household waste turned Chouteau's Pond into a foul cesspool primed to spread disease.

The first hint of a new cholera outbreak reached St. Louis at the start of 1849 when news arrived that the disease was raging through New Orleans. In early January, the first cholera victims arrived in St. Louis on riverboats. Newspapers in St. Louis, though, downplayed the threat. When they reported on cholera at all, they insisted that the disease wasn't endemic in the city but was only present among some riverboat passengers.

Cases of cholera remained relatively low through April, although fears ran high. By May, cholera deaths escalated: in the second week of the month, 181 St. Louisans died from the disease. Religious leaders called for a day of prayer and fasting to stem the immorality driving the epidemic. Not everyone believed that would be enough. One St. Louisan wrote to a relative: "Truly if the 'wicked are turned into Hell' at least St. Louis will be strongly represented there."[2]

When the city erupted in fire on May 17, the pace of the epidemic slowed temporarily, but cholera still claimed 517 lives during the month. One resident wrote, "Death is wielding his scythe among us but a few hours separates the most healthy from death."[3]

A CITY IN PANIC

The city's newly elected mayor, John Barry, assumed office as many residents fled the city to escape the epidemic. Those who could afford to leave did so, which included most of the city council. Those council members would later return just long enough to transfer power to an ad hoc group of citizens who formed the Committee of Public Health to manage the crisis. The new group aggressively attacked the disease, and sanitation practices were a primary target.

The committee established temporary hospitals for cholera victims at schools and assigned doctors and nurses to each. The city hired its first employee to provide sanitation services. His entire job was to collect garbage and tote it to locations where it wouldn't pose a threat to public health. The committee ordered regular purification fires, a common approach at the time to counter the miasma that was blamed for spreading disease. To purify the air of infectious agents, each night at eight p.m., the city burned barrels of coal, sulfur, tar, and wood. The streets filled with dense smoke meant to suffocate the bad vapors that were assumed to be making people sick.

While health officials didn't fully understand the role of fouled drinking water in transmitting the disease, they suspected a connection existed. A network of inspectors scoured the city to drain pools of standing water. The city opened its water hydrants to supply drinking water from its new reservoirs to its poorer citizens. Still, the epidemic raged on.

One of the hardest-hit parts of the city was a poor neighborhood known as Shepherd's Graveyard, an area where poor immigrants lived in shanties. The disease claimed twenty-one people in a single building in the neighborhood. By some estimates, two-thirds of its residents died during the 1849 cholera epidemic. Cholera ravaged entire families. Irish immigrant John Grigg lost all five of his children and his wife to cholera. While the epidemic hit the poorest parts of the city hardest, the disease spread throughout the city and social classes. Residents had to plan for the worst, because if they contracted cholera, they could die quickly.

Despair settled over the city, and not just because of the purification fires. Eliza Keesacker Howard wrote to her sister: "It is indescribable, nothing but death, you may see a person well and hearty and the next day hear of their death, everyday is dull and gloomy no one goes to church, no one to the stores, no one in the streets, but funerals passing all the time."[4]

The death toll was so high that funerals ran nearly nonstop. "The streets are the almost constant scene of funeral trains," one resident wrote, "while the long solemn tolling of funeral bells, announcing that the destroyer is still doing his fatal works, altogether has imparted a feeling of gloom among the citizens, that is a great many of them."[5] The constant tolling of church bells announcing yet another funeral became so overwhelming that city officials asked churches to suspend the practice during the epidemic.

St. Louis residents weren't the only victims. The California gold rush was in full swing, and many prospectors stopped in St. Louis for supplies. Their timing couldn't have been much worse. "Many of the Eastern gold hunters on the way to California have fallen amongst us and the River Banks are becoming strewn with graves."[6]

As the death toll mounted, cemeteries couldn't keep up with the pace of the burials. Bodies stacked up in graveyards. Catholic Archbishop Peter Richard Kendrick waived burial fees for those who couldn't afford to pay.

Children were especially vulnerable to the disease. On some days, one-third of the dead were children under six years old. Many other children lost their parents. There were no social services, so religious organizations took in some orphaned children. The mayor also had the authority to place orphans with new families, an option that Mayor Barry sometimes exercised.

In one case, the mayor appointed a designee to find a new home for siblings—a five-year-old boy and six-month-old girl. The designee ultimately placed them with separate families and compensated them to take the children in. The boy's new family got a woodstove and a rifle, while the girl's family received a horse and cart and clothing. This process happened over and over throughout the epidemic. It's likely that many families today have no idea that one of their ancestors grew up in an adoptive household.

MISERY SLOWLY FADES AWAY

As the epidemic raged on, the city set up a quarantine station to isolate sick passengers coming upriver on steamboats. All steamboats were required to stop. City inspectors boarded every boat and removed any passengers who looked sick. Those passengers stayed at the quarantine station until they recovered, or died.

Deaths peaked in mid-July. On July 9, 145 people died from cholera; 722 died during the week of July 9–15, a quarter of whom were under five years of age. Business slowed to a crawl, especially on the riverfront. Boats landed but couldn't unload. Many of those idled workers were Irish immigrants, and the downtime sparked restlessness and conflict that spilled into the city. Catholic and Protestant Irish immigrants assaulted each other. On July 29, a fight erupted between a group of Irish men and firefighters. People were restless.

By late July, the daily death toll had dropped dramatically: Nineteen people died from cholera on July 25. Cases continued to drop into August. The gloom slowly lifted, and city residents got about the business of getting back to business.

Officially, the city attributed 4,547 deaths to cholera in 1849. That number is almost certainly an underestimate. The final toll was probably closer to eight thousand, which would have been 10 percent of the city's population. Still, it could have been much worse. Between 1847 and 1851, cholera killed one million Russians.

In the 1850s, Englishman John Snow surmised that the prime culprit responsible for the spread of cholera was water contaminated with human waste. During one epidemic, he observed a concentration of cases around a single water source. He ordered the removal of a pump handle—thus making the water inaccessible—and new cases of cholera quickly declined. Over time, cities implemented ambitious programs to filter and treat drinking water supplies. They also built sanitary sewers that separated human waste from drinking water. In 1851, St. Louis drained the polluted mess that was Chouteau's Pond. Transmission of cholera declined.

Still, it took a while for cities to build sanitation systems. There was another cholera epidemic in 1866, mostly in the eastern half of the country, but fewer people died. There was another minor outbreak in the United States in 1873, but cholera was largely gone from the country by 1900. While cholera is no longer endemic in the United States, the disease still affects up to four million people every year and kills tens of thousands in parts of the world where clean water is even now a luxury.

Tormenting Insects

Mosquito-Borne Diseases

DURING A HIKE A FEW YEARS AGO, I MADE AN IMPULSIVE STOP TO WALK to an overlook at Savanna Portage State Park in northern Minnesota. Within a few seconds of hitting the trail, a cloud of mosquitoes engulfed me and I questioned how badly I really wanted to see that view. I ended up running along the trail, quickly snapped a few pictures at the overlook, then ran back to my car.

Mosquitoes are one of the most abundant life-forms on our planet, and not just in northern Minnesota. There are thousands of species of them, and while they all share an attraction to carbon dioxide and a universally irritating buzz, they are a diverse group of creatures. Some species are only active at night, while others prefer the bright of day. Some can't live without blood, while others only suck juice from plants. While most species are no more annoying than a hangnail, a very few are deadly. These outliers may be responsible for more human deaths than just about any other creature, except humans themselves.

A MOSQUITO DOSE

> *[T]he Egyptian plague was not more cruel. . . . This little creature [the mosquito] has caused more swearing since the French came to Mississippi, than had been done before that time in all the rest of the world.*

> —FATHER PAUL DU POISSON, 1727[1]

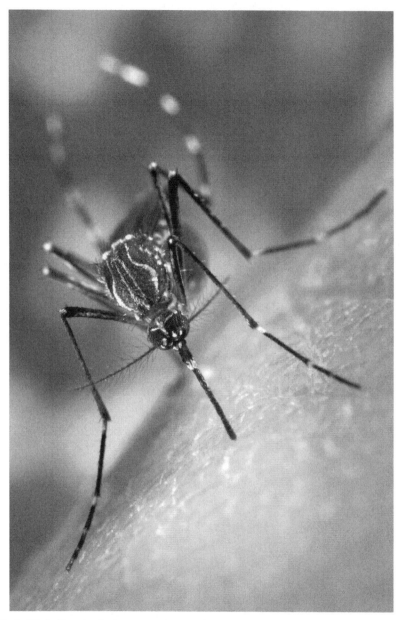

Photo 21.1. Female *Aedes aegypti* mosquito getting a meal.
CDC, PHOTO BY JAMES GATHANY.

Europeans and Americans who traveled along the Mississippi regularly complained about the multitudes of mosquitoes they encountered. Timothy Flint, a writer and Protestant missionary, described his experience along the big river in Arkansas in the early 1800s:

> *The air was excessively sultry, and the musquitoes troublesome to a degree, which I have not experienced before nor since. I was obliged to sleep under a very close musquito curtain. I would soon become oppressed for want of breath under the curtain, and when I drew it up and attempted to inhale a little of the damp and sultry atmosphere, the musquitoes would instantly settle on my face in such numbers that I was soon obliged to retreat behind my curtain again. Thus passed those dreadful nights, amidst the groans of my family, calls for medicine and drink, suffocation behind my curtain, or the agony of musquitoe stings, as soon as I was exposed to the air.[2]*

These thick clouds of mosquitoes inspired some creative coping techniques: "The inhabitants," Flint wrote, "while jesting upon the subject, used to urge this incessant torment as an excuse for deep drinking. A sufficient quantity of wine or spirits to produce a happy reverie, or a dozing insensibility, had a cant, but very significant name,—'a musquitoe dose.'"[3]

Mosquitoes in the genus *Anopheles* are among the most notorious. Females in 30 to 40 of the 430 *Anopheles* species can transmit the *Plasmodium* parasites that cause malaria, a disease that some scientists estimate has been responsible for half of all human deaths since the Stone Age. Female mosquitoes pick up the parasite from a human host, then the parasite migrates from the mosquito's stomach to its salivary glands, at which point the mosquito can pass the parasite to other humans.

Infected people typically get sick one to four weeks after exposure. The most common symptoms of malaria include some combination of fever, chills, sweats, headaches, nausea and vomiting, and aches. In more severe cases, victims can experience seizures, anemia, and organ failure. Even once the primary symptoms have waned, victims often report a deep, lingering fatigue.

In 2019, over two hundred million people around the world contracted malaria. Four hundred thousand people died from it, two-thirds of them children under the age of five. People whose ancestors lived in malaria-prone areas inherit a genetic adaptation, the "sickle-cell" gene, that developed over millennia and hundreds of generations, an adaptation that renders malarial disease less deadly. Individuals who have a single copy of the sickle-cell gene are 90 percent less likely to die from malaria than those without the gene. Unfortunately, inheriting 2 copies of the sickle-cell gene practically guarantees the development of sickle cell anemia, a disease that few people survive beyond their forties to early fifties.

While people exposed to the *Plasmodium* parasites develop resistance to malarial disease, repeated exposure to the parasites is necessary to maintain resistance. Someone who grows up in a malaria-endemic region and moves away for a few years can therefore be just as vulnerable to malarial disease as a person who has never been exposed to the parasite.

Mosquitoes have long been abundant along the Mississippi River— even the *Anopheles* mosquito, in all likelihood—but malaria was unknown in North America before European colonization because the *Plasmodium* parasites weren't present. The first cases probably came to the continent with Hernando de Soto in the sixteenth century. Malaria and other diseases carried by de Soto's army spread throughout the Southeast, killing thousands more American Indians than those de Soto's group killed directly. Malaria eventually ran its course and disappeared from North America for a while, only to reappear when the next round of Europeans returned.

Anopheles mosquitoes thrive in areas where there are standing pools of water and plenty of sunlight. The Mississippi Delta, that vast expanse of floodplain that stretches from southern Missouri to northeastern Louisiana, provided a hospitable home for the *Anopheles* mosquito after plantation farmers cleared forests and converted them to open fields of cotton and rice. Puddles formed throughout those fields as wheel ruts and furrows filled with water. With a favorable habitat and a growing human population, malaria spread quickly along the Mississippi River.

When Charles Dickens visited Cairo, Illinois—the embryonic town in the swamp at the confluence of the Ohio and Mississippi Rivers—he found a community overrun with malaria, "a breeding-place of fever, ague, and death" where "wretched wanderers who are tempted hither, droop, and die, and lay their bones." The people at Cairo, Dickens wrote, were "more wan and wretched than any we had encountered yet."[4]

Malaria hit Arkansas especially hard. Residents contracted the disease well into the twentieth century. Surveys in the 1930s found the parasite present in nearly a quarter of the population in some communities. The disease had been a fact of life for so long that many people self-medicated with quinine and only went to a doctor if self-dosing didn't work.

People have recognized quinine as an effective treatment for malaria for three centuries. It is derived from the bark of the cinchona tree, which is native to parts of South America. The Quechua people in what is now Peru produced a medicine from the bark to treat involuntary shivering. The drug isn't a cure, but it significantly reduces the severity of symptoms. During the Civil War, quinine probably helped Union forces defeat the Confederacy. Union doctors handed out nineteen tons of the drug to soldiers, while Confederate soldiers and civilians faced a chronic shortage of quinine after the Union blockaded Southern ports.

In 1929, a public health expert touring the Missouri River floodplain noticed

> *Quinine in large bottles stood on the clock shelf of every home in the "bottom" lands, together with a tumbler of water containing slippery elk bark. In some families, quinine taking was a daily ritual—not as a preventive, because the people were so rarely free from malaria that there was no question of anything but cure.*[5]

An ambitious public health program eventually reduced the incidences of malaria in the United States, which culminated with the National Malaria Eradication Program in 1947. The primary weapon was a chemical called dichloro-diphenyl-trichloroethane. We know it better by its initials: DDT. Officials blasted the chemical around areas where malaria was widespread, so it would wipe out breeding *Anopheles* mosquitoes.

Other measures that reduced the population of those pesky mosquitoes included draining swamps, introducing *Gambusia* minnows to bodies of water where mosquitoes bred (they feast on mosquito larvae), and putting screens on windows and doors.

All those efforts worked. In 1945, Arkansas reported 2,226 cases of malaria, but just six years later, there were none. Of course, spraying all that DDT around had some terrible unanticipated consequences, such as nearly wiping out America's bald eagles.

The Black Vomit

Malaria wasn't the only mosquito-borne disease that residents of the Mississippi Valley feared. While malaria became a fact of life along the Lower Mississippi, yellow fever terrorized entire communities with sporadic outbreaks that sent city residents fleeing for the country.

Like malaria, yellow fever isn't native to North America. The yellow fever virus probably traveled to the Americas on slave ships from Africa. Female mosquitoes in the species *Aedes aegypti* pick up the virus from infected people and spread it around. In North America, the disease proliferated during the warmer months of the year, typically July to October, although it didn't disappear completely until the first frost that killed the mosquitoes.

There was a common belief at the time that yellow fever was a manageable disease if you took care of yourself, especially if you didn't drink alcohol, ate properly, and lived a moral life. Some newspaper accounts even extolled the benefits of yellow fever infection as "invigorating," claiming that "It reconstitutes and re-organizes the system, and makes a man almost proof thereafter against disease."[6]

People who survived yellow fever did indeed acquire lifetime immunity, although no one really knew what that meant. There was a belief, for example, that Black people had natural immunity to yellow fever, which many White people used as another justification for slavery. Some Christians believed God had given Black people immunity to yellow fever so they could work the cotton fields instead of White people. The idea that Black people had a natural immunity to yellow fever just isn't true, though, and some people at the time obviously knew that. White enslavers often paid more to purchase Black men, women, and children who had survived yellow fever.

A person only acquired immunity by contracting yellow fever and surviving it. That immunity, or what people at the time called "becoming acclimated," carried considerable currency, especially in New Orleans. One newspaper noted that the acclimated resident "walks along the street with a tremendously bold swagger."[7] Acclimated New Orleanians had an easier time landing a decent job or marriage partner. For that reason, some people chose to stick around during yellow fever outbreaks, so they too could become acclimated. It was a risky decision.

About 15 percent of those infected got very sick, usually after the third day. If you were in that unlucky group, your odds of surviving were as good as picking heads on a coin flip. Death from yellow fever was an unpleasant way to exit the earthly plane and the time from the first onset of symptoms to severe illness could be shockingly brief. "Often I have met and shook hands with some blooming, handsome young man to-day," Theodore Clapp recalled, "and in a few hours afterwards, I have been called to see him in the black vomit, with profuse hemorrhages from the mouth, nose, ears, eyes, and even the toes; the eyes prominent, glistening, yellow, and staring; the face discolored with orange color and dusky red."[8]

After the initial bout of fever and general discomfort, a couple of days of muted recovery fooled many into believing that they had survived the worst. When symptoms returned, though, they were much more severe. One of the most terrifying sights was when victims in late stages of the illness vomited black-colored blobs—partially digested blood (hence the Spanish name for the disease, *el vomito negro*). As the disease ran its course, the virus damaged the liver, which caused jaundice that turned its victims' skin the color that gave the disease its English name.

Yellow fever, in its final insult, left the dead looking tormented:

The physiognomy of the yellow fever corpse is usually sad, sullen, and perturbed; the countenance dark, mottled, livid, swollen, and stained with blood and black vomit; the veins of the face and whole body become distended, and look as if they were going to burst; and though the heart has ceased to beat, the circulation of the blood sometimes continues for hours, quite as active as in life.[9]

BECOMING ACCLIMATED

Aedes aegypti mosquitoes thrived in North America's urban environments and did not shy away from daylight. The earliest yellow fever outbreaks raged through the major cities of the Northeast starting at the end of the seventeenth century. Philadelphia and New York routinely lost up to 10 percent of their residents during sporadic epidemics over the next century.

Yellow fever eventually faded away for reasons that aren't entirely clear, but improved sanitation practices and regular use of quarantines probably helped. The northern climate also made it nearly impossible for the *Aedes* mosquitoes to survive long, so an epidemic could only begin when both the mosquito and the disease arrived, usually via ships from the Caribbean. In the South, though, *Aedes* mosquitoes were already abundant when ships from the Caribbean or South America arrived with passengers infected with the disease. Yellow fever found a welcoming home in the American South.

No city suffered the effects of yellow fever more than New Orleans. From 1804 to 1860, New Orleanians endured twenty-two major outbreaks of yellow fever. One of the worst epidemics swept through the city in 1853, a year that had started with great optimism. The city's economy was thriving thanks to record cotton yields and the expansion of railroads that had funneled new commerce into the city. The first cases were identified in May, but it spread slowly through June, the time of year when upper-class residents took their summer leave of the city. June was also a great month to be a breeding mosquito. On June 28, the *Daily Picayune* reported that "A barbarous horde of great, ugly, long billed, long legged, fly away creatures has invaded our streets and houses, and taken possession of our domestic goods."[10]

By early July, the outbreak had picked up steam, and fear was spreading with the virus. By the end of the month, nearly a hundred people were dying every day. "The morning train of funerals, as was the evening's, crowded the road to the cemeteries. It was an unbroken line of carriages and omnibuses for two miles and a half."[11] Charity Hospital filled beyond its capacity, forcing staff to lay some patients on the floor.

Doctors treated some of the sick with quinine. Other medical professionals treated yellow fever victims with cupping or bloodletting. Some physicians even advised the afflicted to drink their own urine or to eat spiders. There wasn't a lot of uniformity in treatment options, though, and sick people were often referred to a physician from their own ethnic group, whose treatment options varied:

> [T]he German, who, after the first course of medicine, when the patient desired food, gave him successfully strong fluid nourishment; another, who prescribed hard-boiled eggs as the most nutritious and digestible in a more advanced stage of convalescence; the French physicians, of equal success, with hot drinks and cold drinks, close covering or no covering at all on the patient; him who administered strychnine with reported success.[12]

As the disease raged through the city, bodies piled up at burial grounds. One resident "saw coffins piled up beside the gate and in the walks, and laborers at work digging trenches in preparation for the morrow's dead. . . . A fog, which hung over the moss enveloped oaks, prevented the egress of the dense and putrid exhalations. The atmosphere was nauseating to a degree that I have never noticed in a sick-room."[13] As the deaths accumulated, the stench of rotting corpses filled the air. Residents covered their noses with rags soaked in camphor or spices to mute the smell.

Gravediggers were in short supply, so family members sometimes had to bury their own dead. Funeral parties often arrived at the same time, which resulted in so much conflict that police had to be stationed at cemeteries to keep the peace. The city eventually hired more people to dig graves (they were paid as much as five dollars an hour and given free liquor) and sped up the process by burying the dead in trenches instead of individual graves.

As the death toll increased to two hundred a day, city officials grew desperate. Some public health officials recommended purifying the air, so the city fired cannons fifty times a day, but the only effect was that New

Orleanians became more agitated. The city discontinued the cannon fire after a couple of days. City officials also set barrels of tar afire, which draped the city in a suffocating, oily fog.

River traffic was down, but the city didn't close the port, so ships continued to dock. Some of those ships brought in fresh groups of immigrants who moved into the city, then contracted yellow fever. In some cases, the disease wiped out entire immigrant families.

On August 20, nearly three hundred people died. The epidemic had peaked. By the time it was over, some 40 percent of the city's residents had been infected, and upwards of eleven thousand had died, most of them newly arrived immigrants. People who left the city as the epidemic raged in New Orleans carried yellow fever up the Mississippi River, contributing to major outbreaks in Baton Rouge, Natchez, and Vicksburg.

On October 13, the city's health commission declared the epidemic over. People returned to the city, and businesses opened back up. The rhythms of life returned to normal, and the newly acclimated walked the streets with a swagger.

AN APPALLING GLOOM

Twenty-five years later, a virulent yellow fever epidemic nearly wiped out Memphis. Founded in 1819 by a group of investors that included future President Andrew Jackson, Memphis was in the homeland of Chickasaw Indians and in the heart of the area where pre-European Mississippian cultures thrived. After the Civil War, Memphis grew rapidly, thanks in part to the migration of Black people from the rural South.

That rapid population growth overwhelmed the city's built environment. Poor sanitation practices—open sewers were common—gave Memphis a reputation as the most foul-smelling city in the country and contributed to the rapid spread of disease. There was no sanitation system for human and animal waste, so most of it flowed down streets and gutters and into a bayou in the middle of town that served as the city's sewer. Garbage and animal carcasses piled up in city streets. Pools of water collected around bridge piers, in basements, and on city streets, which provided fertile breeding grounds for the *Aedes* mosquitoes that spread yellow fever.

Memphis had its first brush with yellow fever in 1855, an outbreak that killed 150 people. Memphians lived through another minor yellow fever outbreak in 1867, although it wasn't trivial for Mary Jones. That epidemic took the lives of her husband and all four of her young children. She moved away from Memphis after that and later gained fame as an activist for working people. She was better known by her nickname: Mother Jones. When yellow fever killed two thousand people in 1873, Memphians had to shed their belief that their more northerly location protected them from significant yellow fever outbreaks. Just five years later, any remaining doubts would be shattered.

In early August 1878, word reached Memphis that Grenada, Mississippi—a town south of Memphis—was being overrun by yellow fever. A few days later, Memphian Kate Bionda took ill and died from the disease. Bionda and her husband ran a food stand on the riverfront. City officials responded quickly.

"Immediately Health Officer Erskine took charge of the building and vicinity," J. M. Keating wrote in his account of the epidemic.

> *The rooms, house, and premises were thoroughly fumigated and disinfected with carbolic acid, copperas, etc. The sidewalk and street for half a square on Front Street, and the same distance back on Adams, were also disinfected. An obstruction or railing was placed across Adams Street at Center Alley, and the locality, No. 212, was fenced in around Front Street to the intersecting alley running east and west. . . . Not only was the building in which Mrs. Bionda died disinfected and isolated, but all adjacent buildings in the block were likewise disinfected, and policemen were stationed to prevent people from visiting the particular locality.[14]*

Those efforts weren't nearly enough, though. Cases spread across the city, and when the Board of Health declared a yellow fever epidemic on August 23, Memphians fled the city. Some people sold their prized possessions—silver, watches, jewelry—to raise the money to leave. Others emptied their bank accounts.

People left town any way they could:

[People traveled] by hacks, by carriages, buggies, wagons, furniture vans, and street drays; away by batteaux, by any thing that could float on the river; and by the railroads, the trains on which, especially on the Louisville Road, were so packed as to make the trip to that city, or to Cincinnati, a positive torture to many delicate women every mile of the way. The aisles of the cars were filled, and the platforms packed. . . . The stream of passengers seemed to be endless, and they seemed to be as mad as they were many.[15]

More than half of the city's fifty thousand residents got out. Some went to the country. Five thousand people lived in temporary camps in Shelby County. Other people escaped to cities presumed to be far enough north to be out of the reach of yellow fever—St. Louis, Cincinnati, Detroit, Chicago. Many communities, though, especially the smaller ones around Memphis, imposed quarantines to keep those Memphis refugees out. Quarantines weren't an unreasonable response, as fleeing Memphians carried yellow fever to some places where they sought sanctuary.

Within days, the city's bustling city streets turned desolate and business ground to a halt. Yellow fever spread swiftly among the twenty thousand who stayed behind. "The king of terrors continues to snatch victims with fearful rapidity,"[16] the *Memphis Avalanche* reported. The mood turned desperate.

Officials spread lime and carbolic acid on streets and sidewalks to douse the smells. "An appalling gloom hung over the doomed city," Keating wrote. "At night, it was silent as the grave; by day it seemed desolate as the desert. The solemn oppressions of universal death bore upon the human mind, as if the day of Judgment were about to dawn. . . . The energies of all who remained were enlisted in the struggle with death."[17]

As the casualties accumulated, signs of loss were impossible to hide. "The small burnt piles of bedding that are seen on every street but tells the passer-by, 'A death has occurred here.' These blackened spots are growing in number daily."[18] Help poured in from across the country. Trains dropped off carloads of food, clothing, and coffins.

People collapsed and died on the street. Many died at home alone. Officials found one man, known as Rivière, in his home, naked and with flies swarming around him. "Women were found dead," Keating wrote, "their little babes gasping in the throes of death, beside the breasts at which they had tugged in vain."[19]

The entire Gregg family—both parents and six children—died in a matter of days. "One of the remarkable features of the disease, as it prevails now," wrote the *Memphis Appeal*, "is, that whole families have been swept out of existence—father, mother, and children have followed each other in rapid succession to the grave, and in some instances several members of a family are lying dead at the same time, having died almost within the same hour."[20]

The epidemic claimed many people, including Jefferson Davis, Jr., the son of the former Confederate president. The disease also took prominent merchant Nathan Menken, one of the city's wealthiest and most generous men. After he died, his body had been thrown onto a pile with other victims. The family asked the undertaker, Louis Daltroof, to sort through the stack of corpses and find Menken's body, so they could bury him according to the traditions of his Jewish faith. Daltroof did just that.

Funerals came to a halt while the epidemic raged. It's unlikely they would have been well-attended, anyway. "The luxuries of woe were dispensed with,"[21] Keating wrote. Burials continued, though, of course. And the work was nonstop. "The county undertaker has four furniture wagons busy all day," the *Memphis Avalanche* reported. "Upon each, the coffins were piled as high as safety from falling would permit. These four great vehicles, doing the wholesale burying business, failed to take to the potters' field all of the indigent dead."[22]

Empty streets and stores. The stench of rotting corpses. The constant parade of wagons carrying bodies to be buried. It was too much for people to bear. Father Denis Quinn later recalled the chilling sense that "The most dreadful sense of horror was the fact that, in a short time, those ghastly sights would fail to inspire terror."

By mid-September, fatalities peaked at two hundred people a day. The end of the epidemic came as it typically did, with the season's first frost. "A heavy black frost," Reverend Quinn recalled, "was the pleasing spectacle that gladdened the sight of the many who were on the lookout for it. . . . This harbinger of returning health to Memphis caused unalloyed joy." A few days later, the Memphis Board of Health declared the epidemic over and invited people to return.

With the crisis over, the city took stock of its losses. Of the nineteen thousand who stayed behind (mostly people who couldn't afford to leave), seventeen thousand contracted yellow fever and over five thousand died. The toll included half of the city's physicians, a quarter of the police force, and two dozen firefighters.

Not everything about the epidemic turned out to be bad news. John Thomas and Beatrice Johnson met while helping people afflicted with yellow fever. They fell for each other and were married after the epidemic was over.

Despite the reassurances from health officials, thousands of people never returned to Memphis. Starved of revenue because of the sudden, dramatic loss of population, the city government could no longer pay its bills. In 1879, the city government dissolved, and the State of Tennessee assigned municipal governance to a special taxing district. That summer, Memphis had another yellow fever scare—587 people died—and the taxing district announced plans for an ambitious program aimed at improving public sanitation, which included construction of a state-of-the-art sewer system.

It took a while, but Memphis recovered. The city did not suffer through another yellow fever epidemic, and people began moving to Memphis again. After seeing its population drop from around fifty thousand in 1878 to just thirty-three thousand two years later, the population grew to sixty-four thousand over the next decade.

Yellow fever is no longer a threat in North America. The last significant outbreak in New Orleans was in 1905. Aggressive efforts to control the mosquito population successfully tamped down the disease. There's still no treatment for yellow fever, but the risk of a new epidemic is very low today, thanks to the development of a highly effective vaccine. A single shot provides lifetime protection for 99 percent of people who get inoculated.

Someone to Blame

Drownings

WHEN DIVERS PULLED JARED DION'S BODY FROM THE CHILLY WATERS OF the Mississippi River in 2004, he was, in one respect, just another person who suffered a tragic end by drowning in the Mississippi River. In another respect, though, he was a symbol, one that people would mourn and agonize over as they tried to understand what his death represented.

Photo 22.1. Riverside Park, La Crosse, Wisconsin
PHOTO BY DEAN KLINKENBERG

He was the seventh college-aged man to drown in the Mississippi at La Crosse, Wisconsin, in seven years, and that fact sparked a search for answers.

People drown in the Mississippi with disheartening regularity. Dozens of bodies are fished out of the river every year, sometimes by barge hands or by someone hoping to catch a catfish who landed a corpse instead. At one time, the Mississippi claimed even more bodies than it does today. In 1855, authorities in St. Louis reported they pulled thirty to forty bodies out of the Mississippi every month.

The river is the final resting place for a lot more people today than we like to acknowledge, but not for the reasons many expect. The primary causes have less to do with the inherent dangers of a big river than with people who make the wrong choice at the wrong time, such as failing to wear a life jacket or drinking excessively while on the river. Put the two together on a big river, and a person can quickly find their life in peril. Anyone who spends a lot of time on the river understands this, including the people who live around La Crosse.

The city anchors a metropolitan area of about one hundred thousand people on one of the most scenic stretches of the Mississippi River. One of the major economic drivers for the region is higher education. The three colleges in the city collectively enroll fifteen thousand students.

Drinking is another staple of the city's economy. In 2004—the year Dion died—thirsty residents had 130 licensed taverns to choose from, one of the highest rates of bars per capita in the United States. Many of those bars clustered in the downtown core along Third Street, and many of them catered to the college crowd. Some bars offered popular all-you-can-drink specials. For just a few bucks, customers could refill their cup until they passed out. Binge drinking is a long-standing problem, but in fairness to La Crosse, it's a problem in many parts of the country, especially among young adults.

The downtown bars are just a few short blocks from the city's beautiful Riverside Park that runs along the Mississippi. When the weather is nice, people flow freely between the bars and restaurants downtown and the riverfront.

Dion's death sparked concerns that public officials couldn't ignore. Until that time, law enforcement and newspaper articles had framed the deaths as tragedies, but they had also subtly assigned blame to the young men. All had been drinking heavily. Toxicology tests found the men had blood alcohol levels (BAC) that ranged from 0.22 to 0.31. (Wisconsin law considers a person too impaired to drive a car if they have a BAC of 0.08 or higher.)

Official reports from the police didn't sway everyone, though, and rumors spread that something sinister might be going on. "I would like to know why it is so far out of the realm of possibility for the La Crosse Police Department, the media, and anyone else who had a say over how this tragedy was presented to the public, to acknowledge that we have had a very odd series of events take place and that these deaths could very well be linked in some way,"[1] wrote one person in a letter to the local newspaper.

Speculation quickly turned to the idea that the young men had been victims of a serial killer. After all, these were well-liked young men, in good shape and with no known mental health issues. How were folks supposed to make sense of that?

Two weeks after Dion's death, Police Chief Ed Kondraki led a meeting at the town hall that was broadcast live on local TV. He wanted to reassure the public that nothing nefarious had happened. He assembled a panel of experts who reviewed the drowning deaths and presented the evidence that convinced them that the drownings were accidental deaths fueled by excessive drinking. The crowd booed.

There were no witnesses to any of the deaths, but some people in the crowd insisted they knew someone who had seen something. One explanation offered at the meeting was that the killer had dressed in a uniform, maybe as a security guard or even a cop, to lure the drunk men away from the crowds. "That's how I feel. I feel somebody is dressing up like them, he or she is doing this, a security guard, anything that has some form of a badge,"[2] one person said. The meeting failed to stop the conspiracy theories. People were still afraid.

Two years after Dion's death, another young man disappeared. Luke Homan's friends and family described him as popular and selfless, and he played on the basketball team at the University of Wisconsin–La Crosse. When police recovered his body from the Mississippi, the drowning deaths at La Crosse became national news. Stories ran in the *New York Times*, the *Washington Post*, and the *Chicago Tribune*. The attention attracted the usual mob of opportunists, attention seekers, and charlatans.

Geraldo Rivera—the journalist whose credibility evaporated thirty years earlier in Al Capone's empty vault—took interest. He brought in two investigators, former New York City detectives Kevin Gannon and Anthony Duarte, who concluded that some of the deaths were homicides. They based their reasoning on the similarities between the victims—all were young, male, White, and fit, and six of the eight had been seen at the same two bars on the night they disappeared. They also based their conclusion on a stunning observation: they had found smiley faces painted near the scenes of some of the deaths.

The detectives spawned new speculation (and alarm) that an unknown serial killer with a fondness for childlike graffiti was responsible and was still on the loose. Maybe there was even a gang of smiley face killers who were secretly killing young men across the Midwest. The smiley face was apparently the key. After all, no one had ever seen a smiley face painted anywhere ever before.

Ultimately, the serial killer theories held less water than a sandpit in the Sahara. The drowning victims' bodies showed no signs of trauma. FBI agents had already reviewed the cases and didn't find any evidence of homicide. The La Crosse police department couldn't find any smiley faces near the scenes where the men had disappeared. But conspiracy theories thrive on uncertainty and fear, not evidence. People in La Crosse were afraid, and some people were working hard to sow doubt about the conclusions of law enforcement. After all, it's more consoling to believe that healthy and smart young men were victims of someone else's demons rather than their own.

Third Street, as the name implies, is just three blocks from the Mississippi River. The Mississippi River is an easy downhill walk from the bar district and, once you get to Riverside Park, you can stroll right into the river. There are no barriers to block your path. And that's exactly what happened in these drowning deaths. A few college men wandered into the river on their own after a night of heavy drinking.

The conspiracy theories became harder to cling to after the next tragic death. On February 14, 2010, video surveillance showed Craig Meyers walking alone late at night. Police dogs followed his scent toward the river where a single track of footprints led through the snow onto the river ice and to the open water where he likely fell in. His body was recovered two days later.

Between the dark of the night and the snow cover that blurred the boundaries between land and river (and alcohol; his BAC was 0.19), he probably had no idea that he had walked into the Mississippi. Every other drowning victim had a blood alcohol level between 0.19 and 0.32. How much alcohol do you have to consume to get to 0.20? About ten drinks in one hour for a 180-pound man. Geraldo found himself another empty vault.

While some people pushed conspiracy theories, others jumped into action. In 2006, after the drowning death of Homan, a group of students organized *Operation: River Watch*. It is a volunteer effort managed by local college students and reserve officers from the police department who stand guard at Riverside Park on busy bar nights (Thursday through Saturday) when the colleges are in session. Even the downtown bars got involved by raising money to support the effort. In 2007, the Sigma Tau Gamma fraternity at the University of Wisconsin–La Crosse assumed management of the program, and they still run it today.

The program has almost certainly saved lives. Not long after the program got underway, a volunteer intercepted a young man who was about to walk into the river. The confused man pointed to lights across the Mississippi and insisted that his apartment near campus was in that direction, when it was actually directly behind him. The man had just stumbled out of a bar downtown and started walking. He believed he was heading home. The only thing that stopped him from walking into the river was that volunteer.

Since the program began, only three men have drowned in the river at La Crosse. One fell off a bridge; a second fell out of a boat; and the third, Meyers, walked onto the river in an area south of where the volunteers patrolled. Volunteers with *Operation: River Watch* have intercepted dozens of people (mostly men) who were about to walk into the river or who had already fallen in and had to be pulled from it. It's enough to make a person want to scratch a smiley face on a wall in gratitude.

Acknowledgements

Libraries! I love them and the amazing people who help connect me to the documents and books that make my work possible. I am deeply grateful to the people who work in the libraries, archives, and historical societies in communities throughout the Mississippi Valley and the creative adaptations they made during a pandemic to connect me with the materials I needed. Completing this book would have been immeasurably more difficult without assistance from the Cuyuna Iron Range Heritage Network, the Iron Range Research Center, and especially the Missouri Historical Society archives staff.

I'm also indebted to Amanda Gesiorski at the St. Louis Visitation Archives, Jeanne Nitz from the Clinton (Iowa) Public Library, and Addie Rose Elliott from the Buffalo County (Wisconsin) Historical Society. Mary Ostby pulled binders of materials about the Sauk Rapids tornado from the collection of the Benton County Historical Society. Andy Bloedorn at the Winona County (Minnesota) Historical Society likewise prepared folders of documents about the city's history with prostitution. Jessie Storlien of the Stearns County (Minnesota) Historical Society kept me busy reading about the history of bootlegging and moonshine in central Minnesota. And my good friends, Teri Holford-Talpe and Laura Godden, at the University of Wisconsin–La Crosse Special Collections kept me busy for a couple of days reading about brothels and sporting girls.

No person earned deeper gratitude than my husband John, and not just for his steady support during my years as a writer. He dutifully read a draft of every chapter and consistently offered insightful comments and reality checks along the way. I couldn't have finished this book without him.

Dean Klinkenberg, St. Louis, Missouri

NOTES

INTRODUCTION: SICKNESS AND DEATH

1 S. L. Latham, *Randolph Recorder*, September 16, 1834. In S. R. Bruesch, "The Disasters and Epidemics of a River Town: Memphis, Tennessee, 1819–1879," *Bulletin of the Medical Library Association* 40, no. 3 (1952), 289.

THE GROUND ROLLED LIKE WAVES

1 David Stewart and Ray Knox, *The Earthquake America Forgot: 2,000 Temblors in Five Months . . . and It Will Happen Again* (Marble Hill, MO: Gutenberg-Richter Publications, 1995), 137.

2 Eliza Bryan, letter to Lorenzo Dow, *History of Cosmopolite, or Four Volumes of Lorenzo's Journal* (Washington, OH: Joshua Martin, 1848), 344.

3 Anonymous, letter printed in *The Reporter* (Lexington, KY), February 1, 1812.

4 Vincent Nolte, *Fifty Years in Both Hemispheres* (London: Trubner & Company, 1854), 180.

5 Stewart and Knox, *The Earthquake America Forgot*, 136.

6 Anonymous, letter printed in *The Reporter*.

7 Samuel Cummings, *The Western Pilot* (Cincinnati, OH: George Conclin, 1847), 138–42.

8 Daniel Bedinger, excerpt from his journal published in *National Intelligencer*, March 4, 1812.

9 Dr. Foster, letter dated January 16, 1812, *Farmer's Repository* IV, no. 205, Feb 28, 1812.

10 William Leigh Pierce, *New York Evening Post*, December 25, 1811.

11 Bedinger, *National Intelligencer*.

12 John Bradbury, *Travels in the Interior of America* (Liverpool, England: Sherwood, Neely, and Jones, 1817), 200.

13 Bradbury, *Travels in the Interior of America*, 204.

14 Foster, *Farmer's Repository*.

15 Stewart and Knox, *The Earthquake America Forgot*, 162.

16 Bradbury, *Travels in the Interior of America*, 206.

17 Bryan, *History of Cosmopolite*, 344.

18 John J. Audubon, *Delineations of American Scenery and Character* (New York: G. A. Baker & Company, 1926), 48.

19 Stewart and Knox, *The Earthquake America Forgot*, 207.

20 "New Madrid Earthquake Account of Col. John Shaw," *Missouri Historical Review* 6, no. 2 (192), 91–92.

21 Stewart and Knox, *The Earthquake America Forgot*, 250.

22 Letter from James McBride to Miss Mary M. Roberts, April 1, 1812, *The Register of the Kentucky Historical Society* 72, no. 4 (October 1974), 400, 401.

23 Bryan, *History of Cosmopolite*, 344–35.

24 Firmin LaRoche, "A Sailor's Record of the New Madrid Earthquake," *Missouri Historical Review* XXII, no. 1 (October 1927), 269.

25 Nolte, *Fifty Years in Both Hemispheres*, 182.

26 William Shaler, letter to Samuel L. Mitchell, 1814, https://www.memphis.edu/ceri/compendium/pdfs/shaler.pdf.

27 Mathias Speed, "Earthquake," *Bardstown Repository*, March 2, 1812.

28 John J. Audubon, *Journal of John J. Audubon* (Cambridge, MA: The Business Historical Society, 1929), 34.

Deadly Winds

1 "Horrible Storm! Natchez in Ruins!" *Weekly Courier and Journal*, May 8, 1840.

2 Dorothy Wagner, "The Camanche Tornado." *Palimpset* 40, no. 12 (December 1959): 37.

3 Wagner, "The Camanche Tornado," 538.

4 Ibid., 539.

5 Ibid., 545.

6 Terry Swails, "The Camanche, Iowa Tornado, June 3, 1860." https://www.tswails.com/single-post/the-camanche-iowa-tornado-june-3-1860.

7 Wagner, "The Camanche Tornado," 542.

8 W. B. Mitchell, undated document at Benton County Historical Society, Sauk Rapids, MN.

9 Bertha Arensberger, interview by Larry Schenk, April 5, 1968, Benton County Historical Society, Sauk Rapids, MN.

10 "Score Still Survive Cyclone 50 Years Ago," unidentified newspaper article, Benton County Historical Society, Sauk Rapids, MN.

11 "Town Half Destroyed."

12 "The Cyclone in Minnesota," *Harper's Weekly* XXX, no. 1532 (May 1, 1886).

13 Julian Curzon, *The Great Cyclone at St. Louis and East St. Louis, May 27, 1896* (St. Louis, MO: Cyclone Publishing Company 1896), 20.

14 Martin Green, "Attack of the Wind," *St. Louis Republic*, May 31, 1896.

15 "The Appalling Disaster That Fell on Fair St. Louis," *St. Louis Post-Dispatch*, June 3, 1896, 11.

16 Curzon, *The Great Cyclone at St. Louis*, 100.

17 Ibid., 43.

18 Ibid., 256.

19 Ibid., 260.

20 A. S. Aloe Company ad, *St. Louis Post-Dispatch*, May 30, 1896, 6.

21 Curzon, *The Great Cyclone at St. Louis*, 277.

22 Ibid., 272.

23 "Love Found a Way," *St. Louis Post-Dispatch*, May 31, 1896, 8.

WATER FROM BLUFF TO BLUFF

1 "Sr. Josephine Barber's History of the Foundation at Kaskaskia till the Move to Cass Ave (Transcribed)," St. Louis Visitation Archives, St. Louis Visitation Monastery records #200, Box 102.2.1, Folder 2.

2 J. Thomas Scharf, *History of St. Louis City and County* (Philadelphia, PA: Louis H. Everts, Co, 1883, vol. 2), 1063.

3 Richard Edwards and M. Hopewell, *Edward's Great West and Her Commercial Metropolis Embracing a General View of the West and a Complete History of St. Louis* (St. Louis, MO: Edwards' Monthly, 1860), 383.

4 "Boats Bumped Eaves in Flood of 1844," *St. Louis Post-Dispatch*, June 5, 1903, X.

5 Lulu Leonard, "History of Union County, IL." In *History of Alexander, Union and Pulaski Counties, Illinois*, edited by William Henry Perrin (Chicago, IL: O. L. Baskin & Company, 1883), 291.

6 "Boats Bumped Eaves," *St. Louis Post-Dispatch*, 1903, X.

7 *Republican*, June 22, 1844, cited in *History of St. Louis City and County* (vol. II) (Philadelphia, PA: Louis H. Everts Company, 1883), 1064.

8 Edwards and Hopewell, *Edward's Great West*, 384.

THE UNAPPEASABLE GOD

1 William Alexander Percy, *Lanterns on the Levee: Recollections of a Planter's Son* (Baton Rouge: Louisiana State University Press, 1941), 4.

2 John Barry, *Rising Tide: The Great Mississippi Flood of 1927 and How It Changed America* (New York: Touchstone, 1998), 199.

3 Pete Daniel, *Deep'n as It Come: The 1927 Mississippi River Flood* (New York: Oxford University Press, 1977), 15.

4 Barry, *Rising Tide*, 203.

5 Helen Murphy, "Overflow Notes," *Atlantic Monthly* 140 (August 1927), 225.

6 Daniel, *Deep'n as It Come*, 19.

7 Ibid., 7.

8 Barry, *Rising Tide*, 277.

9 Ibid., 304.

10 Lyle Saxon, *Father Mississippi* (New York: The Century Company, 1927), 66–67.

THE DUCKS CAME AND MEN DIED

1 A. J. Knarr, "The Midwest Storm of November 11, 1940," *Monthly Weather Review* 69, no. 6 (June 1941).

2 William H. Hull, *All Hell Broke Loose: Experiences of Young People during the Armistice Day 1940 Blizzard* (Edina, MN: Stanton Publication Services, 1996), 227.

3 Harold Hettrick, "Hunting Stories," interviewed as part of the Smithsonian Folklife Festival, July 2, 1998. https://www.youtube.com/watch?v=SY7WYoBs_88&ab_channel =BCHStube.

4 Ben Welter, "Tuesday, Nov. 12, 1940: Armistice Day Blizzard," August 15, 2005, https://web.archive.org/web/20080407143900/http://ww3.startribune.com/blogs/ oldnews/archives/17.

5 Welter, "Armistice Day Blizzard."

6 Lowell Washburn, "The Icy Winds of Death: The Armistice Day Blizzard November 11, 1940," *Iowa Outdoors* 67, no. 5 (September/October 2008), 38.

7 "Leaves Loop at 4:30 p.m., Reaches His Home at 6 a.m.," *Minneapolis Star Journal*, November 12, 1940, 13.

8 Welter, "Armistice Day Blizzard."

9 Hull, *All Hell Broke Loose*, 86.

10 Welter, "Armistice Day Blizzard."

11 Hull, *All Hell Broke Loose*, 85.

12 "Storm's Grip Worse Than '24 Blizzard." *Minneapolis Star Journal*, November 12, 1940, 13.

13 The SPAM Man, "Spam Men and Girls Spread Cheer in Blinding Blizzard," *Minneapolis Star Journal*, November 13, 1940, 20.

14 Hull, *All Hell Broke Loose*, 212–13.

15 Welter, "Armistice Day Blizzard."

16 Hull, *All Hell Broke Loose*, 228.

17 Hettrick, "Hunting Stories," https://www.youtube.com/watch?v=SY7WYoBs_88&ab _channel=BCHStube.

18 Wayne Bell, "Rescue Crew Finds Hunters on River but It's Too Late," *Minneapolis Star Journal*, November 13, 1940, 1.

19 Washburn, "The Icy Winds of Death," 39.

20 Hull, *All Hell Broke Loose*, 210.

21 Ibid., 211.

22 Gordon MacQuarrie, "The Ducks Came and Men Died; Tragedy of River Bottoms," *Winona Republican-Herald*, November 13, 1940, 3.

23 MacQuarrie, "The Ducks Came and Men Died," 3.

24 "Girl, Mother Die Sharing Clothing with Baby Twins," *Minneapolis Star Journal*, November 12, 1940, 1.

25 "The Armistice Day Blizzard," *Minneapolis Star Journal*, November 12, 1940, 10.

26 "4,000 'Blizzard Busters' Broke Grip of Snowstorm," *Minneapolis Star Journal*, November 17, 1940, 5.

27 "No Shortage of Drumsticks Despite High Turkey Loss," *Minneapolis Star Journal*, November 17, 1940, 4.

28 Washburn, "The Icy Winds of Death," 41.

29 "It Takes People to Make a Blizzard," *Minneapolis Star Journal*, November 13, 1940, 18.

The Worst-Case Scenario

1 Dave Nimmer, "Mississippi Court Housewives Keeping Wary Eyes on River," *Minneapolis Star*, April 16, 1965, 3A.

2 Jerry Kirshenbaum, "Youth Saved after 1 ½-Mile Ride on Ice Floe down Mississippi," *Minneapolis Tribune*, April 14, 1965, 1.

3 "River Serpent," Twin Cities Music Highlights, https://twincitiesmusichighlights.net/venues/river-serpent/.

4 Jim Shoop, "Custer Loses Last Battle to River," *Minneapolis Star*, April 16, 1965, 2A.

5 Richard Steele, "Wabasha and Winona Brace for Flood Peak," *Minneapolis Tribune*, April 17, 1965, 1.

6 Steele, "Wabasha and Winona Brace for Flood Peak," 6.

7 Jim Talle, "Winona Awaits Crest with Million Sandbags," *Minneapolis Star*, April 16, 1965, 1.

8 Chris Hubbuch, "The Flood of 1965: An Oral History," *Winona Daily News*, April 19, 2005, https://www.winonadailynews.com/news/the-flood-of-1965-an-oral-history/article_5679903c-e6d1-5d2f-9fec-36b670dcddf8.html.

9 Hubbuch, "The Flood of 1965."

10 Ibid.

11 Ibid.

12 Ibid.

13 Ibid.

14 Ibid.

15 Ibid.

16 Ibid.

17 "Forecasters Again Raise Prediction Flood Crests," *Minneapolis Tribune*, April 17, 1965, 1.

18 Marjorie Blaess, "'Silent Henry' Dies as He Lived—Alone," *Clinton Herald*, April 11, 1966, 2. That was the last flood Steele survived. The following year he was found dead in his cabin after an early spring crest. He had apparently died of a heart attack or stroke two weeks before his body was found. He was buried in a county cemetery. No next of kin were identified at the time of his burial.

19 D. B. Anderson and I. L. Burmeister, *Floods of March–May 1965 in the Upper Mississippi River Basin*, Geological Survey Water-Supply Paper 1850-A, Department of the Interior, Washington, DC: US Government Printing Office, 1970, A108.

The River Kept Rising

1 Fred W. Lindeccke, "River Dug Down Deep, Bored Levee's 300-Foot Tear," *St. Louis Post-Dispatch*, July 24, 1993, 6A.

2 Tim Bryant, "Water Smashes Levee, House," *St. Louis Post-Dispatch*, August 2, 1993, 3B.

3 Lia Nower, "Diving Toward Danger," *St. Louis Post-Dispatch*, August 7, 1993, 8A.

4 Rick Williams, "Ste. Genevieve." In *The Flood of 1993: Stories from a Midwestern Disaster*, edited by Betty Burnett (Tucson, AZ: The Patrice Press, 1994), 169.

Uncomfortably Fragile

1 James T. Lloyd, *Lloyd's Steamboat Directory and Disasters on the Western Waters* (Cincinnati, OH: James T. Lloyd & Company, 1856), 201.
2 Lloyd, *Lloyd's Steamboat Directory*, 137–38.
3 Ibid., 139.
4 Ibid.
5 Stanley Nelson, "'Oh, Mother, He Cannot Save Me!'" *Concordia Sentinel*, December 16, 2015.

Burned to the Water's Edge

1 Michael Chevalier, *Society, Manners and Politics in the United States, Being a Series of Letters on North America* (Boston, MA: Weeks, Jordan and Company, 1839), 221–22.
2 Charles Ellms, *The Tragedy of the Seas or, Sorrow on the Ocean, Lake, and River, from Shipwreck, Plague, Fire, and Famine* (Philadelphia, PA: Carey & Hart; 1841), 350, 353.
3 Frederick Way Junior, *Way's Packet Directory, 1848–1994* (revised) (Athens, OH: Ohio University Press, 1994), 101.
4 Way, *Way's Packet Directory*, 197–98.
5 Ibid., 196.
6 "Grand Republic Gone," *St. Louis Daily Globe Dispatch*, September 20, 1877.
7 Ibid.
8 Ibid.

Primed to Blow

1 James T. Lloyd, *Lloyds's Steamboat Directory and Disasters on the Western Waters* (Cincinnati, OH: James T. Lloyd & Company, 1856), 56.
2 Lloyd, *Lloyd's Steamboat Directory*, 189.
3 Ibid., 213.
4 Mark Twain, *Life on the Mississippi* (Cologne, Germany: Könemann Travel Classics, 2000), 149.
5 Twain, *Life on the Mississippi*, 156.
6 "A Sad Meeting," *St. Louis News and Intelligencer*, June 19, 1958, reprinting of article from *Memphis Eagle and Enquirer*, June 16, 1858.
7 Harriet Elinor Smith, ed., *Autobiography of Mark Twain, Volume 1* (Berkeley, CA: University of California Press, 2010), 276.

Going Home

1 Rev. Chester D. Berry, *Loss of the* Sultana *and Reminiscences of Survivors* (Lansing, MI: Darius Thorp, 1892), 29.
2 Berry, *Loss of the* Sultana, 70.
3 Sally M. Walker, *Sinking the* Sultana*: A Civil War Story of Imprisonment, Greed, and a Doomed Journey Home* (Summerville, MA: Candlewick Press, 2017), 95.
4 Berry, *Loss of the* Sultana, 26.
5 Ibid., 29–30.

6 Ibid., 63–64.
7 Ibid., 60.
8 Ibid., 66.
9 Ibid., 10.
10 Ibid., 41.
11 Walker, *Sinking the* Sultana, 116.
12 Berry, *Loss of the* Sultana, 223.
13 Ibid., 31.
14 Walker, *Sinking the* Sultana, 132.
15 Berry, *Loss of the* Sultana, 26.
16 Ibid., 67.
17 Ibid., 80.
18 Ibid., 80.

LET US ALL DIE TOGETHER

1 Dave Barnett interview, Oklahoma Federation of Labor Collection, M452 Box 5, Folder 2, Western History Collections (Norman, OK: University of Oklahoma), 405.
2 Barnett interview, 406.
3 Ibid., 407.
4 Christopher D. Haveman, "The Removal of the Creek Indians from the Southeast, 1825–1838" (PhD diss., Auburn University, 2009), 349, https://etd.auburn.edu/bitstream/handle/10415/2184/Haveman.pdf.txt?sequence=3&isAllowed.
5 James T. Lloyd, *Lloyd's Steamboat Directory, and Disasters on the Western Waters* (Cincinnati, OH: James T. Lloyd & Company, 1856), 127.
6 Billie Byrd, "An Interview of Elsie Edwards, daughter of Tustenuggie Jimboy, of Ke-oho-ba-da-gee," September 17, 1937, University of Oklahoma Libraries Western History Collections 27, interview ID 7571; 189, https://digital.libraries.ou.edu/cdm/ref/collection/indianpp/id/7754.

SHATTERED REMINDERS OF OUR WEAKNESS

1 Frederick L. Johnson, *The Sea Wing Disaster: Tragedy on Lake Pepin* (Red Wing, MN: Goodhue County Historical Society, 2014), 38.
2 "Drowned! An Awful Disaster at Lake Pepin, Minn.," *Minneapolis Tribune*, July 14, 1890.
3 "A Long List. Further Details of the Horror at Lake Pepin," *Minneapolis Tribune*, July 15, 1890.
4 "Sorrowful Scenes: Victims of the Lake Pepin Disaster Finally Laid Away," *Minneapolis Tribune*, July 16, 1890.
5 Johnson, *The Sea Wing Disaster*, 108.
6 Ibid., 99.

SPORTING GIRLS

1 Duane R. Sneddeker, "Regulating Vice: Prostitution and the St. Louis Social Evil Ordinance, 1870–1874," *Gateway Heritage* 11, no. 2 (Fall 1990): 23.
2 William Greenleaf Eliot, *Missouri Republican*, February 18, 1873.
3 Sneddeker, "Regulating Vice," 33.
4 *La Crosse Tribune*, January 9, 1914, 1.
5 Wisconsin Legislative Committee, "Report and Recommendations of the Wisconsin Legislative Committee to Investigate the White Slave Traffic and Kindred Subjects," 1914, Wisconsin Historical Society, https://content.wisconsinhistory.org/digital/collection/tp/id/26592.
6 Wisconsin Legislative Committee, "Report and Recommendations," 36.
7 Milton Gehle paper.
8 Wisconsin Legislative Committee, "Report and Recommendations," 157.
9 Pat Moore, "Ma's House Was Not a Home," *La Crosse Tribune*, September 12, 1976, 13.
10 Moore, "Ma's House," 13.
11 Ibid., 13.
12 Vi Benicke, "Winona's 'Line' Was Known Nationwide—and Beyond," *Winona Daily News*, October 25, 1976, 5.
13 Vi Benicke, "Errand Boy Remembers His Patrons' Generosity," *Winona Daily News*, October 25, 1976, 5.
14 "Sheriff Padlocks Five Vice Houses," *Winona Republican-Herald*, January 2, 1943, 3.

THE RIVER NEVER RAN DRY

1 Joy Jackson, "Prohibition in New Orleans: The Unlikeliest Crusade," *Louisiana History: The Journal of the Louisiana Historical Association* 19, no. 3 (Summer 1978).
2 John Magill, "'The Liquor Capital of America'—New Orleans During Prohibition," The Historic New Orleans Collection, October 8, 2018, https://www.hnoc.org/publications/first-draft/liquor-capital-america%E2%80%94new-orleans-during-prohibition.
3 Bryan M. Gowland, "The Delacroix Isleños and the Trappers' War in St. Bernard Parish," *Louisiana History: The Journal of the Louisiana Historical Association* 44, no. 4 (Autumn 2003), 411–41.
4 "Bootleggers Get Big Fines, and Sentences," *The New Orleans Item*, May 21, 1922.
5 Tim King, "Bootlegging: Farmers Bootleg to Provide for Family," The Land, March 8, 2002, 18.
6 Elaine Davis, *Minnesota 13: Stearns County's "Wet" Wild Prohibition Days* (St. Cloud, MN: Sweet Grass, 2007), 140.
7 Davis, *Minnesota 13*, 142.
8 Ibid., 144.
9 "Mak'n Moon," *Stearns-Morrison Enterprise*, October 5, 1976, 8.

In the Mississippi River

1 David Ridgen, *Someone Knows Something* podcast, Episode 1, Canadian Broadcasting Corporation, 2007.

2 Elizabeth Sutherland Martinez, *Letters from Mississippi* (Brookline, MA: Zephyr Press, 2002), 218.

3 Ridgen, *Someone Knows Something* podcast, Episode 5.

Hot Coals Rained Down from the Sky

1 John F. Darby, *Personal Recollections of Many Prominent People Whom I Have Known, and Events—Especially of Those Relating to the History of St. Louis—During the First Half of the Present Century* (St. Louis, MO: G. I. Jones & Company, 1880), 5.

2 William H. Belcher, letter to Nathan Belcher, May 21, 1849, Belcher family papers, Missouri History Museum.

3 Fredrick M. Colburn, description of the Great Fire, May 17, 1849, submitted May 17, 1899, St. Louis Volunteer Firemen Collection, Missouri History Museum.

4 Sally Smith Flagg journal (1846–1859), May 18, 1849, St. Louis Volunteer Firemen Collection, Missouri Historical Society.

5 Colburn, description of the Great Fire.

6 Ibid.

7 Frances S. Sublette, letter to her husband, William L. Sublette, May 21, 1849, William L. Sublette papers, Missouri Historical Society.

8 Flagg journal.

9 "How Targee Saved St. Louis from Destruction in Fire of 1849 and Lost His Life Blowing Up a Building in Path of the Flames," *St. Louis Republic*, May 13, 1906.

10 "Conflagration. Immense Loss of Property!" *People's Organ*, May 21, 1849, St. Louis Volunteer Firemen Collection, Missouri Historical Society.

11 "Conflagration. Immense Loss of Property!" *People's Organ*.

12 Colburn, description of the Great Fire.

13 Willis L. Williams, letter dated June 23, 1849, Hamilton R. Gamble papers, Missouri History Museum.

When the Walls Caved In

1 Frank Hrvatin, interviewed May 11, 1976 by Iron Range Research Center, Chisholm, MN, A-87-802.

2 John Fitzgerald, "Milford Mine Disaster, 1924: 'Save Your Breath and Start Climbing!'" *MinnPost*, February 5, 2013, https://www.minnpost.com/minnesota-history/2013/02/milford-mine-disaster-1924-save-your-breath-and-start-climbing/.

3 Berger Aulie, *The Milford Mine Disaster: A Cuyuna Range Tragedy* (Virginia, MN: W. A. Fisher Company, 1994), 36.

4 Hrvatin interview.

5 Aulie, *The Milford Mine Disaster*, 36.

6 Hrvatin interview.

7 Arnold A. Gustafson, *LIFE: 1900–1981* (New York: Vantage Press, 1982), 40.

8 Aulie, *The Milford Mine Disaster*, 48.

9 Hrvatin interview.

10 Ibid.

11 Gustafson, *LIFE: 1900–1981*, 42.

12 Hrvatin interview.

13 Industrial Commission of Minnesota, *Second Biennial Report of the Industrial Commission of Minnesota, 1923/1924* (Minneapolis, MN, 1925), 37.

14 A. C. Bacel, *Minnesota Daily Star*, February 13, 1924, 6.

15 F. L. Pitt, *Minnesota Daily Star*, February 13, 1924, 6.

16 Hrvatin interview.

17 Ibid.

TRAGEDY AT RUSH HOUR

1 Paul Levy, "To the Ballgame, on the Bus, Drivers Plunged into Terror," *Minneapolis Star Tribune*, August 2, 2007, A11.

2 Curt Brown, Kevin Duchschere, and Matt McKinney, "Drivers Dodge Dangers on Bridge, in Water," *Minneapolis Star Tribune*, August 2, 2007, A13.

3 Levy, "To the Ballgame," A11.

4 Ibid.

5 Brown et al., "Drivers Dodge Dangers," A13.

6 "Kids on School Bus Survive Mississippi River Bridge Collapse," *CNN*, August 2, 2007, http://www.cnn.com/2007/US/08/02/bridge.collapse.schoolbus/#cnnSTCText.

7 Heron Marquez Estrada, "A Father-to-Be Survives Fall, Helps Children Flee," *Minneapolis Star Tribune*, August 3, 2007, A6.

8 Patrick Condon, "Body of Last Missing Victim of Bridge Collapse Found," *MPR News*, August 21, 2007. https://www.mprnews.org/story/2007/08/20/last.

DEATH IS WIELDING HIS SCYTHE

1 *The Standard*, South Hanover, Indiana, June 18, 1835; July 2, 1835. In Walter J. Daly, "The Black Cholera Comes to the Central Valley of America in the 19th Century—1832, 1849, and Later," *Transactions of the American Clinical and Climatological Association* 119 (2008), 149.

2 I. H. Headlee, letter to S. H. Headlee, June 13, 1849, Missouri Historical Society collection.

3 E. G., Simons, letter to Simeon Leland, May 9, 1849, Missouri Historical Society collection.

4 Eliza Keesacker Howard, letter to Comfort McJilton, July 4, 1849, Missouri Historical Society collection, A3038-00002.

5 Headlee letter.

6 E. G., Simons letter.

Tormenting Insects

1 Reuben Gold Thwaits, ed., *The Jesuit Relations and Allied Documents: Travels and Explorations of the Jesuit Missionaries in New France, 1610–1791* LXVII (Cleveland, OH: The Burrows Company, 1900), 21.

2 Timothy Flint, *Recollections of the Last Ten Years* (Boston, MA: Cummings, Hilliard Company, 1826), 272.

3 Flint, *Recollections*, 272.

4 Charles Dickens, *American Notes and Pictures from Italy* (New York: Charles Scribner's Sons, 1900), 203.

5 M. A. Barber, "The History of Malaria in the United States," *Public Health Reports* 44, no. 43 (October 25, 1929), 2582.

6 *Daily Delta*, July 20, 1853. In John Duffy, *Sword of Pestilence: The New Orleans Yellow Fever Epidemic of 1853* (Baton Rouge, LA: Louisiana State University Press, 1966), 38.

7 *New Orleans Weekly Delta*, August 7, 1853. In Jo Ann Carrigan, "The Saffron Scourge: A History of Yellow Fever in Louisiana, 1796–1905" (PhD diss., Louisiana State University, 1961), 370.

8 Reverend Theodore Clapp, *Autobiographical Sketches and Recollections during a Thirty-Five Years Residence in New Orleans* (2nd ed.) (Boston, MA: Phillips, Sampson & Company, 1858), 189.

9 Clapp, *Autobiographical Sketches and Recollections*, 189.

10 *New Orleans Daily Picayune*, June 28, 1853. In John Duffy, *Sword of Pestilence: The New Orleans Yellow Fever Epidemic of 1853* (Baton Rouge, LA: Louisiana State University Press, 1966), 17.

11 *The Diary of a Samaritan, by a Member of the Howard Association of New Orleans* (New York: Harper & Brothers, Publishers, 1860), 152.

12 Ibid., 132.

13 *Ibid.*, 187.

14 J. M. Keating, *A History of the Yellow Fever: The Yellow Fever Epidemic of 1878, in Memphis, Tenn.* (Memphis, TN: Howard Association, 1879), 146.

15 Keating, *A History of the Yellow Fever*, 108.

16 *Memphis Avalanche*, September 1, 1878. In Keating, 153.

17 Keating, *A History of the Yellow Fever*, 110.

18 *Memphis Avalanche*, September 11, 1878. In Keating, 159.

19 Keating, *A History of the Yellow Fever*, 111.

20 *Memphis Appeal*, August 28, 1878. In Keating, 150.

21 Keating, *A History of the Yellow Fever*, 112.

22 *Memphis Avalanche*, September 5, 1878. In Keating, 155.

Someone to Blame

1 Douglas J. Swanson, "La Crosse, the River, Denial: A College Town Struggles to Frame Responsibility for River Drowning Deaths," paper prepared for the Mass Communication and Society Division, AEJMC Mid-Winter Conference (Reno, NV: February 23, 2007), 9.

2 Swanson, "La Crosse, the River, Denial," 11.

Bibliography

Selected Books

Aulie, Berger. *The Milford Mine Disaster: A Cuyuna Range Tragedy.* Virginia, MN: W. A. Fisher Company, 1994.

Bagnall, Norma Hayes. *On Shaky Ground: The New Madrid Earthquakes of 1811–1812.* Columbia, MO: University of Missouri Press, 1996.

Barry, John. *Rising Tide: The Great Mississippi Flood of 1927 and How It Changed America.* New York: Touchstone, 1998.

Berry, Rev. Chester D. *Loss of the* Sultana *and Reminiscences of Survivors.* Lansing, MI: Darius Thorp, 1892.

Burnett, Betty, ed. *The Flood of 1993: Stories from a Midwestern Disaster.* Tucson, AZ: The Patrice Press, 1994.

Changnon, Stanley A., ed. *The Great Flood of 1993: Causes, Impacts, and Responses.* Boulder, CO: Westview Press, 1996.

Courtaway, Robbi. *Wetter Than the Mississippi: Prohibition in Saint Louis and Beyond.* St. Louis: Reedy Press, 2008.

Curzon, Julian. *The Great Cyclone at St. Louis and East St. Louis, May 27, 1896.* St. Louis, MO: Cyclone Publishing Company, 1896.

Daniel, Pete. *Deep'n as It Come: The 1927 Mississippi River Flood.* New York: Oxford University Press, 1977.

Davis, Elaine. *Minnesota 13: Stearns County's "Wet" Wild Prohibition Days.* St. Cloud, MN: Sweet Grass, 2007.

Duffy, John. *Sword of Pestilence: The New Orleans Yellow Fever Epidemic of 1853.* Baton Rouge, LA: Louisiana State University Press, 1966.

Gordon, Christopher Alan. *Fire, Pestilence, and Death: St. Louis 1849.* St. Louis, MO: Missouri Historical Society Press, 2018.

Hamer, Richard, and Roger Ruthhart. *The Citadel of Sin: The John Looney Story.* Moline, IL: Moline Dispatch Publishing Company, 2007.

Huffman, Alan. Sultana: *Surviving the Civil War, Prison, and the Worst Maritime Disaster in American History.* New York: Smithsonian Books, 2009.

Hull, William H. *All Hell Broke Loose: Experiences of Young People during the Armistice Day 1940 Blizzard.* Edina, MN: Stanton Publication Services, 1996.

Hunter, Louis C., and Beatrice Jones Hunter. *Steamboats on the Western Rivers: An Economic and Technological History.* United Kingdom: Dover Publications, 1993.

Johnson, Frederick L. *The* Sea Wing *Disaster: Tragedy on Lake Pepin.* Red Wing, MN: Goodhue County Historical Society, 2014.

Keating, J. M. *A History of the Yellow Fever: The Yellow Fever Epidemic of 1878, in Memphis, Tenn.* Memphis, TN: Howard Association, 1879.

Lloyd, James T. *Lloyd's Steamboat Directory, and Disasters on the Western Waters.* Cincinnati, OH: James T. Lloyd & Company, 1856.

Maclean, Harry N. *The Past Is Never Dead: The Trial of James Ford Seale and Mississippi's Struggle for Redemption.* New York: BasicCivitas Books, 2009.

Morris, Christopher. *The Big Muddy: An Environmental History of the Mississippi and Its Peoples.* New York: Oxford University Press, 2012.

Nelson, Stanley. *Devils Walking: Klan Murders along the Mississippi in the 1960s.* Baton Rouge, LA: Louisiana University Press, 2016.

Philip, Cynthia Owen. *Robert Fulton: A Biography.* New York: Franklin Watts, 1985.

Pierce, John R., and Jim Writer. *Yellow Jack: How Yellow Fever Ravaged America and Walter Reed Discovered Its Deadly Secrets.* Hoboken, NJ: John Wiley & Sons, 2005.

Quinn, Rev. Denis Alphonsus. *Heroes and Heroines of Memphis, Or Reminiscences of the Yellow Fever Epidemics that Afflicted the City of Memphis During the Autumn Months of 1873, 1878 and 1879, to which is Added: A Graphic Description of Missionary Life in Eastern Arkansas.* Providence, RI: E. L. Freeman & Sons, 1887.

Rose, Al. Storyville, *New Orleans: Being an Authentic, Illustrated Account of the Notorious Red Light District.* Tuscaloosa, AL: University of Alabama Press, 1974.

Stewart, David, and Ray Knox. *The Earthquake America Forgot: 2,000 Temblors in Five Months . . . and It Will Happen Again.* Marble Hill, MO: Gutenberg-Richter Publications, 1995.

The Diary of a Samaritan, by a Member of the Howard Association of New Orleans. New York: Harper & Brothers Publishers, 1860.

Walker, Sally M. *Sinking the Sultana: A Civil War Story of Imprisonment, Greed, and a Doomed Journey Home.* Summerville, MA: Candlewick Press, 2017.

SELECTED CHAPTERS, ARTICLES, AND REPORTS

"Armistice Day Blizzard of 1940 Remembered." National Weather Service. https://www.weather.gov/dvn/armistice_day_blizzard.

"Collapse of I-35W Highway Bridge, Minneapolis, Minnesota; August 1, 2007." National Transportation Safety Board, Accident Report, November 14, 2008.

"How Targee Saved St. Louis from Destruction in fire of 1849 and Lost His Life Blowing Up a Building in Path of the Flames." *St. Louis Republic*, May 13, 1906.

"New Madrid Compendium Eyewitness Accounts." University of Memphis. https://www.memphis.edu/ceri/compendium/eyewitness.php.

"Sauk Rapids Practically Wiped Off the Map 50 Years Ago This Month." *Sauk Rapids Herald*, April 9, 1936.

"Summary of 1811–1812 New Madrid Earthquakes Sequence." US Geological Survey. https://www.usgs.gov/natural-hazards/earthquake-hazards/science/summary-1811-1812-new-madrid-earthquakes-sequence.

"Survivors of 'Sea Wing' Disaster on Lake Pepin Describe Appalling Catastrophe of 40 Years Ago." *Minneapolis Sunday Tribune,* June 8, 1930.

"The Appalling Disaster That Fell on Fair St. Louis." *St. Louis Post-Dispatch,* June 3, 1896.

"The Cyclone in Minnesota." *Harper's Weekly* 30, no. 1532 (May 1, 1886).

Anderson, D. B., and I. L. Burmeister. *Floods of March–May 1965 in the Upper Mississippi River Basin.* Geological Survey Water-Supply Paper 1850-A, Department of the Interior, Washington, DC: US Government Printing Office, 1970.

Bakst, Brian. "Since I-35W, State Has More Eyes and Sharper Focus on Bridges." Minnesota Public Radio, July 31, 2017. https://www.mprnews.org/story/2017/07 /28/since-35w-minnesota-more-eyes-sharper-focus-bridges.

Benicke, Vi. "Winona's 'Line' Was Known Nationwide—and Beyond." *Winona Daily News,* October 25, 1976.

Bruesch, S. R. "The Disasters and Epidemics of a River Town: Memphis, Tennessee, 1819–1879." *Bulletin of the Medical Library Association* 40, no. 3 (July 1952): 288–305.

Cramer, Chris H., and Oliver S. Boyd. "Why the New Madrid earthquakes Are M 7–8 and the Charleston Earthquake is ~M 7." *Bulletin of the Seismological Society of America* 104, no. 6 (2014): 2884–903.

Daly, Walter J. "The Black Cholera Comes to the Central Valley of America in the 19th Century—1832, 1849, and Later." *Transactions of the American Clinical and Climatological Association* 119 (2008): 143–53.

Davis, Tom. "The Day the Duck Hunters Died." *Sporting Classics Daily,* November 9, 2015. https://sportingclassicsdaily.com/day-the-duck-hunters-died/.

Duggan, Martin. "306 Persons in St. Louis Area Were Killed in 1896 Tornado. Property Damage $13,000,000." *St. Louis Globe-Democrat,* May 26, 1946.

Dunn, Rob. "Why Mosquitoes Like You and Not Me." *Scientific American,* August 13, 2013. http://blogs.scientificamerican.com/guest-blog/why-mosquitoes-like-you -and-not-me/.

Fitzgerald, John. "Milford Mine Disaster, 1924: 'Save Your Breath and Start Climbing!'" *MinnPost,* February 5, 2013. https://www.minnpost.com/minnesota-history/2013 /02/milford-mine-disaster-1924-save-your-breath-and-start-climbing/.

Fueglein, J. N. "Worst Flood in St. Louis History—in 1844." *St. Louis Globe Democrat,* May 21, 1943.

Hillig, Terry. "St. Louis Fire Department Remembers an Early Hero." *St. Louis Post-Dispatch,* December 11, 2001.

Hornbeck, Richard, and Suresh Naidu. "When the Levee Breaks: Black Migration and Economic Development in the American South." *American Economic Review* 104, no. 3 (January 2013): 963–90.

Hubbuch, Chris. "The Flood of 1965: An Oral History." *Winona Daily News,* April 19, 2005. https://www.winonadailynews.com/news/the-flood-of-1965-an-oral -history/article_5679903c-e6d1-5d2f-9fec-36b670dcddf8.html.

Jackson, Joy. "Prohibition in New Orleans: The Unlikeliest Crusade." *Louisiana History: The Journal of the Louisiana Historical Association* 19, no. 3 (Summer 1978): 261–84.

King, Tim. "Bootlegging: Farmers Bootleg to Provide for Family." The Land, March 8, 2002.

MacQuarrie, Gordon. "The Ducks Came and Men Died; Tragedy of River Bottoms." *Winona Republican-Herald*, November 13, 1940.

Marcou, David J. "River Deaths and the Culture of Alcohol." *La Crosse Tribune*, March 13, 2007.

Moore, Bob. "New Perspectives on the Great Fire of 1849." *The Confluence* (Spring/Summer 2019): 43–54. https://www.lindenwood.edu/files/resources/the -confluence-spring-summer-2019-moore.pdf.

Moore, Pat. "The Legend Lingers On." *La Crosse Tribune*, September 12, 1976.

Murfree, W. L. "The Levees of the Mississippi." *Scribner's Magazine* (July 1881): 420–31.

Nelson, Stanley. "The Great Natchez Tornado of 1840." *Concordia Sentinel.* https://web .archive.org/web/20110714155617/http://www.natchezcitycemetery.com/custom/ webpage.cfm?content=News&id=75.

Norris, F. Terry. "Where Did the Villages Go?" In *Common Fields: An Environmental History of St. Louis.* Edited by Andrew Hurley, 73–89. St. Louis, MO: Missouri History Museum, 1997.

Petroski, Henry. "The Minneapolis Bridge." *American Scientist* 97, no. 6 (November/December 2009): 444.

Porter, Cynthya. "The Day They Cleaned Up Second Str." *Winona Post*, December 28, 2008.

Remington, Harry. "When Death Rode a Tornado . . . the *Sea Wing* Tragedy on Lake Pepin." *Minneapolis Sunday Tribune*, November 4, 1934.

Richmond, Todd. "Students Keep Drunks from Drowning in Mississippi River near La Crosse." *MPR News*, April 13, 2012. https://www.mprnews.org/story/2012/04/13 /la-crosse-drinking.

Rusch, Elizabeth. "The Great Midwest Earthquake of 1811." *Smithsonian Magazine* (December 2011). https://www.smithsonianmag.com/science-nature/the-great -midwest-earthquake-of-1811-46342/.

Sharing the Challenge: Floodplain Management into the 21st Century. Report of the Interagency Floodplain Management Review Committee to the Administration Floodplain Management Task Force. Washington, DC, June 1994.

Sneddeker, Duane R. "Regulating Vice: Prostitution and the St. Louis Social Evil Ordinance, 1870–1874." *Gateway Heritage* 11, no. 2 (Fall 1990): 20–47.

Trudeau, Noah Andre. "Death on the River." *Naval History Magazine* 23, no. 4 (August 2009). https://www.usni.org/magazines/naval-history-magazine/2009/august/ death-river.

Wagner, Dorothy. "The Camanche Tornado." *Palimpset* 40, no. 12 (December 1959): 537–47.

Wanko, Andrew. "Great River City: The Social Evil." Missouri Historical Society. https://mohistory.org/blog/great-river-city-the-social-evil.

Washburn, L. "The Icy Winds of Death: The Armistice Day Blizzard November 11, 1940." *Iowa Outdoors* 67, no. 5 (2008): 3441.

MISCELLANEOUS
Ridgen, David. *Someone Knows Something* podcast, Season 3 (2017). https://www.cbc.ca/radio/sks/season3.